Teaching Critical Perfor.

Teaching Critical Performance Theory offers teaching strategies for professors and artist-scholars across performance, design and technology, and theatre studies disciplines.

The book's seventeen chapters collectively ask: What use is theory to an emerging theatre artist or scholar? Which theories should be taught, and to whom? How can theory pedagogies shape and respond to the evolving needs of the academy, the field, and the community? This broad field of enquiry is divided into four sections covering course design, classroom teaching, the studio space, and applied theatre contexts. Through a range of intriguing case studies that encourage thoughtful theatre practice, this book explores themes surrounding situated learning, dramaturgy and technology, disability and inclusivity, feminist approaches, race and performance, ethics, and critical theory in theatre history.

Written as an invaluable resource for professionals and postgraduates engaged in performance theory, this collection of informative essays will also provide critical reading for those interested in drama and theatre studies more broadly.

Jeanmarie Higgins is an Associate Professor in the School of Theatre at the Pennsylvania State University, University Park, USA.

Teaching Critical Performance Theory

In Today's Theatre Classroom, Studio, and Communities

Edited by
Jeanmarie Higgins

Routledge
Taylor & Francis Group

LONDON AND NEW YORK

First published 2020
by Routledge
2 Park Square, Milton Park, Abingdon, Oxon OX14 4RN

and by Routledge
52 Vanderbilt Avenue, New York, NY 10017

Routledge is an imprint of the Taylor & Francis Group, an informa business

British Library Cataloguing-in-Publication Data
A catalogue record for this book is available from the British Library

Library of Congress Cataloging-in-Publication Data
Names: Higgins, Jeanmarie, editor.
Title: Teaching critical performance theory: in today's theatre classroom, studio, and communities / edited by Jeanmarie Higgins.
Description: Abingdon, Oxon; New York, NY: Routledge, 2020. |
Includes bibliographical references and index.
Identifiers: LCCN 2019052865 (print) | LCCN 2019052866 (ebook) |
ISBN 9780367409296 (hardback) | ISBN 9780367409302 (paperback) |
ISBN 9780367809966 (ebook)
Subjects: LCSH: Theater–Study and teaching. | Drama–Study and teaching.
Classification: LCC PN2075 .T425 2020 (print) |
LCC PN2075 (ebook) | DDC 792.02/807–dc23
LC record available at https://lccn.loc.gov/2019052865
LC ebook record available at https://lccn.loc.gov/2019052866

ISBN: 978-0-367-40929-6 (hbk)
ISBN: 978-0-367-40930-2 (pbk)
ISBN: 978-0-367-80996-6 (ebk)

Typeset in Sabon
by Newgen Publishing UK

For Sarah B.B.

Contents

Figures

Tables

Contributors

Angela K. Ahlgren is an assistant professor in Theatre and Film at Bowling Green State University, where she teaches theatre history and performance studies. She is the author of *Drumming Asian America: Taiko, Performance, and Cultural Politics* (Oxford, 2018).

Andrew Belser is Director of the School of Theatre, Film, and Television at the University of Arizona. He is a director, cross-disciplinary researcher, and author of the forthcoming *Translating Neuroscience for Performance: the Four Lenses* (Routledge).

Michael M. Chemers is Professor of Dramatic Literature and Director of Graduate Studies for the Department of Theater Arts at the University of California Santa Cruz. His books and articles cover dramaturgy in relation to monster studies, disability studies, and new media studies.

Maria Enriquez is an assistant teaching professor of Theatre at Penn State Harrisburg where she teaches acting, directing, and theatre history. Her scholarship examines the intersections of race, gender, and performance practices. She is also an actor, director, and deviser who works with local Latinx communities.

Jennifer Ewing-Pierce is a visiting assistant professor at the University of North Carolina-Charlotte. In addition to working as a dramaturg, playwright, and director, she publishes about consciousness studies, critical theory, pedagogy, and artificial intelligence.

La Donna L. Forsgren is an assistant professor at the University of Notre Dame where she teaches courses in theatre history and black theatre and performance. She is the author of *In Search of Our Warrior Mothers: Women Dramatists of the Black Arts Movement* (Northwestern University Press, 2018) and *Sistuhs in the Struggle: An Oral History of Black Arts Movement Theatre and Performance* (Northwestern University Press, 2020).

Kikora Franklin is a cultural arts educator, performer, and associate professor of theatre/dance at the Pennsylvania State University. Kikora's creative work focuses on preserving and sharing African and African-related dance as a means for human development, community building, and education.

Jeanmarie Higgins is an associate professor in Theatre at the Pennsylvania State University, University Park. A new works dramaturg in theatre and dance, Jeanmarie publishes widely about the intersection of performance theory and practice.

Stephanie L. Hodde is an assistant professor of English, Rhetoric and Humanistic Studies at Virginia Military Institute. An arts-based literacy educator by training, Stephanie researches and develops multimodal curricula and performance projects for community and undergraduate learners.

Les Hunter is a playwright and also a scholar of twentieth-century American theatre. He is currently an associate professor of English at Baldwin Wallace University, and the Ohio Regional Representative for the Dramatists Guild of America.

Miriam Kammer is an associate professor and theatre director in the Theatre and Women's & Gender Studies programs at Simpson College. Her publications include studies in ecodrama and ecocriticism, interpretations of Shakespeare, and performance as research.

Noe Montez is an associate professor of Theatre, Dance and Performance Studies at Tufts University, where he serves as his department's Director of Graduate Studies. He is the editor of *Theatre Topics* and ATHE Vice President for Professional Development.

Beth Murray is an associate professor in theatre education and applied theatre at the University of North Carolina-Charlotte. A qualitative researcher, Beth's socially-engaged scholarship centers around multi-modal, multilingual literacies, arts-based assessment and arts-driven storytelling

Jean O'Hara is an assistant professor at the University of Alberta. She has been directing and teaching theatre for the past twenty years. O'Hara's research examines the intersectionality of race, gender and sexuality while also supporting Indigenous theatre, language and sovereignty.

Jen Plants is a faculty associate at the University of Wisconsin-Madison, where she teaches playwriting, dramaturgy, performance studies, and critical race theory. As a director, deviser, and dramaturg, Jen's performance as research focuses on creating community-based, sustainable theatre.

Susan Russell is an actor/activist/playwright and Associate Professor in Theatre at the Pennsylvania State University where she teaches literature and criticism, musical theatre history, and playwriting. Her research addresses the application of arts pedagogy to interdisciplinary teaching and learning.

Michael Schweikardt is a scenic designer working professionally in New York, American regional theatre, and abroad. He is also currently a graduate student at The Pennsylvania State University School of Theatre.

Mike Sell is Professor of English at Indiana University of Pennsylvania. He studies and teaches critical theory, Black American literature and performance, interdisciplinary approaches to the avant-garde, and videogame studies. He is project leader of the IUP Digital Storytelling Project, an outreach initiative that teaches Pennsylvania middle- and high-school students to design interactive digital storygames.

Emma Watkins is a playwright, scholar, and dramaturg. She graduated from Princeton University and was a Fulbright Postgraduate at Cardiff University, where she studied contemporary theatrical (re)creations of myth and folklore. Her plays adapt traditional material, engaging with contemporary conversations surrounding identity, environmentalism, and feminism.

Stacy Wolf is Professor of Theater and American Studies and Director of the Program in Music Theater at Princeton University. She is the author of *A Problem Like Maria: Gender and Sexuality in the American Musical*; *Changed for Good: A Feminist History of the Broadway Musical*; and *Beyond Broadway: The Pleasure and Promise of Musical Theatre Across America*.

Isaiah Matthew Wooden is a director-dramaturg and assistant professor of Theater Arts at Brandeis University. He has published articles and chapters in numerous journals and anthologies and co-edited *Tarell Alvin McCraney: Theater, Performance, and Collaboration* (Northwestern University Press, 2020).

Samuel Yates is a professorial lecturer and artist at George Washington University, where he teaches courses in disability studies, cinema, and drama. He is currently working on a monograph about disability aesthetics and musical theatre, *Cripping Broadway*.

Acknowledgments

This collection began as a roundtable session at the 2018 Mid-America Theatre Conference. I wish to thank Cat Gleason and all the Pedagogy Symposium conveners since for supporting this work over the past two years. I am lucky to have colleagues who gave generously of their time and resources to help me turn this idea into a book. I am grateful to Scott Magelssen for our chats early in this process. Likewise, thanks to Bill Doan who introduced me to some of the exciting scholars included herein; and to Lisa Jackson-Schebetta whose encouragement and advice helps me in big and small ways in all of my work.

Thank you to Richard E. T. White at College Cornish College of the Arts in Seattle, Washington for presenting me with the life-changing puzzle of how and why to teach theory to BFA actors and designers. My Cornish students showed me why theatre artists—whose business it is to create embodied meaning in time and space—are so "good at theory," and how theory fuels new performance. I want to acknowledge the students who continue to show what's possible: Sara Porkalob, Jerick Hoffer, Timothy Smith-Stewart, Chelsea Hanawalt, Sarah Grosman, Les Gray, and so many other artist-scholars who move through this world thoughtfully, sometimes difficultly, allowing thought to shape the form.

I blush at my good fortune when I enumerate the scholars who've taught me. In memory of Herbert Blau, thank you for showing me that good teaching begins with giving students your serious attention. Thank you to Sarah Bryant-Bertail, Eng-Beng Lim, Brian McLaren, Barry Witham, Jennifer Salk, and Odai Johnson for teaching me new ways to think. To the many people who have invited me into their theatres, community spaces, and university departments to teach theatre in its many forms—Lenora Champagne, John Pietrowski, John Frick, Doug Grissom, Rosemary McLaughlin, Lynne Conner, Rick Lombardo—thank you.

To my collaborators in teaching and learning—Elisha Clark Halpin, Michele Dunleavy, Erik Raymond Johnson, Charlene Gross, Gwen Walker, Daniel Robinson, Susan H. Schulman, Malcolm Womack, and Steven Snyder—thanks for the welcome. This project was supported by the Pennsylvania State University College of Arts and Architecture, the Arts &

Design Research Incubator, and the Center for Pedagogy in Arts & Design. Thanks to Tara Caimi and Ann Clements for their friendship and guidance, and to Barbara O. Korner and Mallika Bose for their invaluable support.

To my editor, Ben Piggott, thank you for your enthusiasm and guidance; it is a pleasure to work with you. Finally, thanks to friends and family who supported me in many ways during this process: Sarah Marsh, Lee Gregory, Elizabeth Bonjean, Robin Witt, and John and Laura Trainor. And to my partner, Sebastian, and our dog, Oliver, my love, always.

Jeanmarie Higgins

Introduction

Teaching critical performance theory in today's educational landscape

Noe Montez

In the fall of 2018, I had the pleasure of convening the fourth gathering of the Consortium of PhD Programs in Theatre and Performance Studies at my home institution, Tufts University. The conference, which occurs every three to four years, invited directors of Theatre and Performance Studies PhD programs from across the United States and Canada to come together in exploration of how we're educating graduate students and the academic world that we're training our graduate students to enter. As part of this meeting, I presented data from a longitudinal study that I've conducted on the academic job market from 2011 to the present. This data involves close readings of job advertisements in theatre and performance studies to list the skills that are desired among assistant professors and the courses that colleges and universities want their faculty to teach. In reviewing this information, a significant number of the job ads posted wanted applicants grounded in critical theory. Sometimes this work needed to be grounded in the lived experience and knowledge production of minoritarian identities. In other instances, the universities felt as though they wanted their students to have a more generalized understanding of critical theory in order to be better students of the humanities. Regardless of the reasons that the ads were written in this way, anyone who carefully reviews these academic job postings must come away with the certain knowledge that teaching critical theory in theatre and performance classrooms matters.

But why does theory matter? Critical theory aspires to change society as a whole. It aims to unearth and understand how power and privilege operate within the world. As one of the forbearers of critical theory, Max Horkmeier suggests that critical theory must find a wrong in society, that it must identify the pathways for agents to enact change, and must provide achievable goals for transformation. Similarly, in the essential *Teaching to Transgress*, bell hooks describes theory as a necessary practice that allows the voiceless to speak, allowing women of color particularly to break silences in institutions where women of color are not listened to (1994, 65). Theory, in this case offers scholars and artists the opportunity to give voice to new worlds that allow us to know and understand differently in times of difficulty.

In theatre and performance studies, theory produces alternative ways of looking at how we stage and make work for one another. Those who value theory appreciate the numerous perspectives that it contributes to our understanding of the theatre making and theatre education apparatus from syllabus design, to casting, to the classroom, to the rehearsal room, and into how we see and interpret the performances before us. Theory helps us to take on perspectives that may be different from our own and to provide insight into why patterns emerge so that we might draw perspective about their meaning. Additionally, theory informs the ways that we study questions. Theories are linked to epistemological or ontological traditions—or simply put, ways of knowing and worldviews—and are therefore concerned with the nature of knowledge and our ability to interpret and understand that knowledge. On a practical level, this means that theory instills strong research, writing, and oral skills in students, combined with an understanding of society that will position students to enter a diverse workforce. Thinking critically about theory positions students to understand race and gender in ways that will make them team players who know how to work collaboratively, whether that's in the field of theatre or performance, or in another sector.

Critical theory also suggests ways to solve problems as agents of change. Many of the scholars in this collection use theory with the hope that their findings will solve an existing problem. The Civil Rights Movement, feminism, and more recently, environmental justice, Black Lives Matter, and #MeToo are just some of the countless social movements examined by critical theory. These scholars write from a strong tradition of praxis born of a desire to empower the powerless, and to speak for those who have been denied their own voice. Without doubt, critical theory has made a difference in the scholarship and staging practices of theatre and performance studies. While the extent of critical theory used by academics, practitioners, and students varies widely, theory continues to inspire new questions, stimulate debate, and generate controversy. Critical performance theory matters. This is the core tenet at the heart of *Teaching Critical Performance Theory*, an edited collection drawing together an assortment of scholars working across the variegated facets of theatre and performance studies. This collection is designed to introduce a wide spectrum of ideas that readers might expand upon in their own pedagogical practices and theatre-making experiences.

One of the foremost insights of critical theory is the need to articulate the writers' positionality. In this instance the writers of this text are predominantly scholars working and teaching as theatre artists and scholars in the United States. However, the institutions that we teach in range from major research institutions, classified as Research 1 universities, to small liberal arts colleges. The writers represent a wide variety of racial and ethnic identities, gender expressions, sexual orientations, socio-economic positions, and family backgrounds. The careful reader will see these histories and ways of knowing reveal themselves in any of the perspectives taken in this text. The knowledge presented in this text is grounded in the theatre and practices of the Western world. While every text aspires to be as expansive as possible in scope, it is impossible to cover every perspective. Despite this gap in the authors' chapters, this book has much to offer those working in educational theatre.

The chapters in *Teaching Critical Performance Theory* have emerged from conference papers, book projects, pedagogical practice, and collaborations between scholars working within and across universities. This edited collection includes essays on a range of topics connected to teaching critical theory in Theatre and Performance Studies courses including unpacking the politics of white supremacy and blackness in the curriculum, understanding gender theory though musical theatre, and teaching dramaturgy through an understanding of place and technology. The book represents over a dozen theoretical approaches and considers how those approaches might inform the work that theatre professors do on the stage, in their classrooms, and as a pedagogical methodology. The totality of this text offers a diverse look at the continuing interventions that theatre scholars are making on behalf of their students and with hopes of a better world.

The first section of this collection, Course Design: Imagining the Syllabus, serves as a starting point for thinking through how one can imbed a course's curriculum in critical performance theory. Jennifer Ewing-Pierce draws upon situated cognition, a subfield of cognitive studies. This theoretical foundation serves as the basis for a series of classroom exercises designed to empower students to engage in peer-to-peer learning and trying to solve problems using real world examples. Ewing-Pierce writes about dramatic literature courses that she's taught in order to voice strategies for presenting the sociocultural influences of a dramatic text. In doing so, students take the lead in acquiring knowledge about the ways that theatre artists use the stage to imagine new and better worlds.

Emma Watkins and Stacy Wolf's chapter, "Feminist Musical Theatre Pedagogy," invites readers to consider how teaching the history of the American musical from a feminist perspective can inspire future artists to imagine the work that they create in ways that are respectful to the text, while also imagining new possibilities for interpretation. Analyzing the different elements of performance—book, lyrics, performance and choreography—are common in any musical theatre class, but when those explorations are grounded in an exploration of feminist theory, students gain a deeper appreciation for the musical as a genre, and "a much more profound understanding of how the show has performed gender and other embodiments throughout its countless performances" (34).

Angela K. Ahlgren reimagines the two- to three-semester Theatre History sequence for theatre majors in "Theory Over Time: Asian American Performance, Critical Theory, and the Theatre History Sequence." Given the variegated learning outcomes inherent in a mandatory survey that serves as an essential course sequence for undergraduates, Ahlgren articulates a form of slow teaching that favors a "durational approach to building theory-savvy undergraduate syllabi, one that begins by drawing on one's research areas and accrues more sophistication semester by semester" (39). Drawing on her research on Asian-American performance provides examples of how she engages her students to think about Orientalism, postcolonial discourse, and representations of Asian and Asian-American characters in the history of the world stage. It is a profoundly useful chapter for a new faculty member mandated to transform a department's theatre history curriculum.

Michael Chemers and Mike Sell make the case for what they coin as "systemic dramaturgy," a response to the encroachment of digital and virtual technology in the theatre. The duo seek to train dramaturgs to continue the traditional labors of engaging in the play as well as the historical, social, cultural and political contexts that inform the play's creation and its relevance at the time that it is being staged "in order to help dramaturgs to find their way in a dazzling, rapidly changing media universe that encompasses both traditional theatrical spaces and other embodied, dramatic media like sports, escape rooms, immersive entertainment, roleplaying games, and videogames" (54). This work can take place in specialized dramaturgy courses, or in the traditional theatre history coursework. In each instance systemic dramaturgy creates space for reframing the theatre in accordance with twenty-first-century technologies.

Les Hunter closes this section with "Contemporary Playwriting Pedagogies: A Survey of Recent Introductory Playwriting Syllabi." Hunter appraises approximately thirty introductory playwriting classes taught across the United States and Canada as a way of exploring how the courses challenge dominant ideologies about dramatic form and about the very nature of race, power, class, and gender. In reviewing the strengths and weaknesses of these courses, the careful reader should be able to draw from best practices and avoid pitfalls as a way of thinking through a continuum of theoretical approaches that will not only foster better playwrights, but also better citizens and scholars who consider diversity in all of its many forms.

Whereas the first section of this book considers the ways that critical theory can be incorporated at the stages of curriculum building and constructing classroom syllabi, "Classroom Identities: Engaging Students in Theory" focuses on specific lessons and case studies that the authors have produced as a way of introducing critical race theory, disability studies, and ecocriticism to undergraduates in predominantly white institutions who may not be aware of the privilege that they bring into the classroom. In "Performing Blackness, Ecodramaturgy, and Social Justice: Toward a Radical Pedagogy," La Donna L. Forsgren considers the difficulties in teaching predominantly white liberal students in a predominantly white institution how white privilege operates in the contemporary United States. Drawing upon her experience teaching a course titled Performing Blackness at the University of Oregon and Notre Dame University, Forsgren borrows from theoretical interventions in cognitive studies, ecocriticism, and black feminism to teach a variety of African-American texts ranging from Dutchman to *Get Out.*

Samuel Yates incorporates disability studies into his classroom's study of one of the most-often produced plays of the twenty-first century in his chapter, "Casting Christopher: Disability Pedagogy in *The Curious Incident of the Dog in The Night-Time.*" In the author's own words, "using the novel, Stephens's playscript, webpages for the UK West End Production and the New York Broadway Production, and key readings, students learn key disability studies concepts that prepare them to examine issues of disability representation in commercial theatre, such as: casting able-bodied actors to play disabled characters; marketing disability; audience education and engagement; and how disability impacts elements of stage design" (94). From this close reading of the play, its source texts, and marketing, Yates can engage in discussions about casting, representation, and dramatic structure.

Ecocriticism returns to the forefront of classroom exploration in Miriam Kammer's "Greening the Curriculum: Introducing Ecocriticism and Ecodrama to Students in the Classroom and Rehearsal Studio." Whether working in the classroom or the rehearsal studio, the chapter offers pedagogical strategies for teaching and producing plays through this theoretical framework. Kammer explores how to engage with students who may be politically resistant to discuss climate change and the environment, as well as how to work with students who hold environmentalist tendencies so that they might bring that knowledge to bear on the performances that they are studying. The chapter is instructive in considering the roles that empathy and activism play in helping students develop new ways of seeing themselves in the world.

Finally, African American playwrights are centered in a conversation about the value of theatre training in Isaiah Wooden's "Teaching African American Plays as 'Reality Checks,' or Why Theatre Still Matters." Wooden outlines his classroom adaptation of Harry Elam's pivotal theoretical lens, "reality checks," moments that "brusquely rub the real up against representation in ways that disrupt the spectators and produce new meanings" in order to provoke social engagement and activism (123). Teaching Lorraine Hansberry's *A Raisin in the Sun* and Robert O'Hara's *Barbecue* generates opportunities for his general education students to talk about citizenship, housing discrimination, and other forms of racism from the Civil Rights Era to the present day.

"Studio: Theorizing Praxis" moves from the theatre history, performance studies, and dramatic literature classroom to the stage. Jeanmarie Higgins and Michael Schweikardt draw from their pedagogical experiences in their chapter, "Deep Thought: Teaching Critical Theory to Designers." Design expertise is often framed as a hard skill, because of the knowledge needed to draw, draft, sew, and build. Nevertheless, the authors argue that introducing designers to tenets of critical theory not only enhances their artistic work but develops students' awareness of how structures of power organize the academic and professional theatre fields.

The theoretical strategies taken by Higgins and Schweikardt shift from the design studio to the rehearsal space of the performance classroom in the following chapters from this section. Andrew Belser, Director of the School of Theatre, Television, and Film at the University of Arizona, offers suggestions for revising ideas of presence drawing from recent trends in cognitive neuroscience. Drawing from contemporary theories in this area may help to train actors to "work with, rather than against the innate tendencies of our nervous system" to sort and make meaning through a present moment that is always braided with past and future (148). Belser draws on anecdotes and real classroom experiences to make these ideas legible to a reader who may not be experienced with neuroscience.

Jean O'Hara speaks from her positionality as a genderqueer person who desires her acting students to consider how they perform their genders in everyday life, while also wondering how the theatre can allow for different forms of gender expression in her chapter, "Drag Evolution: Re-Imaging Gender through Theory and Practice." Drawing from her first experiences teaching a course on the politics and history of drag allows her to "interweave queer Indigenous studies, feminist anthropological theory, gender theory, queer theory, and trans theory to examine and interrogate gender, gender roles, and gender performance" (162). O'Hara speaks candidly about the aspects of the class that worked and those areas that need improvement.

Maria Enriquez concludes this section by challenging assumptions about the best methods for casting student actors in order to create a more diverse and equitable educational experience for actors of color. Using a production of *Avenue Q* staged at Penn State Harrisburg empowers her to explore what happens when universities are too reliant on mirroring professional practices in the audition room, and how considering casting from a pedagogical perspective can create a better space for learning as well as a healthier and more inclusive departmental culture. The chapter holds a particular resonance at a time when professional theatres across the United States are coming to understand the biases of their casting systems and how those practices undermine non-white actors.

The final section of this collection, "Communities: Applying Theatre" moves beyond scriptive stage practices to consider the place of performance-based critical theory in devised/ applied theatre and in everyday life. Jen Plants asks readers to consider dramaturgy as a political and social action in "Life First: Interdisciplinary Placemaking for the Theatre." Defining placemaking as "the process of creating quality places that people want to live, work, play, and learn in," (184). Plants invites theatre departments to move away from a professional model that typically relies on filling pre-existing spaces with living bodies and to instead imagine a world in which

dramaturgs can work with their communities and the organizational infra-
structure of a theatre company as they create applied performances.

Beth Murray writes about the process of creating a multi-site applied
theatre project in her chapter, "Growing Applied Theatre: Critical
Humanizing Pedagogies from the Ground Up." She focuses her chapter on
two performance sites where groups of fourth and seventh graders drew
upon pedagogical practices espoused by Paolo Freire and Augusto Boal in
order to explore the relationship between food, clothes and the earth. The
chapter provides a deep dive into the process of creation from the initial con-
ceptualization process, to the development of ideas in the rehearsal room,
and into the performance itself before engaging in a thoughtful assessment
of whether or not the project was able to successfully draw upon critical
pedagogy to teach these students and their parents to think about the environment, citizenship, and the common good.

In "Up Close and Wide Awake: Participation in Anna Deavere Smith's
Social Theatre," Stephanie L. Hodde reflects upon how theatre artists might
stage U.S. culture and politics at this particular moment of Trump-based
crisis and upheaval. Teaching at Virginia Military Institute, Hodde writes of
the institution's desire to develop "citizen-soldiers" before expanding upon
how she uses Anna Deavere Smith's pedagogy of social theatre as a theoretical framework that invites students to give voice to characters with
fluid, empathic intent" (212). The chapter offers ethnographic exercises that
students undertook in the classroom, in addition to suggesting supplemental
readings from Smith and other contemporary American playwrights as a
way of teaching the cadets to become comfortable with their own shifting
identities, as well as those of the individuals that they might encounter in
their future work.

Finally, Susan Russell and Kikora Franklin give advice and insight as
women working within the academy in their chapter, "Tricksters in the
academy: 'Find the Gap, Then Look for the People.'" The chapter takes a
dialogic form as the two scholar-artists envision themselves as both inside of
and outside of the academy, using their positionality to confront the systems
of power that they have encountered over the course of their careers. For
both Russell and Franklin, this way of seeing the world has created moments
of dissonance and discomfort, but it has enabled them to create interdisciplinary collaborations that would have otherwise been impossible within the
constraints of a university department and opened up a space for them to
feel freer in body and spirit. Their autoethnography closes out the book in a
spirit of generosity and welcoming.

In totality, these chapters concentrate on teaching critical performance
theory specifically in theatre and performance studies classrooms. The
readings in this collection offer up revelations about the unconstrained
nature of theory and how it can make students better creative minds in
addition to individuals who learn to interpret and evaluate dominant ideologies that underlie social injustice. The chapters featured illustrate the varied

issues and insights that critical lenses can mine from text and performance. Although *Teaching Critical Performance Theory* provides examples of many critical theories at work, they invite the reader to consider how they might draw upon their own knowledge of critical theory in the classroom, in artistic work, and in their communities.

References

hooks, bell. 1994. *Teaching to Transgress: Education as the Practice of Freedom.* New York: Routledge.
Horkmeier, Max. 1972. *Critical Theory.* New York: Seabury Press.

Part I

Course design

Reimagining the syllabus

1 Doing things with theory
Situated cognition and theatre pedagogy

Jennifer Ewing-Pierce

In *Teaching to Transgress*, bell hooks (1994) describes theory as a liberatory practice, but if and only if we ask that theory to *do* something, to assist in a struggle. "Theory," she writes, "is not inherently healing or revolutionary. It fulfills this function only when we ask that it do so and direct our theorizing toward this end" (61). hooks is also quick to remind us that the hegemon enlists theory in the opposite struggle—the struggle to maintain the status quo and protect hierarchical power structures, particularly in the classroom where autocratic privilege tends to be the reigning model of pedagogy (62). In this chapter, pedagogy enlists the help of cognitive science to reorient the classroom toward greater openness in structure as well as content, for the structures of our classrooms teach more than their content. Specifically, I will look at situated cognition, a field founded by Lucy Suchman (a key figure in cognitive science and not frequently cited in cognitive studies within theatre) and the situative approaches to learning in education Suchman has inspired. Furthermore, I will show that using second-generation cognitive science to inform our pedagogy allows for a metacognitive practice that teaches the theory implicitly, while also achieving learning outcomes for teaching dramatic literature. Finally, throughout, situated cognition is positioned as having inherent links with critical theory, providing a hermeneutic of continuity between critical theory and second-generation cognitive science, rather than the hermeneutic of rupture posited by early forays into cognitive science within theatre studies.

Early cognitive science presented the brain as a machine that processes discrete tokens of information, a paradigm that inspired early computer design. As computer science advanced, and models of artificial intelligence failed to achieve verisimilitude, however, it became clear that the brain was a far more complex system than initially theorized. "Second-generation cognitive science" is a specialist shorthand toward the more complex and embodied models of cognition that are leading today. This revolution in thought within Artificial Intelligence and Philosophy of Mind has a continuing impact on the humanities and literary studies, including theatre studies, where over a decade ago an official movement formed on the idea of a "cognitive turn" in theatre and performance studies (McConachie and Hart 2006).

As literary studies had before it via Varela, Thompson, and Rosch's *The Embodied Mind* (1991), theatre studies attached to the idea of embodied cognition and its overlap with phenomenology. The keyword "embodiment" appealed to theatre studies at an intuitive level, primarily because theatre is experienced as an embodied practice, distinguishing it from printed literature. Furthermore, however, embodiment had been one of the formational concepts of performance studies and continues to inform the field with and without cognitive theory. Before McConachie and Hart's adoption of cognitive theory as an official orientation in the field, performance studies scholars were decentralizing text and centralizing embodiment. As one example among many, Judith Hamera, a scholar whose dance training is constitutive of her scholarly orientation, wrote about form, gender, and culture, and "body building" in the classroom (2002, 122). Specifically, feminist theory within performance studies, most prominently through Jill Dolan, Elin Diamond, and Peggy Phelan, made questions of embodiment central to performativity. So much so that cognitive theorist and robotics artist Simon Penny questioned cognitive studies's failure to make connections to feminist theories of embodiment in his primer on theories of embodiment, computation, and the arts (2017, 209–10). It is an elision all the more baffling in fields claiming a connection to performance studies, which was profoundly shaped by feminist theory in the 1980s and 1990s.

Germane to this collection, one might also question whether cognitive studies, as practiced in theatre studies to date, is "critical theory." If we understand "theory" to be a system of ideas with explanatory power, undoubtedly cognitive theory does the work of "theory," small "t," but it has rarely—if ever—done the work of Critical Theory, writ large, as in the work of the Frankfurt School. In fact, at moments, it seeks to destabilize that work, by asserting the primacy of "science." As McConachie and Hart point out in the preface and introduction of *Performance and Cognition*, many of the articles contained therein aim to prove that the truth claims of critical theory were built on scientifically unstable foundations, demonstrably proved incorrect by cognitive theory. Aiming at Freudian psychoanalysis, Saussurean semiology, and Marxism (among others), McConachie and Hart posit that the "cognitive framework" is a more vital field than critical theory because "the validity of cognitive studies rests on the empirical assumptions and self-correcting procedures of cognitive science" (x). As such, seeking scientific "realism" and a higher truth claim, cognitive science, as adopted within theatre studies, frequently evades the questions that critical theory was originally designed to address: questions of power, privilege, capital, race, class, and gender.

Consider, then, that cognitive theory within theatre and performance studies has mostly neglected the work of Lucy Suchman, one of the founding theorists of situated cognition. An anthropologist of science and technology, Suchman's 1987 text, *Situated Actions: The Problem of Human-Machine Interaction*, employed ethnomethodology to reveal that the human lives in a networked world of dynamic interactions between other bodies and the physical and social world. This human–environment dynamism is remarkably like Maurice Merleau-Ponty's environment and organism dialectic, described in *La structure du comportement,* translated into English in 1983, which inspired the bulk of Varela, Thompson, and Rosch's *The Embodied Mind* published in 1991, making the omission of Suchman curious. Similarly, taking its cue from literary studies, which built its foundation on Varela, Thompson, and Rosch, theatre studies have by and large cathected to the idea of embodied cognition, but it is Suchman's situated cognition that is parent to the child. Situated cognition is the genus, embodied cognition is the species (Robbins and Aydede 2009, 3).

Rhonda Blair and Amy Cook's exceptional collection *Theatre, Performance, and Cognition: Languages, Bodies, and Ecologies* does take on situated cognition, understanding it through 4e cognition. "4e" cognition combines four dominant views in cognition: embodied, enacted, extended, and embedded. All of this is to say that cognition is *situated.* Evelyn Tribble has applied situated cognition to analyze not Shakespeare as an individual man of genius but as part of a complex system that produced him and that he helped to produce (2016). Tribble calls these systems "cognitive ecologies," describing what has fallen into the realm of complexity theory in computer science and has impacted psychology, economics, and sociology. In the same collection, Sarah E. McCarroll focuses on the participation of material environment in situated cognition, literally through material as she looks at what she calls "the historical body map" through clothing. While Suchman's work has gone unexamined, the powerful paradigm shift she enacted is finding its way into the work of theatre studies. Of further note, works such as Tribble's and McCarroll's establish connections to prior work in the field through discourses of feminist materialism.

For this chapter, I assert less the novelty of cognitive theory than establish a hermeneutic of continuity with larger, still ongoing discourses in theatre studies inspired by the Frankfurt School. While certain aspects of embodied cognition have allowed some to theorize that the reality of our embodiment has more power than the social and cultural constructions that condition our use and reception of language, the parent concept of situated cognition has far more in common with the Frankfurt School than difference. Both the Frankfurt School and situated cognition take as a non-negotiable starting point that there is no cognition without culture and no culture without cognition. The Frankfurt School focused on social, political, economic, and societal conditions as a matrix for social change. Situated cognition focuses on the dynamic interactions between social, political, economic, societal, and physical environments as being constitutive of the individual and how the individual acts within systematicity. Therefore, there is a stronger potential for a hermeneutic of continuity with the endeavors of the Frankfurt School than a hermeneutic of rupture. Rather than embodiment coming to mean a hardwired brain that operates at an individual level based on its biology independent of cultural construction, embodied cognition now means that cultural, social, and physical influences network with individual brains. In short, embodied cognition comes to mean the study of complex systems. As we will see, classroom communities are complex communities that benefit from this scientifically grounded continuation of the Frankfurt School project.

A field that *has* adopted situated cognition and used it as a liberatory practice is education. In education, situated cognition has evolved into what some refer to as situated learning; others object to that nomenclature because it implies that some learning is *not* situated, and situated learning scientists believe all learning is situated (Sawyer and Greeno 2009, 348). Instead, adherents refer to situative approaches to learning to acknowledge that learning is always and everywhere situated, that is, conditioned by the social, cultural, and physical environment as much as by any individual hardwiring in the individual learning mind.

At stake is the power of situative approaches to provide a liberatory pedagogy that destabilizes autocratic classroom design. Furthermore, it offers a metacognitive component that performatively teaches the theory of situated cognition. However, it is not surprising to learn, and germane to this discussion, that performance is a fundamental paradigm that situated cognitive scientists study. As Sawyer and Greeno write about studies of musicians and actors, "the interactions of some activity systems, such as jazz or improvisational theatre groups are not decomposable," and provide this as a model of what situativity looks like in a classroom (350).

Individualist versus situative

> That's the difference education as the practice of freedom makes. The bottom-line assumption has to be that everyone in the classroom is able to act responsibly. That has to be the starting point—that we are able to act responsibly together to create a learning environment. All too often we have been trained as professors to assume students are not capable of acting responsibly, that if we don't exert control over them, then there's just going to be mayhem.
>
> (hooks 1994, 152)

Contrasting the situative approach to the individualist approach that typifies most classrooms is helpful to understanding situativity in learning:

Situative learning researchers acknowledge that learning never happens in solitude. Even learning that occurs in an environment where the body is physically "alone," the individual is engaging with socially and culturally produced objects such as computers, books, and other learning materials that were created by others. All learning is networked (Sawyer and Greeno 2009, 364). In summary, deep learning is most effective when students work

Table 1.1 Individualist learning versus situative learning

Individualist	Situative
Continual accumulation of knowledge	Gradual appropriation through guided participation
Knowledge is possessed by the individual mind	Goal-directed toward socially situated activities and practices
Directed toward formal abstract thought	Culturally specific in process and outcomes

collaboratively within a system, trying to solve real-world problems or engaging in purposeful, rich tasks (Table 1.1).

One might ask in a dramatic literature class, what are the tasks that students are attempting to perform? What real-world problem are they trying to solve? In adopting a situative approach to teaching literature, I take two different approaches. One is to treat a potential theatre production of the play as a "problem" that a team of students must solve. The other is to present the sociocultural influences on the literary text as the puzzle. Out of concern for scope, I will focus on the details of the latter approach. The latter approach is more broadly applicable to students of dramatic literature from all majors, as the former approach requires the specialized interest, experience, and knowledge of students who engage in production work.

Key to the work is what hooks has identified as education as the practice of freedom. Letting students control the depth, breadth, and level of discussion, exploration, and experimentation as an organic outgrowth of a community is paramount to the success of the model.

The puzzle of sociocultural production and reception

Walter Benjamin, in "Literary History and the Study of Literature," wrote:

> What is at stake is not to portray literary works in the context of their age, but to represent the age that perceives them—our age—in the age during which they arose. It is this that makes literature the organon of history; and to achieve this, and not to reduce literature to the material of history, is the task of the literary historian.
>
> (2004, 464)

Thinking with Benjamin, I would add that he also defines the task of the teacher of dramatic literature and what that means, in no uncertain terms: the students are the primary perceivers of the texts, not the instructor. To create an environment where this is served well through situative environments that support student research teams is the primary "organon" of dramatic literature.

The goals of situative approaches to learning are inherently sociocultural and are, therefore, also well-suited to sociocultural approaches to literature. A primary goal is to promote social interactions and the appropriation of role-based and task-driven activities in the learning process (Ares and Peercy 2003). To empower students' peer-to-peer social learning, working in student-driven pods that later re-connect as a single class promotes more peer-to-peer interactions over student-instructor interactions. Furthermore, working in pods in social situations is a form of intervention into the isolating features of digital activities. While encouraging the use of digital tools, environments, and media projects, it encourages students to do so in parallel rather than in isolation.

One of the challenges of situativity is that in order for a classroom to function as a situative learning system, it must be modeled, as students usually arrive in classrooms expecting vertical, individualistic models, for example, teacher at the head of a class delivers information that the student must accumulate and then in some way regurgitate to demonstrate mastery. Situative learning works best if students work in three- to four-person pods that each work on a separate play ending in a mini-conference, in which the pods present their work to the class. However, it is crucial to work through one play as a class first, in order to model modes and manners of working. Some students take to this work immediately. Some students require more guidance. Most important, the classroom becomes a lab space. By focusing the majority of their working time during class time, the instructor can observe and guide the process. Solving the "puzzle" of the social, cultural, and political environment in which the plays are produced allows the instructor to model situative learning. Therefore, the critical concept of situated cognition is communicated through the content of the assignment and through the form the assignment takes. The following is a map to a unit that can be done over three to four weeks, depending on the number of students enrolled.

Class 1: form your teams

Form the pods that will work together on the unit. Experiment with a variety of approaches. I have tried three means: team formation through a digital random selection tool, allowing students to form their own pods, and skills-based pods. The first two are self-explanatory. I describe the approach I take to skills-based pods below.

Skills-based pods: each pod needs a researcher, a writer, and a media director, with students doubling for one role in four-person pods. During each phase of the project, each job can take the lead, so there is equal opportunity for leadership. I write a job description for each role as seen in Table 1.2.

The instructor distributes these descriptions in advance. In class, they project or write them on a board, then ask students to perform a self-assessment that matches their strengths to the roles listed. The instructor then asks students to sign up under one of these three roles and then reviews

Table 1.2 Situative learning team roles

Researcher

- Lead team in establishing the critical research questions for the play
- Collect and report on information the pod has determined is important and relevant
- Assign and delegate research tasks to other team members as appropriate
- Maintain a resource bibliography for the project
- Document all work assignments for the team for accountability

---

Writer

- Lead team in identifying all writing tasks in the project
- Edit and proof all media created for the project
- Write and wordsmith copy
- Assign and delegate writing tasks to other teammates as appropriate

---

Media director

- Lead team in establishing what media (sound files, video, slides, written handouts, live performance) will be used
- Create a "look" for all materials, collaborating with team members
- Produce all media for the project
- Assign and delegate media-related tasks to other teammates as appropriate

---

to see how evenly distributed the students are among the three tasks. (If there is a lack under one job, the instructor may ask students if someone has overlapping skills and if they might consider switching.) Then, the class forms the pods based on the skills, placing one or two students into each pod from each role. Best practices dictate that the pods not exceed four or five. It is ideal to keep them to three or four.

At the end of the class, the instructor assigns a play to each pod (or lets the students choose their play from a list by discussing among themselves) and assigns puzzles the students are to examine in their pods concerning the play. Here is an example of a puzzle list I have created for students to solve and present on.

Project Puzzle List:

- *What is the summary of the action in the play? Who are the major characters? What time period and what geographic setting is involved in the play? Do you think the characters and the time and setting are close to or contrasting to the audience likely to have seen the play? What would be familiar? What would be foreign?
- Who is the playwright? What is their ethnic, national, and gender identity? What are their other plays? Are there common themes in their other plays? Was this play created early or late in their career?

- Where was the play first performed? What audiences may have attended? Was it a professional theatre? Regional theatre? Did it win any awards?
- What was the critical reaction to the play? Are there representative reviews that are informative? What controversies surrounded the play? What sociopolitical issues does the play address? If it is an older play, what sociopolitical conditions make the play still relevant? Does the play have anything important to say about ethnicity, class, ability, or gender? Does the play exhibit any racist, classist, ableist, sexist, or anti-LGTBQ+ qualities?
- Who were the artists involved with notable productions of this play? Were there any innovations or creative uses of design involved in key productions that are worth noting?
- Are there any difficulties or barriers to understanding this play that may need an explanation? For example, was it set during a particular war that may or may not be a familiar political situation to the class? Are there cultural circumstances that may need an explanation? Is there language that is difficult or is it a multilingual play?
- Can your pod identify and solve any additional puzzles about this play not named here?
    * This question MUST be included in every presentation and cannot be omitted.

    Students are encouraged to volunteer personal responses grounded in their own biographical experiences and positions and include them in the research of the play.

Class 2: establish workflow

By this class, the pods are firmly established, and roles are assigned. Now the students establish workflow for the project. This is a crucial step for them in forming their small-group community; it establishes trust about equal distribution of labor and general team spirit. This is also the time where the instructor should begin doing informal assessments, not for grading but for guidance. Do some groups need help in mediating and negotiating? Do some groups have interaction problems? I try to be aloof but present, ready to step in, but also allowing difficult situations to work themselves out.

Class 2 objectives:

- Establish the tasks to be accomplished
- Establish who is accountable for which tasks and who will be doing what during which working session
- Construct a timeline backward from the deliverable date to make sure the scope of your project is manageable

- Establish who is responsible for what during the presentation. Will you divide it up? Or will one person present? Does someone need to "run tech" during your presentation?

This handout can be posted in a Learning Management System (LMS), printed and distributed, or projected onto a smartboard:

- The mini-conference will be held in class on November 11. All materials must be submitted to the LMS by this date. We will assign a time-slot for presentations at random.
- You will be given three full class periods to work with your teams.
- Keep in mind the constraints of time in determining the scope of your project. Which puzzles can you solve? Can you do all of them? Or do you want to focus more in-depth on one aspect of the play's puzzle?
- Record your workflow plan and timeline; present it to the instructor.
- Your final presentation should be fifteen to twenty minutes long.

Classes 3, 4, and 5

Classes 3, 4, and 5 are in-class working sessions where students work according to the plan they laid out in the workflow session. The professor is available for guidance only.

Class 6 (and 7, if needed)

Mini-conference presentations and assessments.

The journal: metacognitive reflection

Learning researchers Rogers Hall and Andee Rubin discovered three modes of learning that need to work in concert to maximize gradual appropriation of task-specific skills in situative learning environments: private activity, local activity, and public activity (Figure 1.1).

These three levels strike a balance between group learning and individual learning. A journal is a component of the unit and goes into the final assessment. The student is asked to keep a journal online in the LMS that is private between only the student and the instructor. The student is asked to make a 250- to 500-word journal entry after each work session during the unit, reflecting on how they think the assignment is going and what they are learning about the play. Students should be instructed to write about interpersonal conflicts that they are finding unresolvable or any other mitigating circumstances they think might impact their performance on the task. In some cases, when the entries were of poor quality, I have offered prompts. The purpose of the journal is to encourage metacognition, or critical evaluation of one's own competencies, as well as to reinforce skill and knowledge

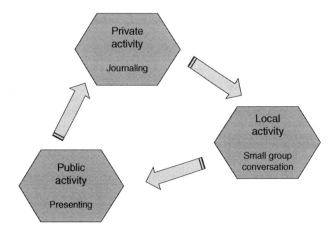

Figure 1.1 Illustration, private/local/public activity flow.

appropriation through critical self-reflection. It also serves as a teacher-student communication tool that allows the instructor to step in and provide guidance and coaching on issues with which the student is struggling. Some examples of metacognitive prompts I have used include:

- What are some strategies and skills you are using to complete this assignment effectively and on time?
- Am I doing an effective job at communicating with others and welcoming their points of view?
- Is there an example of a time where you saw a play differently than another member of your pod?
- Did you find out anything about the play, the playwright, or its context that surprised you?
- Are there aspects of this work that you find unsatisfactory or frustrating? Why or why not? Do any aspects of the pod conversation feel exclusionary? To you? To others?

I also ask the students to make a final entry on the structure of the classroom environment. In asking them to reflect on the situated and socialized nature of the work in the classroom, I am implicitly teaching the concept of "situated cognition" and the idea of dramatic literature being a social and culturally influenced practice.

Notes on assessment

In addition to the journal assignment, I offer each of the students the opportunity to self-assess and to challenge my rubric assessment if it differs from theirs. Another option is allowing peer, rubric-based assessment and averaging the numbers for the final grade. Table 1.3 is an example of a rubric to employ for situated learning assignments like these.

The journal will sometimes express mitigating circumstances that might allow the instructor to change the rubric-based grade. This can also allay student anxieties about being graded on other people's work. The journal is best graded pass/fail based on the length of the entries. Either they are done and of appropriate length or they are not.

Although the soft skills of social interaction, group participation, and media design can seem to bring us far afield of dramatic literature, the situative approach is the concrete consequence of adhering to second-generation cognitive science theoretical orientations about the nature of embodied consciousness. It is the social interactivity of the classroom as a cultural system that teaches more than the content of the course itself. What is understated in presenting these materials in print is the highly specific and culturally responsive results achieved through using these socially driven models of learning in the classroom. Recall the italicized statement in the Puzzles handout: *students are encouraged to volunteer personal responses grounded in their own biographical experiences and positions and include them in the research of the play.*

Encouraging students to bring their own experiences to bear on the text can produce some of the most meaningful exchanges in the pods and the ones most likely to reappear in the private activity journal.

As a final note, perhaps the most challenging aspect of this model is releasing the professorial role of instructor-as-expert. The instructor's expertise is best employed through the pod-driven process and through the interactions at the mini-conference through reciprocal teaching strategies: questioning, summarizing, clarifying, and asking students to predict (Wertsch 1998). The natural outflow of adopting these strategies in interacting with student work is that students begin to question, summarize, clarify, and predict based on their peers' work.

Discussion: pedagogy that is grounded in critical theory

The definitive inclusion of body, material artifacts, sociocultural conditions and practices, and other body-minds in our understanding of mental processes has concrete implications for pedagogy in theatre studies and humanities study in general. The introduction of situated cognition, the parent concept to embodied cognition, has created a revolution within learning theory best understood through two competing paradigms in learning "acquisition" and "understanding in practice." Acquisition relies on the idea that mental processes are manipulating discrete tokens of information, separate from the body and the world. It imagines learning as a disjunctive cognitive function distinct from performing tasks. When we specialize in something such as "teaching dramatic literature," we imagine that we are leading students to

Table 1.3 Situative learning assessment rubric

Component	3 (Sophisticated)	2 (Established)	1 (Emerging)
Teamwork	Student worked well within the team within a specific framework. Student valued others' input and exhibited mutual respect.	Student overcame occasional breakdowns in communication to establish strong work flow. Student was mostly respectful to others.	Student frequently contributed to breakdowns in communication and interrupted workflow. Student exhibited sub-optimal communication skills.
Contribution	Student contributed above and beyond expectations, completed all assigned tasks and helped others to achieve their best.	Student met expectations on all tasks assigned.	Student didn't always meet pod expectations or complete tasks on time. Student didn't make up for work missed during absences.
Subject knowledge	Student's final project exhibited strong subject knowledge in broad strokes and in detail.	Student exhibited strong general knowledge of the subject matter	Student exhibited some subject knowledge but missed some basic information.
Media collateral	Student used a wide variety of media genres to communicate information.	Student used one or two varieties of media to communicate information.	Student only used one medium to communicate information.
Composition	Student's materials were cohesive, effective and employed a strong sense of design.	Student's materials were neat and organized and delivered the information effectively.	Student's materials sometimes delivered information effectively but were sometimes disordered and poorly executed.
Sources	Student's project employs a wide variety of valid sources, well documented.	Student's project employs an adequate variety of valid sources.	Student doesn't use enough valid sources or document them.

acquire knowledge of the canon. It treats literature as objects to be acquired or possessed or, in a related concept, as something the instructors *transmit* (Lave 1997, 19).

But, as Lave points out, Karl Marx, Pierre Bourdieu, and Anthony Giddens, among others, "take as crucial the integral nature of relations between persons acting (including thinking and learning) and the social world, and between the form and content of learning-in-practice" (Lave 1997, 20), further demonstrating the clear connection between critical theory and cognitive science's projects. The alternative paradigm, that of "understanding in practice," proposes "cognitive apprenticeship" as a more satisfactory model. Although thinking of an apprenticeship at a theatre—a student working among people who do their job exceedingly well, as a form of learning—is helpful, it is not exactly what "apprenticeship" means in curricular design. It is a concept, as Lave put it, "to think with." Thinking with a cognitive apprenticeship in designing curricula means *situating* our students in socialized situations that have task-specific orientations. As mentioned earlier, modeling these pods is highly dependent on doing a project with the students first. Instead of preparing a lecture and bringing it to class, the instructor can prepare the lecture in real-time *with* the students, just as they will be asked to do in their pods later. Lave joins social anthropologist James V. Wertsch and several others in pointing out the relationship of these learning theories (Lave 1997, 20).

Perhaps the most promising aspect of situated learning theory is its cultural specificity. Take, for example, Lave and Hass's ethnographic study of a bilingual classroom. Specifically, the bilingual students used their native language to communicate with each other to circumvent the inadequacies and inefficiencies of the teacher's proposed methods of problem-solving. The students not only developed efficient problem-solving strategies, humorously, they also developed strategies for producing work that gave the illusion of having been done according to the teacher's strategies (Kirshner and Whitson 1997). Lave and Hass's ethnography illustrates what social anthropologist Wertsch has connected to Mikhail Bahktin's work on alterity that within situated discourses, a dialogic space opens up to provide more relevance to alterity in learning environments. When knowledge is treated as a static token that needs to be transmitted, alterity presents as a distraction or tangent to the classroom process. The situative approach to classroom experience design, as well as curricular design, is a powerful tool in building culturally responsive, equitable, and inclusive classrooms.

In conclusion, situated cognition offers another tool within critical theory that contributes to the design of performative classroom spaces—performative in the sense of calling into being a classroom that bears the implicit hallmarks of critical theory: applying humanities and social science to the reflective, metacognitive evaluation of society and culture. The structure of the situative classroom itself is a reflective assessment of culture and society; in particular, it performs a critique of the typical classroom.

Jürgen Habermas is widely understood to be the inheritor of the Frankfurt School tradition. His work has employed a strong focus on embodiment, cognition, and speech and has specifically made a call for "reconstructive sciences" that will bring critical theory into the realm of the social sciences (1984, 10), which have arguably embraced situated cognition more than any other interdisciplinary field. Rather than disjuncture, situated cognition and its offshoot embodied cognition provide rich potentials in carrying on the tradition of the Frankfurt School. This fulfills hooks's provocation to use theory that *does* things for our students, providing not only justification for the unfettered study of situated cognition in theatre pedagogy, but for the continued dialogue between these new areas of discourse and the Frankfurt School, continuing the work of critical theory implicitly and explicitly in the theatre classroom, in both content and form.

References

Ares, Nancy M., and Megan M. Peercy. 2003. "Constructing Literacy: How Goals, Activity Systems, and Text Shape Classroom Practice." *Journal of Literacy Research* 35 (1): 633–62. https://doi.org/10.1207/s15548430jlr3501_4.

Benjamin, Walter. Rodney Livingstone, Michael William Jennings, Howard Eiland, and Gary Smith, eds. 2004. *Walter Benjamin: Selected Writings Volume 2.* Cambridge, MA: Harvard University Press.

Blair, Rhonda, and Amy Cook, eds. 2016. *Theatre, Performance and Cognition: Languages, Bodies and Ecologies.* London: Bloomsbury Methuen Drama.

Habermas, Jurgen. 1984. *The Theory of Communicative Action, Vol. I: Reason and the Rationalization of Society.* Cambridge, UK: Polity Press.

Hall, Rogers and Andee Rubin. 1998. "There's Five Little Notches in Here: Dilemmas in Teaching and Learning the Conventional Structure of Rate." In *Thinking Practices in Mathematics and Science Learning.* New York: Routledge.

Hamera, Judith. 2002. "Performance Studies, Pedagogy, and Bodies in/as the Classroom." In *Teaching Performance Studies*, edited by Nathan Stucky and Cynthia Wimmer, 121–30. Carbondale: Southern Illinois University Press.

hooks, bell. 1994. *Teaching to Transgress: Education as the Practice of Freedom.* New York: Routledge.

Kirshner, David, and James Anthony Whitson, eds. 1997. *Situated Cognition: Social, Semiotic, and Psychological Perspectives.* Mahwah, NJ: Lawrence Erlbaum.

McCaroll, Sarah E. 2016. "The Historical Body Map: Cultural Pressures on Embodied Cognition." In *Theatre, Performance and Cognition: Languages, Bodies and Ecologies*, edited by Rhonda Blair and Amy Cook, 141–58. London: Bloomsbury.

McConachie, Bruce A., and F. Elizabeth Hart, eds. 2006. *Performance and Cognition: Theatre Studies and the Cognitive Turn.* London: Routledge.

Merleau-Ponty, Maurice. 1983. *The Structure of Behavior.* Pittsburgh: Duquesne University.

Penny, Simon. 2017. *Making Sense: Cognition, Computing, Art, and Embodiment.* Cambridge, MA: MIT Press.

Robbins, Philip, and Murat Aydede, eds. 2009. *The Cambridge Handbook of Situated Cognition.* Cambridge: Cambridge University Press.

Sawyer, R. Keith, and James G. Greeno. 2009. "Situativity and Learning." In *The Cambridge Handbook of Situated Cognition*, edited by Philip Robbins and Murat Aydede. Cambridge: Cambridge University Press.

Suchman, Lucille Alice. 1987. *Plans and Situated Actions: The Problem of Human-Machine Communication*. Cambridge: Cambridge University Press.

Tribble, Evelyn B. 2016. "Distributed Cognition, Mindful Bodies, and the Arts of Acting." In *Theatre, Performance and Cognition: Languages, Bodies and Ecologies*, edited by Rhonda Blair and Amy Cook, 133–39. London: Bloomsbury.

Varela, Francisco J., Evan Thompson, and Eleanor Rosch. 1991. *The Embodied Mind: Cognitive Science and Human Experience*. Cambridge, MA: MIT Press.

Wertsch, James V. 1998. *Mind as Action*. New York: Oxford University Press.

2   Feminist musical theatre pedagogy

Emma Watkins and Stacy Wolf

Overture: revisiting *Oklahoma!*

A classroom of students sits in the dark with pencils poised, waiting patiently for the projector to warm up. Finally, with a hum, the screen is flooded with a blue sky, framed by the wispy branches of willow trees. A demurely dressed Ado Annie fixes her eyes on the ground as she speak-sings, "I'm just a girl who cain't say 'No,' / I'm in a terrible fix! / I always say 'Come on, let's go,' / Just when I oughta say 'Nix!' "[1] Gloria Grahame's performance in the 1955 film version of *Oklahoma!* is bashful and confused, struggling to reconcile her romantic impulses with society's expectations of women. The students giggle with disbelief at this ludicrous performance of femininity.

The second clip they watch comes from the Tony Awards performance of the 2019 Broadway revival of *Oklahoma!*[2] Ali Stroker, who made history as the first wheelchair user to win a Tony, belts out the opening lyrics of "I Cain't Say No" with confidence and sauciness—clearly, this is an Ado Annie who relishes the sound of her own voice (Salam 2019). After a leisurely beginning, the music accelerates under Stroker's powerful voice as she dances across the stage, flirting with audience members as she goes.

When the professor pauses the video mid-performance, an audible sigh of disappointment rises up from the captivated class.

"I know!" she says, "It's terrible to stop it! But let's talk about it. What did you see? What struck you?"

"Well, to start off with, the orchestra sounds completely different in the 2019 clip," one student, a composer and classical music conductor, answers. "And I just Googled it, and it looks like they completely re-orchestrated the score for this revival. They took twenty-eight musicians down to a seven-person band!" (Culwell-Block 2019).

"And Stroker's performance—obviously, it's a completely different interpretation of the song," an actor and computer science major chimes in. "She's costumed differently, in jeans and a tank top, and the way she's singing it is new and sort of subversive. It feels like this Ado Annie doesn't believe the words she's saying."

"Why do you think the creative team chose to tell the story that way in 2019?" the professor prompts. "And why should anyone want to see a revival of *Oklahoma!* here and now?"

Using the contrasting videos as a jumping-off point, the class dives into a close analysis of both performances, examining the song structurally and lyrically, while paying close attention to each actor's performance of femininity. After an hour or so of discussion, the class takes a quick break. As the students stretch their legs, the conversation continues in the hallway. Two directors debrief as they meander toward the vending machine: "Had you heard *Oklahoma!* before class today?" one asks. "Yeah! I memorized it when I was, like, five," the other laughs. "My older sister was in it when she was in high school, and I idolized her. When I listened to it again when I was in high school, I kind of wrote it off because of the way it deals with gender and race. But maybe this revival addresses some of those issues."

Historical perspective, contemporary reverberations

In some theatre and musical theatre curriculums, a historical perspective is overlooked and undervalued, sidelined in favor of practical course-work in acting, dance, or vocal technique. But as this classroom discussion shows, studying musical theatre history from a feminist perspective can be an essential tool for inspiring and informing a rising generation of theatre-makers, producers, performers, and academics. Prepared with new methods and vital historical context, these students are enabled, encouraged, and emboldened to approach their own theatrical work in a way that is simultaneously respectful and critical. They become informed fans of musical theatre and its most thoughtful critics. As both the consumers and the creators of future musical theatre work, these students become self-reflexively conscious of how the genre performs gender, race, and other embodiments.

The contemporary moment is an exciting and historic one for musical theatre, as more stories featuring and created by women and people of color are being told on Broadway stages. In 2016, *Waitress* made history as the first musical on Broadway with an all-female core creative team (Cox and Cox 2015). Two years later, Broadway's first all-female design team was announced. (Rickwald 2018). In an article titled "Who Calls the Shots on Broadway? She Does," the *New York Times* celebrated the female producers leading some of the 2019 season's most prominent musicals (Paulson 2019). Of course, there is still a long way to go before the Great White Way reflects the gender and racial diversity of the city surrounding it. A study by the Asian American Performers Action Coalition, for example, found that 95 percent of all plays and musicals in Broadway's 2016–2017 season were written by Caucasian playwrights, while 89 percent of playwrights produced on Broadway were male ("Ethnic Representation on New York City Stages" 2017, 3). But although there is a significant amount of work still to be done, problems of inequity and representation are now being voiced and discussed on a range of platforms—from online chat rooms to Broadway's biggest stages. When Rachel Chavkin won the 2019 Tony Award for Best Director of a Musical, she used her acceptance speech to champion diversity. "There are so many women who are ready to go. There are so many artists of color who are ready to go," Chavkin said in her speech.

> We need to see that racial diversity and gender diversity reflected in our critical establishment, too. This is not a pipeline issue. It is a failure of imagination by a field whose job is to imagine the way the world could be.
>
> (Chavkin 2019)

As the movement toward inclusivity and intersectionality gains momentum on Broadway stages, undergraduate theatre programs have an opportunity and an obligation to study, and indeed, to model a more diverse future for musical theatre. A feminist perspective provides an essential lens through which to study one of America's most popular artistic forms, with an eye toward how gender, race, sexuality, and class have been scripted and performed throughout history. In this curriculum, undergraduates use their knowledge of what musical theatre has been in order to imagine what it could be. Then, they are enabled to catalyze that change within and beyond the classroom—from their local high schools to New York stages.

This essay offers some thoughts on the teaching of the musical theatre canon through a feminist lens. In co-writing this piece, we have considered this pedagogical approach from the perspectives of both teacher and student. I (Emma) first met my mentor Stacy Wolf when I enrolled in her musical history course during my first year of college. Although I was already a long-time musical theatre fan and performer, I had never analyzed a musical in a classroom setting. Stacy's class enabled me to apply a critical and creative approach to one of my favorite art forms, a practice that I have carried forward into my work as both a student and a playwright. Since that first class, we have collaborated in the classroom and in a scholarly context. By sharing the perspectives of two generations of feminists and musical theatre scholars, we hope to demonstrate how musicals provide an invaluable medium through which to analyze our history and imagine our future.

Musical theatre at the undergraduate level

Arguably, the popularity and prevalence of musical theatre in American culture make it one of the most accessible modes of theatre available for study. Despite this, college and university drama curriculums have long deemed musical theatre a trivial or guilty pleasure, too popular and commercial for "serious" academic study, never to be listed on a syllabus alongside the works of Shakespeare or Chekhov or Arthur Miller. Only since the early 2000s has a significant body of critical musical theatre scholarship emerged, signaling and supporting academic engagement with musicals, both as texts (librettos and scores) and as performances. The extensive scholarship dedicated to the work of composer and lyricist Stephen Sondheim is in itself enough to warrant several university-level courses. However, many musical theatre scholars are broadening their scope beyond the rarified niche of Sondheim studies. In *The American Musical and the Formation of National Identity*, which was among the first serious academic studies of musicals (and the first of two volumes by the author), Raymond Knapp explores the musical as a distinctly American art form, "answering to specifically American demands and shaping American experiences more directly than arts imported from Europe could ever have managed to do" (Knapp 2005, 4). Bud Coleman and Judith Sebesta's essay collection, *Women in American Musical Theater*, provides an expansive perspective on the contributions of female musical theatre creators throughout history (Coleman and Sebesta 2008). In the *Oxford Handbook of the American Musical* and the *Routledge Companion to the Contemporary Musical*, as well as a number of other anthologies, scholars examine the whole musical theatre canon through a range of academic lenses, exploring dynamics of gender, politics, race, and class, alongside questions of historiography, performance, and reception (Knapp, Morris, and Wolf 2011; Sternfeld and Wollman 2019). As the scholarly engagement expands and diversifies, so do potential topics of conversation in musical theatre history classrooms. As Scott McMillin writes in his detailed analysis of musical theatre's conventions and forms, *The Musical as Drama*, the question is not

> if the musical is up to the standards of the university but if the standards of the university are up to dealing with the musical. Can we bring our ways of academic thinking … [and] use our methods of analysis— historical, musical, literary, philosophical— and still get this form of popular entertainment right?
>
> (McMillin 2014, xi)

A feminist lens is a useful tool in the study of this popular and collaborative art form, which encourages a rigorous approach, blending scholarship and practical knowledge with the embodied ethnographic observations of the students in the class.

Entr'acte: a (re)visitation

In 2007, I (Stacy) published "In Defense of Pleasure: Musical Theatre History in the Liberal Arts [A Manifesto]," in which I argued for the importance of including musicals in the study of drama and theatre.³ I suggested that professors need not be experts in all of the fields of musical theatre's component parts—theatre, music, dance, design—to teach musicals to undergraduates. Following David Savran's "Towards a Historiography of the Popular," which launches my article, I asserted that musical theatre is the perfect performance genre through which to study US history, politics, and culture (Savran 2004). At the time, I had just started teaching courses that embedded musicals in their social context, and I was, as I admit early in the essay, surprised that my students did not see musical theatre as an unworthy topic for academic study.

In the more than twelve years since I wrote that article, that sense— that it's entirely appropriate for musical theatre to be studied in college— has grown stronger. The cultural and aesthetic hierarchies, which students refused and which baffled me when I wrote that article, continue to be irrelevant for students, but I'm not surprised anymore. Across the country, musical theatre history, including a critical approach that goes beyond facts and famous people, is integrated into many (although not all) theatre programs' curriculums. More courses include musicals in "regular" dramatic literature and theatre history courses, which is good. But for the most part, musicals are relegated to their own courses (not unlike other genre-oriented curriculums).

More than that, interest and involvement in musical theatre exploded after Disney's *High School Musical*, *Glee*, "talent" competitive reality TV shows, film musicals of the 2010s, and Broadway musicals like *Hamilton*, *Dear Evan Hansen*, and *Mean Girls*, to name a few. Also, access to bootlegs and clips of musicals—professional and amateur—means that more students arrive at college with significant musical theatre experience and knowledge. Typically, though, they tend to be less equipped to engage in analysis and critique, since most high schools and community theatres must focus their energy on just getting the show up.

From the start, my work was (and is) feminist, and every class discussion of every musical included analyses of gender and race, but I didn't begin to teach classes explicitly focused on representations of gender and sexuality until 2010 or so, when I was nearly finished writing *Changed for Good*.⁴ By then, "feminism" was no longer the "f" word, as it had been in the earlier 2000s, and my students (of all genders) arrived in my classroom with strong feminist sensibilities and exceedingly sharp analytical skills developed in their daily lives as media consumers. The project, then was to prod them to marry their feminist critiques with their passionate engagement with musicals. Perhaps because they derived such pleasure from performing in, working backstage on, or seeing musicals, they might have needed "permission—or legitimation from a professor?—to embrace the contradictions that a feminist critique of musical theatre necessitates.

When I wrote the article, I was more concerned with acknowledging and respecting students' love for musicals and taking musicals seriously. At this juncture, I feel the need for every encounter to be explicitly feminist and anti-racist, for every examination of every musical to ask what ideological work it does, why it matters politically, and so on. In terms of the inclusion/foundation/perspective of gender, musical theatre was and is fundamentally built on gender and gender distinctions. As I argue in *Changed for Good*, gender is as elemental to musical theatre as music and lyrics, text, and choreography. We really can't talk about musicals without talking about gender.

From both of our perspectives, we also need to talk about gender because many students of musical theatre identify as women or as non-binary, and musicals are a source of pleasure and power for them. Many roles in musicals are retrograde in terms of both gender and race. Musical theatre remains fairly rigidly heteronormative, but there are some glimmers of difference, in, for example, *Wicked*'s queer couple; *Kinky Boots*; gay and lesbian characters in *Rent* and *Spring Awakening*. We need to develop critical and creative tools to navigate, resist, and revise this repertoire, which includes a more expansive, nuanced, and non-binary view of gender and an approach that moves between critical and creative, that fosters new ideas, while acknowledging the constraints of licensing.

A feminist approach enacted

When preparing my syllabus for this musical theatre history class, I (Stacy) chose to spend an entire seminar session on *Oklahoma!* because I wanted to explore the musical's pivotal role in propelling what some label the "Golden Age of the Broadway Musical." But before exploring the ways in which *Oklahoma!* broke artistic ground, I first needed to situate the show in musical theatre history. *Oklahoma!* opened on Broadway in 1943 as the first collaboration between Richard Rodgers, then the successful composer who had already written twenty-eight musicals with Lorenz Hart, including *Pal Joey* (1940) and *The Boys from Syracuse* (1938), and Oscar Hammerstein II, son of an impresario and lyricist for the groundbreaking *Show Boat* (1929), with music by Jerome Kern. *Oklahoma!* effectively launched the team that would go on to define the American musical through the Cold War and beyond with *Carousel, South Pacific, The King and I*, and *The Sound of Music* (Green 2019).

According to standard musical theatre histories, *Oklahoma!* broke with a number of conventions of this form of entertainment that still, in 1943, displayed its roots in vaudeville and minstrelsy. By ignoring certain typical performance practices of musicals in the early 1940s, *Oklahoma!* installed new ones that remain part of the "rule book" for musicals to this day. Lingering on *Oklahoma!* would allow students to note, foreground, and analyze those conventions.

Archival material, including production photos from 1943 and later revivals, the 1955 film, and clips from several revivals over the years, help students to explore embodiments of femininity since the 1940s. Ado Annie, the musical's comic female lead, is desirous and unapologetically sexual, the potential threat of her aggressive pursuit of men typically undercut by what might be seen as her ditzy, silly personality. But recent performances, especially Stroker's remarkable, joyously lustful rendition of the song in *Oklahoma!*'s 2019 revival, convey a contemporary, feminist approval of female desire and agency.

The occasion of this revival, which featured not only Stroker's award-winning performance but equally strong and vibrant performances by Rebecca Naomi Jones as Laurey and Mary Testa as Aunt Eller, opened a conversation about revivals and how classic musicals can and should speak to contemporary audiences. Although auteur director Daniel Fish changed not one word of the script (he did get permission from the Rodgers and Hammerstein Organization to revise the score for a country western band), his concept, casting, and direction, in collaboration with designers and the actors created a production that felt entirely of our time. As Sarah Larson wrote in her *New Yorker* review, when *Oklahoma!* made its debut in 1943,

> it brought joy and a sense of American identity to the citizens of an anxious nation at war. Daniel Fish's vivid, stripped-down revival […] similarly offers audiences a vision of themselves. Seventy-five years ago, we were at war with foreign powers; now the enemy is within.
>
> (Larson 2018)

Oklahoma! is at once old and new, groundbreaking and conventional, traditional and radical—an invaluable touchstone with which to begin a class on the history of musical theatre.

Following their snack break, the class reassembles under the humming projector. At the front of the room, a small team of students has arrived early. While one opens up a PowerPoint, another distributes a printed handout: the sheet music for *Oklahoma!*'s opening number, "Oh, What A Beautiful Morning." This randomly selected group, made up of first years and seniors alike, has been designated the leaders of the afternoon's continued discussion about the classic Rodgers and Hammerstein musical.

As anyone who has set foot backstage knows, the creation of a musical takes a small army, including (but not limited to) the show's writers, composers, producers, designers, production crew members, stage managers, directors, and performers. Because collaboration is at the heart of every musical, the study of musical theatre is best served by a classroom dynamic that encourages every voice and experience in the room. A feminist approach informs both the practice and the content of a musical theatre history course, creating a classroom experience built upon dialogue, engagement, and equity. Empowering all students to prepare and lead discussions based on their interests is just one way in which a classroom can model the inclusivity it hopes to inspire. This is especially vital in a liberal arts environment, in which students enter the room with a wide range of interests and skills, ranging from history to economics to environmental studies. These developing areas of expertise and diverse perspectives can be applied to the study of musicals, resulting in a more wide-reaching classroom discussion than could ever be facilitated by a single professor—regardless of their degree of expertise.

"There's a bright, golden haze on the meadow, / There's a bright golden haze on the meadow," the baritone voice of the cowboy Curly lilts from the classroom sound system. As the cast album recording of "Oh, What A Beautiful Morning" plays, the class pours over their sheet music handouts. As noted earlier, *Oklahoma!* made several groundbreaking innovations in terms of aesthetic and form. For example, the opening number of a musical is typically a rousing song featuring the entire ensemble, which helps the audience to get situated in the world of the musical (Wolf 2011, 17). But as the class listens to the *Oklahoma!* score, it becomes clear that "Oh, What A Beautiful Morning" defies many of the conventions of a traditional opening number. By reading along with the sheet music, the class discovers that Curly's first lyrics are sung a cappella and from offstage. With just four measures to go before the song's recognizable chorus, the stage directions reveal that Curly finally enters the stage.

As the recording ends, the discussion leaders transition seamlessly into their carefully constructed talking points. They prompt their classmates to analyze the different elements that work together to create the performance—including the show's script, lyrics, acting, characterization, and its blocking and choreography (or lack thereof).

"Imagine—you're sitting in a theatre in 1943," a discussion leader, a biologist and singer begins. "And you hear that voice singing from offstage. The only person you see onstage is the actress playing Aunt Eller, churning butter. But what things do you know about the identity of Curly, the person who's singing?"

"Well. He's probably male," one student offers.

"He's a big guy, with a voice like that," another chimes in. "And he's singing about wide open fields of corn and cattle—it's kind of the epitome of the American West."

"Great," the discussion leader looks excitedly to her peers. "Now we're going to do a little performance for you, inspired by a revival of *Oklahoma!* that I saw at the Oregon Shakespeare Festival."

With that, she exits the room. Her fellow discussion leaders set up a semblance of a butter churn, using an old stool.

"I'm Aunt Eller," one says, sitting down behind the prop churn. Suddenly caught out, the final discussion leader gets down on all fours, announcing, "And I'm a cow!"

As the newly appointed "Aunt Eller" begins churning, a beautiful soprano voice rings out from outside the door, singing, "There's a bright, golden haze on the meadow, / There's a bright, golden haze on the meadow."

A miniature performance of "Oh, What A Beautiful Morning" unfolds in front of the class as the discussion leader, now acting the part of a female cowboy, swaggers into the room. She surveys her fields of corn and cattle. When the song comes to an end, the actor turns to address her classmates.

"The production that I saw at the Oregon Shakespeare Festival used cross-gender casting. Laurey and Curly were both played by women. And Ado Annie became Ado Andy," she says. "So … based on what you just saw, how does a voice—a solo, offstage voice—signify a character's gender and race? What happens when you upset the expected staging of a song?"

With this, the discussion turns to non-traditional casting, and the importance of including non-gender conforming actors in musical theatre. By the time class has come to a close, the students have gleaned not only a deeper appreciation for *Oklahoma!* as a musical, but also a much more profound understanding of how the show has performed gender and other embodiments throughout its countless performances.

Outmarch: beyond the classroom

Even as students make their way out of the classroom, the day's lessons continue to resonate.

One student plans his final project for the class, inspired by the clip from the radical revival of *Oklahoma!*. As a software engineer, he hopes to create a website to benefit his high school theatre program and others like it. He said, "every show I did in high school tried to mimic the Broadway production. We studied everything we could find about the professional performance, and we took it as law. But what I'm realizing is that Broadway isn't always right. And even at the high school level, we can engage with musicals in a way that is responsible and informed."

A director leaves the classroom with ideas that she will carry into the upcoming rehearsals for a musical she's developing: "It's so important for everyone to feel like they have a voice. I want to run my rehearsal room more like this classroom."

Inspired by the ways revivals adapt and revise classic material, I (Emma) began to think of musical theatre as a medium through which to rewrite familiar stories from previously unheard perspectives. I returned to snippets of Welsh mythology that my father had shared with me as childhood bedtime stories. Eager to revitalize the outspoken but marginalized female characters in these tales, I wrote a new play with music expanding upon one character's voice and experience. Her story became a narrative lens through which to explore contemporary conversations surrounding identity, feminism, and environmentalism.

Like many of my peers, I have gained invaluable perspective and tools in my study of the history of musical theatre, which have influenced both my creative and critical work. With this skill set, we are not only more able to critically engage with the theatre that we experience, but we are better equipped to make new work, and to aid our friends in their creative processes as collaborators and dramaturgs.

After this lively and engaging class on *Oklahoma!*, I (Stacy) am nonetheless reminded that while a feminist perspective can fuel class discussion, it should also be center of mind when I select the shows and artists that we study in my musical theatre history courses. My syllabi are often filled with history's most commercially successful or critically acclaimed shows, but I acknowledge that such courses perpetuate a canon dominated by the work of white male creatives. I now aim to balance canonical shows with musicals created by women and people of color, both to honor their work and to legitimize their shows within the popular and critically studied canon. Teaching a musical encourages students to read its libretto, listen to its cast albums, and maybe buy a ticket to a production—creating a new canon of work by underrepresented communities whose contributions to the form might otherwise go overlooked. What's more, student artists who don't see themselves reflected in the predominantly white male canon of musical theatre creatives find inspiration and solidarity from the role models they encounter through coursework. Representation in academic environments is a vital means by which to shift the demographic of those who feel entitled to create new musical theatre.

As a commercially driven art form, Broadway's musical theatre is beholden to marketing and tourism industries, as well as historically entrenched and institutionalized systems of casting and producing that slow down movement towards diversity and inclusivity. Thus, while these changes are happening in New York, they are not happening quickly enough. In order to present a more expansive and inclusive understanding of what the world can be, Broadway will rely upon a new generation of theatre-makers, empowered to thoughtfully and subversively engage with the materials of the past and to create novel musicals that reflect their contemporary surroundings. With feminist courses in musical theatre, undergraduate institutions can become the home of the resistant and engaged dramaturgy that will change Broadway and shape the future of musical theatre.

Notes

1 This and other lyric selections from *Oklahoma!* are drawn from the musical score (Rodgers and Hammerstein 2004). Descriptions of film are drawn from the 1955 musical film, directed by Fred Zinnemann (Zinnemann 1955).

2 This production, directed by Daniel Fish, premiered at St Ann's Warehouse in 2018. It ran on Broadway from April 2019 to January 2020. Descriptions of Stroker's performance are drawn from the 2019 Tony Awards (Fish 2019).

3 See Wolf (2007). Also see Cermatori (2015).
4 See Wolf (2011).

References

Asian American Performers Action Coalition. "Ethnic Representation on New York City Stages." 2017. www.aapacnyc.org/uploads/1/1/9/4/11949532/aapac_2016-2017_report.pdf.

Cermatori, Joseph. 2015. "How to Make Sense of Music in the Theatre: A Primer for Beginners." *Theatre Topics* 25 (1): 67–76.

Chavkin, Rachel. 2019. "Best Director of a Musical Acceptance Speech." *Tony Awards*. CBS.

Coleman, Bertram E., and Judith Sebesta, eds. 2008. *Women in American Musical Theatre: Essays on Composers, Lyricists, Librettists, Arrangers, Choreographers, Designers, Directors, Producers and Performance Artists*. Jefferson, NC: McFarland.

Cox, Gordon. 2015. "'Waitress' Musical Serves Up Broadway's First All-Female Creative Team." *Variety* (blog). December 1, 2015. https://variety.com/2015/legit/news/waitress-musical-all-female-creative-team-1201651168/.

Culwell-Block, Logan. 2019. "Stripping Down *Oklahoma!* With a Brand New Sound for the Broadway Revival." *Playbill*. March 14, 2019. www.playbill.com/article/stripping-down-oklahoma-with-a-brand-new-sound-for-the-broadway-revival.

Fish, Daniel. 2019. "The Tony Awards 2019: *Oklahoma!*" *Tony Awards*. CBS. www.facebook.com/TheTonyAwards/videos/433285037505283/.

Green, Jesse. 2019. "Listen to the Sound of Love Reinvented in 'Oklahoma!' (Headphones On)." *The New York Times*, July 10, 2019, sec. Theater. www.nytimes.com/2019/07/10/theater/oklahoma-musical-songs.html.

Knapp, Raymond. 2005. *The American Musical and the Formation of National Identity*. Princeton University Press.

Knapp, Raymond, Mitchell Morris, and Stacy Ellen Wolf, eds. 2011. *The Oxford Handbook of the American Musical*. Oxford Handbooks. New York: Oxford University Press.

Larson, Sarah. 2018. "Daniel Fish's Dark Take on 'Oklahoma!,'" October 15, 2018. www.newyorker.com/magazine/2018/10/22/daniel-fishs-dark-take-on-oklahoma.

McMillin, Scott. 2014. *The Musical as Drama: A Study of the Principles and Conventions behind Musical Shows from Kern to Sondheim*. Princeton, NJ: Princeton University Press.

"Oklahoma!" by Richard Rodgers and Oscar Hammerstein III, directed by Bill Rauch, Oregon Shakespeare Festival, April–October 2018, Agnus Browner Theatre, Ashland, OR.

"Oklahoma!" by Richard Rodgers and Oscar Hammerstein III, directed by Daniel Fish, April 2019–January 2020, Circle in the Square Theatre, New York, NY.

Paulson, Michael. 2019. "Who Calls the Shots on Broadway? She Does." *New York Times*, August 14, 2019, sec. Theater. www.nytimes.com/2019/08/14/theater/broadway-women-producers.html.

Rickwald, Bethany. 2018. "Broadway's First All-Female Design Team Announced for The Lifespan of a Fact." *TheatreMania*. June 20, 2018. www.theatermania.com/broadway/news/lifespan-of-a-fact-first-all-female-design-team_85638.html.

Rodgers, Richard, and Oscar Hammerstein. 2004. *Oklahoma! Vocal Selections.* Rev. ed. [New York]: Milwaukee, WI: Williamson Music; Distributed by Hal Leonard.

Salam, Maya. 2019. "Ali Stroker Makes History as First Wheelchair User to Win a Tony." *New York Times*, June 9, 2019, sec. Theater. www.nytimes.com/2019/06/09/theater/ali-stroker-oklahoma-tony-awards.html.

Savran, David. 2004. "Toward a Historiography of the Popular." *Theatre Survey* 45 (2): 211–17.

Sternfeld, Jessica, and Elizabeth L. Wollman, eds. 2019. *The Routledge Companion to the Contemporary Musical.* New York and London: Routledge.

Wolf, Stacy. 2007. "In Defense of Pleasure: Musical Theatre History in the Liberal Arts [A Manifesto]." *Theatre Topics* 17 (1): 51–60.

Wolf, Stacy. 2011. *Changed for Good: A Feminist History of the Broadway Musical.* New York: Oxford University Press.

Zinnemann, Fred, dir. 1955. *Oklahoma!* Twentieth Century Fox.

3 Theory over time
Asian American performance, critical theory, and the theatre history survey

Angela K. Ahlgren

The theatre history survey operates under multiple and competing imperatives within many theatre programs; its delivery is therefore complex and labor-intensive. Among other things, the survey may function as the primary set of courses in which students are asked to read a large number of plays; learn about period characteristics, styles, and genres; understand dramatic structure and major developments in design and technology; and be exposed to major strands of theatrical criticism. In some programs, theatre history is taught separately from dramatic literature, while in others, Theatre History functions as a survey of both dramatic literature and historical developments, taught over two or three semesters, one of which may be a separate "world theatre" course. Where does critical performance theory fit within these demands? As if the list above did not represent a daunting number of learning outcomes for one course or sequence, those of us invested in teaching critical theory in the theatre history classroom may find ourselves stretched thin.

Time-related pressures on faculty in the neoliberal academy weigh heavily on scholars in all fields and at all levels, from undergraduate students to tenured faculty. As Stephannie Gearhart and Jonathan Chambers write in their edited volume, *Reversing the Cult of Speed in Higher Education: The Slow Movement in the Arts and Humanities*, while academia in general is "profoundly affected by social acceleration," the arts and humanities "are commonly the targets of criticism" for university metrics that value instrumentality over contemplation (2019, 2). Margarita Rayzberg and Blake Smith, in their contribution to the volume, acknowledge that in the absence of structural change in the university, taking one's time—making an individual choice to move slowly—is less a sustainable solution than a "multitude of custom-made dodges, short-cuts, and escapes by which scholars find ways to survive," an embrace of queer temporalities (2019, 63). In many theatre departments, the task of delivering a two- or three-semester history sequence often falls to a single faculty member who may or may not be granted occasional relief from this duty and who may or may not also be involved in production or asked to deliver other aspects of the curriculum, such as acting, script analysis, or non-major theatre courses. This is, of course, in addition to research and service demands, which can vary widely according to institution and position. For women and faculty of color, the demands proliferate.[1] There is much we cannot control about academic labor, but I offer here my "custom-made dodge" that—while not an antidote to larger structures that value speed and market value—may prove a sustainable strategy through which to develop strong, theoretically informed theatre history syllabi over time.

"Theory Over Time," then, is not necessarily an argument for privileging theory over chronology, although I do privilege concepts over coverage. Rather, this chapter advances strategies for integrating critical performance theory into the undergraduate theatre history classroom over time and advocates for scholars to play to their own theoretical strengths as a way to build strong syllabi, especially when a curricular overhaul is not an option. This durational approach is influenced by Robert Boice, whose research reveals that faculty who work with moderation achieve more success than those who work in frenzied bursts.[2] Particularly, but not exclusively, for newly-minted PhDs in their first job, getting a theatre history sequence up and running not only requires an overwhelming amount of class prep, but may also chafe against the theoretical and historiographical acumen accrued during graduate study. While some departments are re-imagining the role of theatre history and historiography in undergraduate majors (and I applaud them), it is difficult for faculty to undertake a curricular overhaul in their first years in a new position, should they even be allowed to do so. At the same time, I operate under the assumption that many of us find critical theory useful, if not crucial, in teaching theatre history, and that few of us want to teach straight out of the available textbooks and anthologies in the long term, even if they provide a general basis for course design. Thus, this essay is aimed at those for whom the history sequence remains firmly part of—and often performs multiple functions within—the undergraduate theatre major, and who want to imagine a theory-forward approach to theatre history without burning out or sacrificing other professional goals, such as research.

In the following pages, I describe how theories that undergird my research on contemporary Asian American performance practices inform not only how I teach units on post-1965 Asian American theatre, but also how (and in what sequence) I teach topics such as Sanskrit drama, classical Japanese theatre, popular twentieth-century Japanese performance, and the Modernist movements influenced by Asian forms. Using practical examples from my experience teaching theatre history in a range of formats, I model an approach to Asian and Asian American theatre that readers might adopt in their theatre history classrooms. Finally, acknowledging the impossibility of crafting "the perfect" theatre history survey, I advocate for a durational approach to building theory-savvy undergraduate syllabi, one that begins by drawing on one's research areas and accrues more sophistication semester by semester.

Beyond the anthology: critical theory and post-1965 Asian American theatre

Many students enrolled in Theatre History are preparing to become theatre-makers, and introducing them to critical theory—particularly concepts that critique Orientalist (read: racist) assumptions at the heart Western historical narratives—equips them with stragegies for making artistic choices in a profession that is undergirded by racism. While I typically spend only one week a year teaching "Asian American Theatre," critical theory at the intersections of Asian American studies and theatre and performance studies informs not only the way I organize the course schedule and select plays, but in fact influences my entire approach to teaching theatre history. As for many scholars and their areas of expertise, the kinds of issues I raise and concepts I introduce across a range periods and genres are informed by the political and intellectual force of Asian American cultural critique. I am transparent with my students about my choices, and I cite the scholars whose work has influenced my thinking. Below, I model this approach as I briefly discuss the key theoretical concepts, play choices, and syllabus structure I have used in teaching Asian American theatre in a survey context.

My research to date has focused on Asian American performance, especially taiko, a physically demanding ensemble drumming form that originated in Japan and was taken up by Japanese Americans in the late 1960s and early 1970s. The theories I elaborate here come from Asian American studies as well as performance studies, both of which suggest that not only texts, but acts—bodies in their fleshy specificity in quotidian and staged contexts—constitute crucial sites of analysis. Three theoretical strands wind through the remainder of this brief essay, not necessarily in this order: that Orientalism is both a way to understand play texts and an epistemology that frames many strands of theatre history; that theatre artists theorize through the artistic work they produce and the choices they make, including but not limited to play texts, movement vocabularies, company mission statements, and activism; and finally, that because history is inextricably entwined with theories of time, time can be a window to theoretical thinking, from ideas about how we use time to prepare for class to how much time we cover in a survey to ways we might "slow down" by lingering in a particular period or moving quickly through others.

The wave of Asian American cultural critique published in the late 1990s and early '00s provides key insights into the relations among literature, popular culture, performance, and the ways Asian Americans have been constructed not only in representational but also in social and political, terms. Many of these scholars take up ideas developed by Edward Said in his 1978 work, *Orientalism*, in which he explicates the nexus of political power, hegemonic forces, and cultural and aesthetic imperatives that structure and support Western conceptions of and dominance over "the Orient" in the nineteenth and twentieth centuries. Said's ideas, along with those of other postcolonial, poststructuralist, and psychoanalytic theories, influence the ways these writers examine Asian American politics and culture. Lisa Lowe's *Immigrant Acts* articulates how understanding the "heterogeneity, hybridity, and multiplicity" of Asian American experience in the United States helps to break down the fiction of the "dominant, 'orientalist' construction of Asian Americans," one that, among other things, views all Asian Americans as the same despite vastly different histories among Americans of Asian descent (Lowe 1996, 67). Robert G. Lee's work on "Oriental" stereotypes in popular culture across the decades of the twentieth century illustrates how a range of stereotypes reflects and shapes dominant political exigencies. Theatre and performance studies scholars like James Moy, Josephine Lee, Karen Shimakawa, and Dorinne Kondo draw on these and other theories to specifically address how race and gender, as well as historical and social forces, are brought to bear on Asian American theatre and performance. Yutian Wong's *Choreographing Asian America* provides a crucial intervention to these works, insisting that dancing bodies are always central to issues of race, agency, and Asian American critique.

I teach Asian American theatre as a theatrical movement with its own history, defined by those who invested in and created it, an approach influenced by Esther Kim Lee's historical work on the topic (2006). Like Lee and others, I am not interested in reifying the category "Asian American theatre" or parsing what does or does not belong under its rubric, particularly given my positionality as a white woman. Moreover, as ethnomusicologist Grace Wang writes, "the conceptual coherence of the term *Asian American* continually fractures under the weight of its heterogeneity" (Wang 2015, 19). Instead, I focus on the cultural work Asian American theatre, as a movement, has done and continues to do. Because the very term "Asian American" gained traction more or less simultaneously with the first Asian American theatre companies in the 1960s, it is useful to discuss with my students what the newly formed category enabled, both in and out of the theatre, and how it was and continues to be contested.

I typically deliver a lecture structured around three types of cultural work Asian American theatre does: (1) critiques racist stereotypes and performance traditions, (2) writes and performs Asian American histories, and (3) explores the complexities of Asian American identities a la Lowe's formulation of heterogeneity, hybridity, and multiplicity. This structure provides a context in which to introduce the legacy of yellowface performance and racist casting practices; and allows me to discuss (although not read) a wide variety of plays, so as to counteract the idea implicit in the available anthologies that there are merely one or two plays by Asian American playwrights worthy of attention. Moreover, by focusing not just on plays, but other developments, I consider how actors' protests and theatre companies' mission statements were a form of theorizing about how casting, staging, and playwriting re-produced racist structures.

Critical theory at the intersection of Asian American studies and performance studies informs how I select and present Asian American plays in Theatre History. I have taught Asian American plays in a range of contexts: within Introduction to Theatre general education courses, theatre history surveys for both majors and non-majors, and focused graduate and undergraduate Asian American Theatre and Performance seminars. I mention these multiple contexts, despite my focus on theatre history in this essay, because I believe that some plays are more appropriate in a seminar context, where it is possible to discuss how they engage in an ongoing conversation, than in a survey, where Asian American theatre gets perhaps a week of the students' attention. Below, I discuss the cultural work and theoretical implications of David Henry Hwang's *M. Butterfly*, Wakako Yamauchi's *And the Soul Shall Dance* (1990), and Michael Golamco's *Cowboy Versus Samurai*, in a theatre history survey context.

If one assigns plays only from anthologies typically used in theatre history courses, the sole choice is David Henry Hwang's 1988 play, *M. Butterfly*.[3] Hwang's quasi-Brechtian send-up of the Orientalist assumptions at the heart of Puccini's opera *Madama Butterfly* and Belasco's play *Madame Butterfly* tells the story of Rene Gallimard and his love affair with opera singer Song Liling in the decades leading up to the war in Vietnam, using vignettes that represent fragments of Gallimard's memory as he sits in a jail cell. I have deep reservations about accepting this play as "the" Asian American play available for study in a survey course, to the exclusion of all others. The first difficult issue is its re-staging of Orientalist spectacle through Peking Opera scenes, the glamorous Anna Mae Wong inflected cross-dressing of Song, and Gallimard's Butterfly drag at the end of the play. Each of these spectacles is dismantled and critiqued through dialogue and through what was in its original staging a shocking theatrical reveal of Song's gender. *M. Butterfly* has invited a number of theorists to consider the role of re-staged stereotypes in Asian American theatre, some arguing that Hwang's re-creation of the "butterfly" stereotype effectively dismantles it (Shimakawa 2002; Kondo 1997), while others assert that its power is re-invigorated through yet another iteration (Moy 1993; Josephine Lee 1997).[4] My students' responses to *M. Butterfly* have been mixed, some running parallel to those of newspaper critics, who were "so thoroughly transfixed by [the play's] bizarre (homo)sexual story that the drama's incisive racial critique is in danger of vanishing" (Eng 2001, 143), and others connecting with the play's critique of racial and gender stereotypes and their consequences. Second, the play's use of Asian theatrical conventions in its staging may reinforce the false notion that Asian American playwrights have a natural affinity for Asian performance forms. Given the ways the Asian American body continues to be conflated with the Asian—or worse, a stereotyped "Oriental"—body on stage in the United States, the tacit connection this play provides between Asian American theatre and Peking Opera and other Asian performance forms is likely to reinforce the conflation of Asianness with Asian Americanness.

M. Butterfly undoubtedly invites a thorough discussion of Orientalism, but in the absence of other examples of Asian American theatre, it also suggests that Asian American playwrights are deeply and consistently influenced by Asian art forms. Although some Asian American playwrights do find inspiration in Asian theatre, there is nothing more inherent or natural about Asian Americans' use of them than, for example, Paula Vogel's use of bunraku conventions in *The Long Christmas Ride Home*. In discussing her play *36 Views*, which also critiques Orientalist attitudes through Japanese staging techniques, playwright Naomi Iizuka herself notes in an interview that Kabuki is no more familiar to her, being half Japanese, than it is to her audiences, who are presumably majority white (Wren 2002, 32). I can understand resistance to what I have said here: *M. Butterfly* offers a compelling theoretical stance of its own, and indeed many students have enough theoretical sophistication to parse out its subtleties. At the same time, I regularly encounter students and colleagues alike who hear the term "Asian American theatre" and think "Kabuki." In my view, it is worth moving beyond the anthology to explore plays that do not conflate twentieth-century Asian American theatre and classical Asian forms.

One play I have taught several times in Theatre History, and which I want to advocate for, is Wakako Yamauchi's 1977 *And the Soul Shall Dance*.[5] The play is written in the realist genre, and as such, focuses on social issues faced by the play's characters, the neighboring farming families, the Muratas and the Okas, first- and second-generation Japanese Americans in Imperial Valley, California, in 1935. Gritty details of bathing, food preparation, farming, drinking, and domestic abuse emphasize the humanity of the characters, the effects of the racist laws and social norms they face, and the pressures of intergenerational family dynamics, rather than focusing on the spectacle and fantasy that surrounds the Japan of mainstream cultural production.[6] In this sense, the play avoids the "re-Orientalizing" that some theorists claim *M. Butterfly* indulges.

The central character, eleven-year-old Masako Murata, observes the behaviors of her parents and their neighbors as she negotiates her family's Japanese customs and assimilation into her American school. The play deals with racism, not necessarily as its core message, but as part of the given circumstances of the action: that is, the characters' actions are shaped by their status as Japanese immigrants not eligible for naturalized citizenship. Josephine Lee writes that Yamauchi's plays, including this one, "foreground family problems rather than race relations ... the racist conditions of immigration and settlement for Japanese Americans are undeniably the causes of the family problems" (1997, 153). The play highlights the racial discrimination the characters face, not only through narrating encounters like not being served at a restaurant while traveling but also through attention to the Alien Land Laws, which prevented Japanese people from owning land in the United States, a given circumstance in the play that keeps these families locked in precarious financial and social relations. In its engagement with historical circumstances faced by first- and second-generation Japanese

Americans, *And the Soul Shall Dance* opens up opportunities to teach aspects of American history that are often left out of mainstream curricula.[7] Furthermore, while the play does not focus on the performance of gender via theatrical conventions, as does *M. Butterfly*, *Soul* does attend to structural gender inequalities through attention to women's work, the coming-of-age struggles of two adolescent girls, and dialogue about appropriate gendered behaviors.

I sometimes teach *And the Soul Shall Dance* in sequence with Maria Irene Fornes's *Fefu and Her Friends*, another play set in 1935, written by a woman of color playwright in the late 1970s. Together, these plays offer contrasting glimpses of the year 1935 in the United States, the midst of the Great Depression. In *Soul*, the characters subsist despite racist immigration and land ownership laws, while in *Fefu*, the characters' affluence and whiteness shelter them from Depression-era poverty even as they suffer at the hands of patriarchal institutions. Each play critiques the structures (medical, juridical, educational) its characters navigate using different dramaturgical modes. Why linger in one year in U.S. history when there are thousands of years and vast geographies to cover? The temporal links between the two plays prompt an inquiry about how dramaturgical choices, such as when a play is set, enact their own kind of theory, challenging or reinforcing dominant approaches to that historical moment. Practically speaking, the choice to linger in 1935 is also temporary and can be changed the following year. The point is not to achieve static syllabi but to experiment on a small scale, building theoretical frameworks and critically sound choices over time.

Michael Golamco's 2006 *Cowboy Versus Samurai* is yet another choice, a play whose comic treatment of Asian American identity crises provides opportunities to discuss theoretical concepts that are easy for students to relate to.[8] A romantic comedy, it provides relief from a semester of plays heavy on tragedy and existential angst, and its humor allows relatively easier access to its critiques of racism and exoticism than the other plays I have discussed. At the same time, it theorizes how events in Asian American history affect characters' emotional lives. The play follows three Asian Americans living in the otherwise all-white town of Breakneck, Wyoming. Based loosely on Edmund Rostand's *Cyrano de Bergerac*, *Cowboy* revolves around new-in-town Korean American Veronica Lee and the three men who fall for her: Chester, an adopted Asian of unknown national origin who lives in his parents' basement; Travis, a Korean American high school teacher in exile from Los Angeles; and Del, a white, handsome Breakneck native, an "all-American cowboy."

Cowboy Versus Samurai sends up Orientalist stereotypes in ways different from *M. Butterfly*, which critiques stereotype by re-staging its most spectacular and tragic dimensions, albeit with a dark, sardonic wit. Golamco critiques stereotype through playful dialogue and broad comedy and replaces stereotypes with realistic (if comic) Asian American characters.[9] The play's message that stereotypes influence identity construction are largely delivered via the character Chester, an adoptee who does not know "what kind of Asian he is" (Golamco 2007, 249). To address this lack, Chester constructs endless iterations of his identity performed through a pastiche of cultural representations: he prays to a poster of Bruce Lee, dons ninja attire, and reads about Yellow Power. The psychic toll of crafting an identity from cultural remnants erupts in an exchange between Travis and Chester:

TRAVIS: You call yourself Asian, but you don't know a thing about it. You read magazines and books, you wear costumes and you call that your identity—
CHESTER: IT'S ALL I'VE GOT. (*Travis slowly lets him go. Chester is sobbing and blubbering now.*)

(Golamco 2007, 277–278)

Chester's "sobbing and blubbering" may be comic, but they manifest for the character as grief for the genealogy lost to him in the event of transnational adoption. In this scene, to use Anne Cheng's terms, Chester's racial grievances manifest on stage as racial grief (Cheng 2000, 18). Moreover, the play exemplifies Lisa Lowe's observation that, "one of the more important stories of Asian American experience is about the process of critically receiving and rearticulating cultural traditions in the face of a dominant national culture that exoticizes and 'orientalizes' Asians" (1997, 65). Chester's racial grief and his process of "rearticulating cultural traditions" from various Asian cultures is something college students might easily relate to, since university life often asks them to understand themselves in new ways.

Moreover, the play highlights historiographical thinking when Chester attempts to re-write (Asian) American history by protesting a museum tour commemorating the anniversary of the completion of the Central Pacific railroad. Arming himself with papier-mâché limbs, fake blood, and picket signs, Chester lays himself on the railroad track where the commemorative train will ride through town, calling attention to the history of Chinese laborers whose work on the railroad was cropped out of photographs and out of history. The scene foregrounds the ways Asian American and other minoritarian histories have been suppressed in favor of a triumphant, white American past. Chester's protest signs (which say, among other things, "INDENTURE THIS," and "FUCK YOU"), gesture to the performative modes of protest used by Black Power and Yellow Power activists of the 1960s and 1970s (and which, in 2019, have been re-activated). Disguised as romantic fluff (it reads more like Steve Martin's *Roxanne* than Rostand's *Cyrano*—not that any of my students are familiar with either), in the context of theatre history, the play creates opportunities to discuss the role of performance in Asian American activism, the performative dimensions of racial identity, and revisionist histories in the theatre history classroom.

Chronology over geography: syllabi and organization

Some choose to teach "world theatre" separately from Western theatre history, or even to move through theatre history by continent or other geographic designation. These approaches have been critiqued for reinforcing an Orientalist mindset, so I present theatre traditions from Asia, Africa, and elsewhere together within a linear chronology to reinforce the fact that they have specific histories, as opposed to being merely "ancient," "traditional" or unchanging.[10] Rather than teach Noh, Kabuki, and Bunraku as a single unit on classical Japanese theatre, I teach them according to the periods in which they developed. Linear chronologies are not groundbreaking, of course; both the Norton and Wadsworth anthologies organize their plays chronologically. But teaching European, North and South American, Asian, and African theatre histories alongside one another—as opposed to in isolated geographical blocks with self-contained historical narratives—makes room for thinking about transnational flows and points of intersection among these traditions, rather than rendering them isolated from one another. As many theatre historians do, I assign theoretical readings alongside plays and historical readings. Selections from Zeami's "Teachings on Style and the Flower" and the Natyasastra, for example, not only provide information about the ways Noh and Sanskrit may have been practiced at a particular moment in their development, but also provide alternative approaches to dramatic structure in a field that is dominated by Aristotelian dramaturgy.

Postcolonial theory influences the way I present Modernist movements of the late nineteenth and early twentieth centuries. An aspect of avant-garde movements often sublimated in textbook readings is how modernists appropriated African and Asian forms in service of their aesthetic innovations. (Well-known examples here are Picasso's use of African mask aesthetics in his cubist paintings and Ezra Pound's harnessing the minimalism and imagery of Noh in his poetry.) Rather than see it as an unfortunate side effect of Modernism, I present appropriation as a key strategy of many Modernist approaches to theatre and art-making that reinforce Orientalist notions of Asian and African art as raw material for Western innovation. In this light, William Butler Yeats's *At the Hawk's Well*, for example, can be seen as part of a larger *zeitgeist*, rather than a novel re-purposing of noh conventions for the modernist stage.

While highlighting the cultural appropriation at the heart of Modernist work, it is also important to clarify that global flows are not unidirectional. Asia does not merely provide raw material for Western innovation, but Asian artists are also influenced by European and American aesthetics. My inclusion of the all-women's theatre troupe, Takarazuka, in my theatre history course emphasizes this point. The Takarazuka performance troupe and academy was founded in 1913 by entrepreneur Ichiro Kobayashi in the Osaka, Japan, suburb of Takarazuka. Created as a way to recover his losses after his luxury resort built near the Takarazuka rail stop failed, the organization has continued for over a century as a beloved performance tradition that attracts many ardent fans. Recognized for lavish productions that culminate in finales with performers in glittering costumes and oversized feathery headdresses descending grand staircases *en masse*, Takarazuka delivers programs that include repertoire from classical Japanese forms like Kabuki and Kyogen, large-scale renditions of regional Japanese and Southeast Asian folk dances, and spectacular musical revues influenced by Parisian cabaret and Broadway musicals. More recent performances stage adaptations of popular manga and anime stories, as well. As such, Takarazuka stands as an example of a Japanese theatre phenomenon with explicitly Western influence, and provides an opportunity to discuss the rapid Westernization of Japan in the twentieth century.

While my focus in this essay is on Asian American critical theory, it is worth noting the opportunities Takarazuka provides for introducing (or revisiting) gender theory and drag performance. Jennifer Robertson's 1998 ethnography, *Takarazuka: Sexual Politics and Popular Culture in Modern Japan* provides a robust introduction to the group's history, culture, and gender politics, and more recent essays provide some updates to Robertson's research.[11] Performers begin their careers as students in the academy, admission to which is highly competitive. A significant dimension of their training is the way student performers (all cis-gender women) are segregated by gender—that is, by those who will perform male roles (*otokoyaku*) and those who will perform female roles (*musumeyaku*). Thus, Takarazuka prompts a discussion of gender performance in which women not only inhabit male roles, but also learn to embody masculinity, a shift from the relentless number of classical theatre traditions in which male performers maintain ownership of female roles. Additionally, Takarazuka's primary audience is women, and their attendance of live shows, consumption of ephemera, and active participation on fan sites presents ample opportunity to engage with ideas of spectatorship. As one example of Japanese performance that is not considered "classical" or "ancient," Takarazuka's links with drag, vaudeville, Broadway, as well as classical Japanese forms make it a pleasurable phenomenon on which to linger.

Theory over time: concluding thoughts

This chapter has articulated some of the ways that critical theory at the intersection of Asian American studies and performance has shaped how I teach the undergraduate theatre history survey. What I teach now, in 2019, has evolved significantly over time: the way I select, organize, and present material shifts each time I teach the course, even though I sometimes circle back to earlier choices. Yet, the theoretical frameworks that inform my research on taiko as Asian American performance consistently undergird structural aspects of my syllabi, as well as inform the specific ways

I approach Asian American theatre. In other circumstances, I might have written about how feminist and queer theory enter into my theatre history courses; certainly, scholars whose theoretical strengths lie in other areas will produce syllabi in which critical theory appears in different ways.

What I hope comes through here is that I advocate for focusing on strengths as the place at which to begin transforming the theatre history survey. Particularly for those just beginning full-time teaching or those wanting to introduce more theory to an existing course, I suggest that it may reasonably begin with expertise. After my first term teaching theatre history in my first teaching position after graduate school, I told the senior historian in my department that I wanted to scrap it and start the next term with a completely new approach. He kindly suggested that the class was probably fine the way it was and advised me to make incremental changes instead. Choose three lectures that you want to overhaul every semester, he said, and make do with the rest.[12] I followed that advice, more or less, and over time my teaching improved without having to start over again. Building sophisticated syllabi over time not only leaves room for other pursuits, but it also allows for judiciousness about when and how to include it, and what to prioritize in a particular semester.

As I write in 2019, my home department is contemplating bigger changes. Students in the Department of Theatre and Film at Bowling Green State University have spearheaded critical conversations about racism in casting, season selection, and curriculum. Some students' understanding of these issues outpaces faculty members', while for other students, confronting racism is very new. My hope is that a theoretically grounded theatre history classroom can be part of a larger strategy to foster critical thinking about issues like racism, sexism, and other ethical debates in the field. My suggestion to take time to develop sophistication is not a way of downplaying the urgency of undoing racist (and sexist and other) practices. The pressure on history courses to teach a range of skills and content cannot be overestimated, and sometimes a curriculum-level or even course-level overhaul *is* necessary. I believe, however, that small changes, grounded in critical theory, can make a large impact on equipping students to grapple with difficult questions about theatre practices, both in the university classroom and beyond.

Notes

1 See, for example, Mariam B. Lam, "Diversity Fatigue Is Real," *The Chronicle of Higher Education*, September 23, 2018 and Kerry Ann O'Meara, "Constrained Choices: A View of Campus Service Inequality from Annual Faculty Reports," *Journal of Higher Education*, January 27, 2017.
2 See Boice (2000).
3 *M. Butterfly* appears in both the *Norton Anthology of Drama, Volume 2*, and the *Wadsworth Anthology of Drama*. See also David Henry Hwang, *M. Butterfly* (New York: Plume Books, 1988).

4 For discussions of how the play dismantles stereotypes, see Shimakawa (2002, 125) and Kondo (1997, 48). For discussions of the play's failure to dismantle stereotypes, see Josephine Lee (1997, 118–119) and Moy (1993, 5).

5 *And the Soul Shall Dance* was adapted from Yamauchi's short story of the same name and premiered at East-West Players in 1977.

6 My analysis is based on the version of the script published in *Between Worlds: Contemporary Asian-American Plays*, edited by Misha Berson. It is also available in *The Creative Spirit: An Introduction to Theatre*, edited by Stephanie Arnold (McGraw-Hill, 2015).

7 Other plays from the 1970s and 1980s that offer realist, or selective realist, approaches that delve into Asian American histories include, but are not limited to, Philip Kan Gotanda's *The Wash* and *Song for a Nisei Fisherman*, Genny Lim's *Paper Angels*, and Hwang's *The Dance and the Railroad*.

8 *Cowboy Versus Samurai* premiered at the National Asian American Theatre Company in New York City in November 2005, and had a subsequent production in March 2006 at Theater Mu in Minneapolis. Since then, the play has been produced frequently by Asian American and Asian Canadian theatre companies.

9 For a discussion of replacing the stereotype, see Moy (1993).

10 The approach taken in Zarilli's *Theatre Histories* is also effective in its thematic approach to theatre history, and I occasionally excerpt some of its critical theory selections for class.

11 See Robertson (1998). For more recent scholarship, see Chen (2010).

12 Thank you to Bill Condee at Ohio University for being such a kind and supportive mentor in my first academic post. His advice resonates with Robert Boice's advocacy for making mindful, unhurried choices in teaching and university life. I have found Boice's *Advice for New Faculty Members* (2000) to be an indispensable read for those in their early (and probably all) years of university teaching.

References

Boice, Robert. 2000. *Advice for New Faculty Members: Nihil Nimus*. Boston: Allyn and Bacon.

Chen, Yilin. 2010. "Gender and Homosexuality in Takarazuka Theatre: *Twelfth Night* and *Epiphany*," *Performing Ethos: International Journal of Ethics in Theatre and Performance* 1 (1): 53–67.

Cheng, Ann Anlin. 2000. *The Melancholy of Race: Psychoanalysis, Assimilation, and Hidden Grief*. New York: Oxford University Press.

Eng, David. 2001. *Racial Castration: Managing Masculinity in Asian America*. Durham, NC: Duke University Press.

Gearhart, Stephannie S. and Jonathan Chambers. 2019. "Contextualizing Speed and Slowness in Higher Education." In *Reversing the Cult of Speed in Higher Education: The Slow Movement in the Arts and Humanities*, edited by Stephannie S. Gearhart and Jonathan Chambers, 1–35. New York: Routledge.

Golamco, Michael. 2007. *Cowboy Versus Samurai*. In *New Playwrights: The Best Plays of 2006*, edited by D.L. Lepidus and Chungmi Kim, 243–296. New York: Smith and Kraus Publications.

Hwang, David Henry. 1993. *M. Butterfly*. New York: Penguin.

Kondo, Dorinne. 1997. *About Face: Performing Race in Fashion and Theater*. New York: Routledge.

Lee, Esther Kim. 2006. *A History of Asian American Theatre*. Cambridge, MA: Cambridge University Press.

Lee, Josephine. 1997. *Performing Asian America: Race and Ethnicity on the Contemporary Stage*. Philadelphia: Temple University Press.

Lee, Robert G. 1999. *Orientals: Asian Americans in Popular Culture*. Philadelphia: Temple University Press.

Lowe, Lisa. 1996. *Immigrant Acts: On Asian American Cultural Politics*. Durham, NC: Duke University Press.

Moy, James. 1993. *Marginal Sights: Staging the Chinese in America*. Iowa City: University of Iowa Press.

Rayzberg, Margarita and Blake Smith. 2019. "Queerness Over Time: Slowness, Speed, and the Chronopolitics of Scholarship." In *Reversing the Cult of Speed in Higher Education: The Slow Movement in the Arts and Humanities*, edited by Stephannie S. Gearhart and Jonathan Chambers, 55–65. New York: Routledge.

Robertson, Jennifer. 1998. *Takarazuka: Sexual Politics and Popular Culture in Modern Japan*. Berkeley: University of California Press.

Said, Edward W. 1978. *Orientalism*. New York: Vintage Books.

Shimakawa, Karen. 2002. *National Abjection: The Asian American Body Onstage*. Durham, NC: Duke University Press.

Wang, Grace. 2015. *Soundtracks of Asian America: Navigating Race through Musical Performance*. Durham, NC: Duke University Press.

Wong, Yutian. 2010. *Choreographing Asian America*. Middletown, CT: Wesleyan University Press.

Wren, Celia. 2002. "Navigating Alien Worlds: An Interview with the Playwright." *American Theatre* 19 (2): 32.

Yamauchi, Wakako. 1990. In *Between Worlds: Contemporary Asian-American Plays*, edited by Misha Berson, 133–174. New York: Theatre Communications Group.

4 From systemic dramaturgy to systemic pedagogy

Rethinking theatre history and technology

Michael M. Chemers and Mike Sell

In our book *Systemic Dramaturgy: From Zeami to The Legend of Zelda*,[1] we make the case for a revised theory and practice of dramaturgy. "Systemic Dramaturgy" is the name we give to a critical, creative, collaborative process that is shaped by, on one hand, a desire to sustain time-honored traditions of dramaturgy and, on the other, the need to respond effectively to the challenges and opportunities of emerging technologies, critical theory, and the rapidly changing field of performance and theatre studies. But we have yet to address a critical question: How do we teach our students to be systemic dramaturgs?

What is a dramaturg? As Michael explains in *Ghost Light: An Introductory Handbook for Dramaturgy*, a dramaturg "is a member of the artistic team of a production who is a specialist in the transformation of a dramatic script into a meaningful living performance"(Chemers 2010, 5). He observes that dramaturgical practice applies to three phases of theatrical production: analysis of the "aesthetic architecture" of the text or texts of the performance; broad and deep research that facilitates the company's efforts to make the performance relevant to the audience; and the practical application of those critical and scholarly efforts in the artistic work of the company. We highlight this time-tested conception of dramaturgy as particularly pertinent to the task of teaching critical performance theory in classrooms, studios, and the wider communities that intersect with our work.

First, we note that all three phases are implicitly concerned with education. The dramaturg's analytic, scholarly, and creative work is always oriented toward answering questions, improving comprehension, providing information, or challenging assumptions. Second, we note that all three phases of dramaturgy can and should be informed by rigorous critical thinking, particularly the methods and insights of what can be broadly termed "critical performance theory." Whether the dramaturg is analyzing a text, pursuing research that facilitates theatrical conception, or providing insight that enables an engaging, moving, beautiful production, the dramaturg fulfills their duties by asking good questions. These questions concern the dramatic text, of course. But they can and should also encompass the broader political and social contexts of production, inside and outside the company.

Our concept of systemic dramaturgy sustains these time-tested traditions, but also responds to several urgent concerns having to do with the role and impact of technology in all aspects of theatre, the limitations of traditional ideologies regarding the relationship of technology and theatre, and the ways that the methods and insights of dramaturgy can be productively applied beyond the theatre to new performing arts made conceivable and accessible by digital and computational technology. In *Dramaturgy: From Zeami to The Legend of Zelda*, we explore several examples of this extensive, interdisciplinary, cross-media dramaturgy. And we describe the kinds of analytic, scholarly, and practical insights that dramaturgs can provide to, for example, the designers and players of videogames (see below). In this, we affirm and encourage the long-lived dramaturgical tradition of interdisciplinary inquiry and collaboration across the arts.

To sum up, a systemic conception and practice of dramaturgy encourages dramaturgs to think about their work within a set of critical-theoretical frameworks defined, broadly speaking, by the question of technology. These frameworks don't just affect the way we do dramaturgy. If dramaturgs are always educators and critical thinkers, then it would be naïve to presume that changing how dramaturgy works wouldn't affect how we understand learning and, therefore, how we teach. Our argument is that a systemic conception of dramaturgy should inform and be informed by a systemic conception of theatre pedagogy, one that promotes active, interdisciplinary, inquiry-based learning and that enables budding dramaturgs to engage critical themes in theatre studies and critical challenges to production. The end goal of this systemic pedagogy would be a dramaturg who can articulate their own ideas about theatre but also engage intelligently the historical, social, cultural, economic, and political systems in which theatre is made and experienced. In this essay, we will describe a pedagogy that reframes the relationship of performance to technology, re-historicizes the relationship of performance and technology, and reorganizes our topics to highlight the dramaturgical challenges shared across time and place.

The way we do then, now

> Theatre is life.
> Film is art.
> Television is furniture.

As this "old" industry aphorism suggests,[2] theatre folks have tended to look down on other, putatively more technologically sophisticated performance media, especially those that record, distribute, and display performance electronically. As enthusiastic as we are about new technologies, we can't help but share some of that anxiety. There is something about digital reproduction that feels distancing from (if not threatening to) the joyful and profound connection that theatregoers have long believed is the whole point of dramatic art. After all, contemporary concerns about the ways that technology is reshaping theatre—its forms, its themes, its audiences—have been expressed by lovers of theatre for thousands of years.

How might such a rethinking affect the way we approach traditional dramaturgical texts? Western dramaturgy draws its most fundamental assumptions about theatre from Aristotle's *Poetics:* its insistence on the centrality of *mimesis* to human learning, its recognition of the therapeutic efficacy of profound emotional engagement with embodied and action-based storytelling, and its identification of the facility of theatre to increase the human capacity for empathy and compassion. Because he prioritizes moral and psychological education in dramatic art, Aristotle ranks the constituent elements of a performance, placing the play's plot and themes at the top, and the particulars of its staging (what he calls "spectacle") at the bottom.

But for us, Aristotle's dismissive attitude towards spectacle is problematic because of what it implies about theatre's relationship to technology. He seems to consider the technical dimensions of material production to be, at best, superfluous, and at worst, a threat to the essential purpose of dramatic art: the eliciting of powerful, life-changing emotions. Staging seems to be a problem to be managed and mitigated if the great work of *katharsis* is to be achieved in the most salutary fashion. Because of his prominence, Aristotle's attitude toward the mechanics of staging has shaped discussion of dramatic literature in the West ever since. It has informed the so-called "anti-theatrical prejudice" of church fathers and moralizing pundits from across the ages, in both Christian and Islamic cultures, who deemed the embodied illusions of the theatre a threat to the soul and the state. It haunted the debates surrounding the 1876 production of Richard Wagner's *Der Ring des Nibelungen* in Bayreuth, Germany, with its enchanting backdrops, faltering gas lighting, and clever simulation of the river in which the *Rhinemaidens* swim (Salter 2010, 1–4). And it can be seen on the many university campuses in the United States where dramatic literature is taught one way in the English Department (typically, with little reference to theatre history or stagecraft) and another way in the Theatre Department (where critical theory, especially critical performance theory, typically remains underdeveloped).

This is why we say that the original problem of theatre is technology. Not only do we need to think in more critical ways about what theatre technology is (i.e., that the performer's facial expressions, gestural language, and dialogue are no less "technological" than an LED projector[3]), but we also need to think about the history of theatre itself. For us, that means spending less time with our students on *katharsis* and more on why Aristotle looked down his nose at the mask-makers and stagehands. A few small changes to how we approach the instruction of basic theatre history promise real benefits for budding dramaturgs trying to find their way in a dazzling, rapidly changing media universe that encompasses both traditional theatrical spaces and other embodied, dramatic media like sports, escape rooms, immersive entertainment, roleplaying games, and videogames. In addition to helping students understand the applicability of their dramaturgical skills within and beyond conventional theatre, a critically minded engagement with the discourses and practices that have informed the relationship between theatre and technology now, in the past, and around the world promises broader benefits.

As theatre historians, we are certain of two things. First, humanity as we understand it would not exist without drama, theatre, and performance. Second, drama, theatre, and performance would not exist without the scientists and engineers who devised counterweight cranes, dragon-pulled chariots, hellmouths, *hanamichi, ringgit,* vampire traps, Pepper's Ghosts, the astonishing automated stages that made Schiller's work performable, the skilled realistic artistry that did the same for Ibsen, and the electric lighting that added glamor to Gilbert and Sullivan. From Vitruvius to Hatsune Miku, the story of theatre is the story of audiences taking instruction and delight from stage magic. Despite this, the theatre also fulfills its promise to be a special place where people gather to witness an embodied story and be entertained (and hopefully edified) by it. Despite the fears of theatre-lovers and hopes of theatre-haters, technology has neither obviated nor eliminated the ancient relationship between audience and actors. When used judiciously, thoughtfully, cleverly, with an awareness of the manifold systems that surround that precious moment of encounter between artists and audience, technology has instead enhanced that relationship. This much we regularly teach.

But despite this, theatre critics and makers still express anxieties about technology, a bias reflected in the general absence in our curricula of critical-theoretical work on technology, technoculture, *techne*, post-humanist theory, and disability theory.[4] This is especially worrying in light of the intensifying and expansive growth of computational, digital, surveillance, and prosthetic technologies. How can dramaturgs—whether in rehearsal rooms or classrooms—address this gap in critical, historical, and practical instruction?

Backward-and-forward compatibility

We tend to think of technology as almost exclusively forward-looking, as a set of shiny, networked solutions to never-before-encountered problems or, alternately, as sleek, user-friendly, sustainably designed ways of dealing with long-lived challenges. But technology is not a new thing—and new technologies often reveal things about our past that we never suspected. Ancient cultural myths like the Greeks' Prometheus or the Maori's Māui show that the very conception of the human being is intimately connected to tools and making. Furthermore, not only is technology not a new thing, it develops at different rates, in different ways, in different forms, in different places—as do attitudes toward and understandings of technology. The story of Prometheus reflects a very different set of concerns about power, humanity, nature, and technology than the story of Māui. Technology isn't just about the things we make—it's also about the stories we tell about it, how we think and feel about it, and the social and cultural practices that surround it. Systemic dramaturgy is based on a concept of technology that is historically expansive, culturally diverse, and critically minded. But first and foremost, a systemic dramaturgy affirms the pragmatic spirit of theatre artists around the world and across time.

That combination of critical thinking and get-it-done pragmatism, which Aristotle called *phronesis* (Chemers 2010, 5–6), should inform not only how we make theatre, but how we teach it. For example, we might adapt to our teaching the practices of engineers who are tasked with designing systems and products so that they can be used alongside older tech and in synch with local codes and customs. Engineers call this design principle—and the things it produces— "backward compatibility." Similarly, the term "forward compatibility" is used to describe systems or products that are designed to anticipate new evolutions in technology. We've found that "compatibility" is a great way to reframe and catalyze a student's critical and creative relationship to technology. This is a crucial first step toward complicating their thinking about how theatre relates to all the things we associate with technology: innovation, commodification, exploitation, modernity, sustainability, cultural chauvinism, colonialism, obsolescence, embodiment, prosthesis, inclusiveness, exclusiveness, and so on. We've also found that exploring different ways of "doing" compatibility can help our students (and us!) find new attitudes towards and uses for specific technologies. Theatre is a perfect example of a backward-and-forward-compatible technology. As we know, the word "theatre" derives from the Greek *theatron* (θέατρον, from the root verb "to view" in Greek), "seeing place," in both a literal and conceptual sense. Architects, designers, and choreographers collaborated with playwrights and actors to produce those early spectacles, regardless of Aristotle's attitude toward them.

As teachers, we want to communicate to our students how *strange* is the notion that our humanity can be shown and witnessed, and how that notion changed and continues to change the very experience and understanding of being human. Not incidentally, the creation of this technology of showing and witnessing—this system of words and bodies and space and things— brought with it a raft of new issues, especially for cultural and political authorities. Greek theatre artists and their supporters among the social and political elites—virtually every one of them men, slaveholders, and misogynists—were anxious about theatre's tendency to provoke strong emotional responses in spectators, so they devised strict rules about when and where theatre could happen, who could watch and who could perform it, what was worthy of theatrical representation and what deserved either no or highly distorted representation. If theatre were invented tomorrow, we could anticipate congressional hearings and pulpit-banging sermons to follow.

Thus, for the systemic dramaturg, backward-and-forward compatibility is not only a question of how we engage with new technology but also of how we think about and with theatre as a medium. We want to communicate to our students both the thrill of innovation and our concerns about discrimination and access when technology is not ethically managed. This means that we cannot teach the history of technology in theatre as corollary of its social, cultural, political, and aesthetic significance, but rather as one of its fundamental determinants. Furthermore, we cannot teach that history in evolutionary terms, as if theatre artists across eons and around the world were reaching towards some platonic ideal of theatre as opposed to devising a particular solution for the particular problems they faced at a particular time (in other words, the central phronetic concern of the working dramaturg). The most technologically bleeding-edge theatre companies—the Wooster Group, Dumb Type, the Builders Association, Blast Theory—use tools and techniques developed hundreds, even thousands of years ago alongside the latest Arduino. The last thing in the world we want is for students to think of the theatre of Ancient Greece, Japan's Muromachi period, or 1920s Mexico with the same sense of mythic distance as they do King Arthur or telephones with rotary dials.

One of our favorite examples of backward-and-forward compatibility comes from a relatively recent moment in theatre history. In 1971, The Performance Group, led by Richard Schechner, was invited to develop a production at a brand-new theatre at the University of Rhode Island. Rather than being delighted by the technological wonders at their disposal, they were horrified by what they encountered: an amalgam of backward-and-forward compatibility. Here they saw the traces of the Greek amphitheatre, there the vomitoria of the Roman stadium, and there and there the wagons of the medieval pageants, the fly systems of the Italian renaissance, the orchestra pits of nineteenth-century opera, and the turntable of the early twentieth. "These theaters," Schechner wrote at the time, "are like old trees weighted down by so many branches that they break," he cried, punctuating his despair with, "Pity the poor student actor!" In the face of a theatrical technology that he felt would fatally distort his company's desire to return to a fundamental relationship among the actor's body, the performance space, the dramatic text, and the audience's sense and sensibility, Schechner and his company chose the theatre's scene shop instead, "an honest, large, irregular space that could be made into anything" (Schechner, 32–3).

This is a perfect teachable moment for a developing dramaturg. It can be tempting to read Schechner's rejection of URI's cutting-edge theatre as a rejection of technology *per se*. But we would urge our students to consider the possibility that the URI's effort to achieve historical technological synthesis is not *a priori* monstrous, just not the right thing for all purposes. Although they couched it in the language of anti-technology, Schechner and the Performance Group were actually rejecting a certain *idea* about technological systems, driven by their explicit desire to devise and develop their own—which Schechner called "environmental theatre"—representing a different creative process, conjuncture of page and stage, and relationship of spectator to action. Both the designers of the URI theatre and the Performance Group applied the methods that would best support performance and witnessing, so this was essentially a technological question—a question of attitude about performance technique. In other words, these were different responses to the facility of theatre as a backward-and-forward-compatible medium.

How might we design a dramaturgy curriculum that teaches this problem, that reflects a more capacious understanding of technology that holds space for both the capacious compatibility mindset that informed the design of a stage like the one at URI *and* the rigorously minimalist approach of the Performance Group? How might we present the challenges of staging in a way that enables learners to identify and work not only with the practical problems of a particular space and set of constraints and affordances, but also with the social, cultural, philosophical, environmental, and economic systems in which they are working? A systemic approach to dramaturgy requires a systemic approach to pedagogy.

Zeami the Constructivist: reorganizing our topics

A pedagogy informed by a systemic approach to dramaturgy frames interdisciplinary, historically grounded, theoretically rigorous and culturally diverse research within an inquiry-based, collaborative, problem-solving approach whose goal is the creation of a meaningful performance. While reframing and re-historicizing the relationship of theatre and technology are crucial components of a critically attuned approach to dramaturgy, their benefits will be undermined unless we reorganize the topics we cover in our courses. A systemic approach to dramaturgy isn't particularly well-served by the traditional approach of dividing a year's instruction of theatre history into "Ancient Theatre History," followed by "Renaissance and Romantic," then "Realism," then "Contemporary." This chronological approach imposes an unnecessarily teleological narrative and an unhelpfully Eurocentric focus on our subject matter. Further, it tends to emphasize the finished product—playscripts and productions—at the expense of process, which has a side effect of marginalizing community-based and politically-charged theatre in favor of big-ticket productions that use a lot of technical expertise. In other words, it tells the story of the solutions to the problems rather than the story of how those problems were identified and the processes by which they were solved. We encourage a curriculum that focuses first and foremost on questions (What is a human? What is a body? How is empathy created? How does a person communicate that they are *performing*?), techniques (codified gestures, presentational performance, breath control), tools (masks, make-up, lighting, stage blood), and dramatic actions (sex, murder, confession) across performance cultures and periods.

On its face, this reorganization of the topics of theatre history might appear to emphasize practical concerns over critical thinking. Quite the contrary. A curriculum built around a systemic approach to dramaturgy is inquiry-based and deploys a diverse range of genealogies, rigorous comparative thinking, and speculative theatrical practice to encourage both effective making and critical reflection. It provides emergent dramaturgs a richer range of examples to put into their own practice. It encourages students to develop a repertoire of critical-thinking methods that enables them to contextualize their practice, to reflect on what they and their teams are doing, and to ask smart questions to ensure the best possible staging. In sum, a systemic approach to dramaturgical education promotes a dialogical relationship between critical thinking and creative practice that embraces technological production systems alongside hermeneutic and heuristic ones.

What might this look like in the classroom? One example of a technology-focused genealogy that encourages inquiry-based critical thinking about performance concerns one of our favorite theatrical technologies: the puppet. A focus on puppetry has the potential to reshuffle assumptions about theatre history and raise profound questions about the ways human beings have thought about the performer's body, about what makes a human human, and how Western historians have understood theatre in unhelpfully restrictive ways.

We begin our three-part unit with the Polish director Jerzy Grotowski, the Polish Laboratory Theatre, and the notion of "Poor Theatre." Students begin with Grotowski's essay "Towards a Poor Theatre," identifying the reasons why he focuses on the performer as the artistic and moral center of theatre. We watch selections from James MacTaggart's film of the PLT's *Akropolis* to articulate theory and practice. We highlight the ways that production treats the actor's body as a symbolic form; in particular, the way the performers deploy their bodies to communicate emotion and create a compelling sense of stage reality in the absence of almost all the usual technological accoutrements of theatre. And we work with students to physicalize those exercises, which helps them to understand the way Grotowski's actors approached character and the relationship of performer and audience.

From there, we turn to the single most important influence on Grotowski, the avant-garde Soviet-era director Vsevelod Meyerhold, whose work Grotowski discovered while he pursued research in the classified files section of Russia's State Institute for Theatre Arts. Theatre historians conventionally associate Meyerhold with technophilic, aggressively modernist avant-garde trends like Futurism and Constructivism and frame his theory and practice of Biomechanics as a theatrical adaptation of the industrial efficiency theories of Frederick Winslow Taylor. We don't deny that association, but we also encourage our students to consider why Grotowski, whose work is anything but technophilic and industrial, would be so inspired by these techniques. To answer that question, we read selections from Meyerhold's writings, watch film recordings of biomechanical exercises, and practice those exercises. We ask our students to identify shared values (i.e., the desire to transform the actor's body into an expressive tool), shared forms, and their experiences as biomechanical performers (Meyerhold 2016, 176; Braun 1995, 128).

Meyerhold loved puppets and deeply admired puppeteers. And among those he loved the most were the ones used in Japanese theatre. In contrast with the industrial framing of Biomechanics, we emphasize Meyerhold's passionate appreciation for Japanese theatre, particularly kabuki and bunraku (Tian 1999). We expose students to both of these genres—ideally, by watching live performances, and, ideally, by enabling them to practice a few of these forms' core techniques. Again, we encourage them to identify similarities and differences between the practices, to construct a rich set of historical, critical, and comparative relationships.

And that's where we encounter Zeami Motokiyo, the fifteenth-century actor, playwright, and dramaturg whose writings and practice deeply influenced noh, kabuki, and bunraku. We ask our students to read selections from his 1424 treatise *Kakyo* ("The Mirror Held Up to the Flower") in which Zeami uses the imagery of a puppeteer to describe what an actor does:

> This constructed puppet, on a cart, shows various aspects of himself but cannot come to live of itself. It represents a deed performed by moving strings. At the moment when the strings are cut, the figure falls and crumbles. *Sarugaku* too is an art that makes use of just such artifice. What supports these illusions and gives them life is the intensity of mind of the actor.
>
> (Rimer and Masakazu, 97–8)

With Zeami, kabuki, and bunraku in mind, we take another look at Meyerhold's biomechanical exercises and Grotowski's *Akropolis*. If we've done our job well, those will now look very different, and our students will be able to identify and reflect upon the ways that a performance-focused, technology-conscious approach to theatre history can reveal surprising, fascinating, even inspiring connections among theatre artists and traditions that, on their face, appear to have little in common with each other. Except, of course, a shared concern with the human experience.

Conclusion: the principles of systemic dramaturgy

A reframed, re-historicized, and reorganized approach to the relationship of theatre and technology is just the start to a theatre education that enables students to engage critically with the technology available to them right here, right now. Ultimately, we must enable our students to ask the kinds of questions that pertain to the productions that are happening in the world around them. History, after all, must serve the present or be nothing worth. What questions should the critically informed dramaturg be asking about the digital, the cyber, the virtual, the robotic, and the prosthetic in relation to the process of creating engaging, memorable live performance? How can the systemic dramaturg help directors, designers, and audiences think critically about technologies both old and new, technologies that can not only create memorable experiences in the theatre but facilitate creation and collaboration by those who want to make those kinds of experiences?

The perspicacious professor's task is less about helping the next generation of theatre makers become comfortable with new technologies than it is about helping them recognize their positionality in respect to technology as history, practice, and ideology. We want to promote a generation of dramaturgs who understand that the questions we're asking about technology today are hardly new—and the solutions of the past are not irrelevant simply because they were made out of rope and cloth instead of microcomputers and high-definition digital projectors. A history of world theatre that understands technology as the original problem of theatre—rather than a problem pertaining only to a thin temporal and geographical slice of modernity—suggests a different set of problems and solutions, if not an entirely different ethical orientation. The reframed, re-historicized, and reorganized theatre history that we've described here recognizes that digital tech doesn't threaten theatre any more than an *ekkyklema* did. On the contrary, it expands the horizons of our art form and our pedagogy.

We advocate, then, a dramaturgical pedagogy that is guided by and inculcates five core principles:

1   Although dramaturgical theories emerge from historical understandings of performance and the technologies that informed them, they are not in any way beholden to them.
2   It is the responsibility of the dramaturg to thoroughly interrogate those historical understandings to ensure that the ideological conceptions— the *tekne*—that govern particular historical or cultural understandings of technology do not interfere with the critical exploration and application of those technologies.
3   The emergence of new technologies of performance does not render obsolete older technologies. Likewise, new conceptions of technology do not render obsolete older conceptions.
4   The incorporation of new technologies into the production process and staging of live performance is not a threat to but an extension of human experience into new imaginative, aesthetic, and entertainment

territories. Further, it affirms a history of creative problem-solving that is shared across cultures.

5   Advances in digital technology have not only expanded the experience of human subjectivity, but alert us to a history of technology that complicates how we understand technology as both a concept and a repertoire of techniques and tools.

We hope that our students will come to understand that the relationship of performance to technology is now and always has been dynamic, complex, and problematic. The systemic dramaturg should be able to understand and engage the relationships between the actor and the performance, the natural and the artificial, the real and the virtual, and the mediated and the immediate not as set states but as commingled parts of a fluid and contingent system. In that way, the dramaturg should be capable of crafting specific dramaturgical solutions for their creative team that enables innovative, practical solutions and, just as importantly, prioritizes inclusiveness, diversity, and the deconstruction of unhelpful orthodoxies. Ultimately, a systemic dramaturg should be a systemic educator, capable of empowering themselves, their teams, and their audiences to make theatre that is beautiful, memorable, powerful, and smart.

Sample syllabus: *Systemic dramaturgy: An introduction*

Course description

This course introduces the student to a new approach to the study of dramaturgy and theatre history, specifically as it concerns the adoption of new technologies in performance art. The course asks three questions:

1   To what extent are traditional dramaturgical theories and practices changed by digital, robotic, and social technologies?
2   How do new technologies alter the way we conceptualize, make, stage, and experience live performance? *Vice versa*, how can live performance change the ways we understand and experience technology, whether old or new?
3   How do new technologies alter our understanding of the human as such—especially, our capacity to perceive, think, feel, reflect, and communicate?

It is the responsibility of the dramaturg to thoroughly question and comprehend those historical notions for themselves and their creative team. After all, technology isn't just tools but a way of thinking, an ideological conception—what the philosophers call *tekne*. We will investigate how the incorporation of new technologies into performance at various ages and places extends human experience into new imaginative, aesthetic, and entertainment territories. Ultimately, this course will help the budding dramaturg better understand the history of theatre, better comprehend how technology shapes theatre, and, most importantly, how to think and make with the emergent technologies of our own moment.

Course goals

Upon completion of the course, the student will be able to do the following:

1   Define and identify technology as both a repertoire of theatrical tools and techniques as well as a conceptual framework (i.e., *tekne*) that shapes how we understand the script, the stage, the actor, the audience, and other aspects of the theatre as medium.
2   Identify, compare, and evaluate multiple examples, applications, and conceptions of technology in diverse historical, cultural, and aesthetic contexts.
3   Identify, apply, and evaluate specific technologies and technologies applications that respond effectively to practical theatrical challenges.
4   Articulate critical questions that prioritize inclusiveness and diversity and that challenge assumptions that undermine communication, collaboration, and creation.

Course schedule

UNIT ONE. *Tekne and its discontents.* Students dive into a classic dramaturgical text with an eye towards how it envisions material production.
Read: Aristotle, *Poetics* (the constituent elements of Tragedy).
Read: Aeschylus, *Prometheus Bound:* Students read this with a critical eye on the role technology plays in the script but also on how to stage the events the play describes in the text.
Do: Masked performance workshop, with masks provided by the instructor or, even better, crafted by the students.
Do: Devise staging strategies for *Prometheus Bound.*

UNIT TWO. *The anti-technological as technological.* Students leap to the recent past to consider how two of the most celebrated directors of the 20th century respond to the explosion of theatre technologies.
Read: From Schechner, Richard. 1973. *Environmental Theatre.* New York: Applause Books.
Read: From Grotowski, Jerzy. 1968. *Towards a Poor Theatre.* New York: Grove.
Watch: Clips from Grotowski's *Akropolis* (1964), The Performance Group's *Dionysus in 69* (1969), or similar.

Do: Identify a space for an environmental theatre performance of *Prometheus Bound*, highlighting the specific aspects of that place that align with the play's themes and dramatic action.

UNIT THREE. *From Bunraku to Biomechanics.* Students are introduced to critical historiography by mapping conceptual and formal connections between two very different artists and artistic cultures.

Read: Zeami (1984) from *Kakyo* – "Connecting All the Arts through One Intensity of Mind." In *On the Art of the No Drama: The Major Treatises of Zeami.* J. Thomas Rimer and Yamazaki Masakazu, trans. Princeton, NJ: Princeton University Press.

Read: Meyerhold, Vsevelod. (1917) 2016. "The Stylized Theatre," and "The Actor of the Future and Biomechanics." In *Meyerhold on Theatre*, 4th ed. Edward Braun, ed. New York: Bloomsbury Methuen.

Watch: *The Lover's Exile: The Artistry of the Legendary Bunraku Puppet Theatre* (Marty Gross, 2011), and Jörg Bochow's *Meyerhold's Theatre and Biomechanics* (2003).

Do: Biomechanical exercises.

Do: Puppet performances.

UNIT FOUR: *Dramaturgy beyond the theatre: videogames.* Students explore the application of dramaturgical techniques beyond theatre.

Play: Cardboard Computer, *Kentucky Route Zero*

Watch: Tamas Kemenczy, "The scenography of *Kentucky Route Zero*"

Read: Haley, Jennifer. 2009. *Neighborhood 3: Requisition of Doom.* Los Angeles: Samuel French.

Do: Devise staging strategies for *Neighborhood 3*.

UNIT FIVE: *Engaging the argument.* This unit immerses the student in a contemporary controversy concerning technology and asks them to locate themselves within it.

Read: From Phelan, Peggy. 1993. *Unmarked: The Politics of Performance.* London: Routledge.

Read: From Auslander, Philip. 2008 *Liveness: Performance in a Mediatized Culture*, Second Edition. London: Routledge.

Read: Chemers, Michael and Mike Sell. Forthcoming. "*Sokyokuchi*: Towards a Theory, History, and Practice of Systemic Dramaturgy," *Theatre History Studies*, vol. 39.

Watch: Blast Theory's *2097: We Made Ourselves Over* (2017); Builders Association's *Continuous City* (2007) or *Super Vision* (2005); Dumb Type's *S/N* (1994); or similar.

Do: Participate in a debate concerning whether electronic and social-media technology damage the audience experience.

UNIT SIX: *Full circle.* Students revisit Aristotle by looking at a modern "systemic" production of an ancient Greek play that emphasizes cultural diversity, technological facility, and creative innovation.
Watch: Julie Taymor's *Oedipus Rex* (1993).
Do: Devise staging strategies for *Prometheus Bound* that utilize digital, computational, social-media, or robotic technologies.

FINAL PROJECTS

Students work in small teams to generate a production concept for Kan'ami's noh drama *Matsukaze.*

Students work individually to compose a dramaturgical statement about that production that explains and justifies their production choices on a philosophical level.

Notes

1 Forthcoming from Southern Illinois University Press.
2 No record of this "old" saying appears prior to its first known use in an article in the Chicago *Sun-Times* of 10 Jan 1993 (53) by Janet Kidd Stewart entitled "You Don't Have to Go Broke to Go Out." Stewart coins this phrase, then, in the middle of the late-twentieth-century controversies about the merging of electronic tech with live performance art.
3 When we had the opportunity to present this research at the Humanities Center of the University of Pittsburgh (26 September 2019), dramaturg Meghan Monaghan Rivas and film and media professor Neepa Majumdar helped us to clarify the definition of "technology" to include performative language and gesture.
4 Which is not to say such works do not exist, only that they are not yet widely adopted in undergraduate curricula. Our bibliography contains sources for teachers looking to bone up on the subject.

References

Bay-Cheng, Sarah, Jennifer Parker-Starbuck, D.Z. Saltz. 2015. *Performance and Media: Taxonomies for a Changing Field.* Ann Arbor: University of Michigan Press.

Bay-Cheng, Sarah, C. Kattenbelt, A. Lavender, R. Nelson, eds. 2010. *Mapping Intermediality in Performance.* Amsterdam: Amsterdam University Press/ University of Chicago Press.

Bloom, Gina. 2018. *Gaming the Stage: Playable Media and the Rise of English Commercial Theatre.* Ann Arbor: University of Michigan Press.

Braun, Edward. 1995. *Meyerhold, A Revolution in Theatre.* Iowa City: University of Iowa Press.

Causey, Matthew. 2006. *Theatre and Performance in Digital Culture: From Simulation to Embeddedness.* London: Routledge.

Chemers, Michael M. 2010. *Ghost Light: An Introductory Handbook for Dramaturgy.* Carbondale: Southern Illinois University Press.

Chemers, Michael M. and Mike Sell. Forthcoming. "*Sokyokuchi*: Towards a Theory, History, and Practice of Systemic Dramaturgy." *Theatre History Studies* 39.

Dixon, Steve. 2007. *Digital Performance: A History of New Media in Theatre, Dance, Performance Art, and Installation.* Cambridge, MA: MIT Press.

Eckersall, Peter, Helena Grehan, and Edward Scheer, 2017. *New Media Dramaturgy: Performance, Media, and New-Materialism.* New York: Palgrave MacMillan.

Grotowski, Jerzy. 1968. *Towards a Poor Theatre.* New York: Grove.

Meyerhold, Vsevelod. (1917) 2016. "The Actor of the Future and Biomechanics." In *Meyerhold on Theatre.* Edward Braun, trans. and ed. New York: Bloomsbury.

Parker-Starbuck, Jennifer. 2011. *Cyborg Theatre: Corporeal/Technological Intersections in Multimedia Performance.* New York: Palgrave Macmillan.

Rimer, J. Thomas, and Yamazaki Masakazu. 1984. *On the Art of the No Drama: The Major Treatises of Zeami.* Princeton, NJ: Princeton University Press.

Salter, Chris. 2010. *Entangled: Technology and the Transformation of Performance.* Cambridge, MA: MIT Press.

Schechner, Richard. 1973. *Environmental Theatre.* New York: Applause.

Tian, Min. 1999. "Meyerhold Meets Mei Lanfang: Staging the Grotesque and the Beautiful." *Comparative Drama* 33:2; 234–69.

5 Contemporary playwriting pedagogies
A survey of recent introductory playwriting syllabi

Les Hunter

Introduction

The discourse of performance studies and theory has generally viewed the authorial "text" with suspicion. As Henry Bial points out in his introduction to *The Performance Studies Reader*: "[Richard] Schechner and others suggested a de-emphasizing of literary, text-based criticism in favor of performance-based analysis" (2016, 5). This exclusion extends to the traditional craft of script creation, playwriting. The word "playwriting," for instance, appears only three times in Schechner's 377-page *Performance Studies: An Introduction*, last updated in 2013 (2013). However, as W. B. Worthen has noted in his own oft-cited essay "Disciplines of the Text/Sites of Performance," "texts are not what is really at issue, but how they are construed as vessels of authority, of canonical values, of hegemonic consent" (1995, 14). Furthermore, as Schechner has observed, projects within the field of performance studies and related areas "often act on or act against settled hierarchies of ideas, organizations, and people" (2013, 4). If then, power— its forms, uses, and misuses—is within the purview of the field of critical performance theory, then a look at the way power is being authorized by the text within the classroom could be considered as an apt area of study.

Given these concerns, it stands to reason to examine, within this discourse, dramatic texts, their various strategies of creation, and the way they function in the classroom. Moreover, Jill Dolan argues in her genealogy of performance studies, "The Polemics and Potential of Theatre Studies and Performance," that the field grew out of a desire to question and critique the "objectivity and empiricism of traditional theatre departments" in order to create students who are "not only scholar/artists but citizen/scholar/artists" (2006, Chapter 28). In this view, an evaluation of playwriting pedagogy could productively yield information on not only the way that playwriting— and traditional dramatic creation—is currently being taught in the United States, but could also point out ways that contemporary pedagogy practices both succeed and fail to question assumptions about power, race, gender, class, and canon. This study yields, for instance, data that suggest both that most introductory playwriting classes in America rarely set out to question traditional forms of dramatic creation, and that more often than not questions about power and canon are not brought up in compelling ways.[1] This study will additionally look at the tension between the writing and the reading of plays. Plays operate in the classroom as both a text—a site of analysis—but also as a discursive site of creative invention with its own conventions, methodologies, and historical context. These too can be seen as acting for— or against—"settled hierarchies of ideas, organizations, and people," and thus are open for survey and analysis within the field of performance studies.

Institutions of higher education actively engage in the instruction of playwriting. According to *Peterson's* online college guide, twenty-seven schools in the United States and Canada offer degrees in playwriting and screenwriting (Peterson's 2017). This volume of instruction has sparked an increasing body of literature on what *should* be taught in the playwriting classroom. This corpus ranges from *Playwrights Teach Playwriting*, edited by Joan Herrington and Crystal Brian (2006); to essays on ideal playwriting pedagogy like Anne García-Romero and Alice Tuan's "Teaching Playwriting in the 21st Century" (2013) and Jonathan Levy's "Why Teach Playwriting?" (2001, 13–15) as well as quantitative high school classroom studies like Paul Gardiner's "Playwriting Pedagogy and the Myth of Intrinsic Creativity" (2016, 247). Yet despite this growth in interest in playwriting pedagogy, there is little information available on what contemporary college playwriting courses actually teach. To engage with this problem, I conducted the following analysis to ground this discourse in an understanding of the kind of instruction that generally takes place in the contemporary playwriting classroom. I wanted to see if that instruction suggests anything about academe's positioning of playwriting within its curriculum, or indeed if it says anything about how burgeoning playwrights and other theatre makers are introduced to playwriting practice. At the core of the analysis was a survey of thirty playwriting syllabi from across the country. I used the following questions to guide my analysis: (1) What are the stated primary goals in courses that focus on an introduction to playwriting? (2) What kinds of assignments do these courses employ? (3) What kinds of texts are used? (4) Do the texts challenge students to become, in Dolan's words, "citizen/scholar/artists"? (2006, Chapter 28). (5) How do these courses consider diversity (national, temporal, ethnic, cultural, racial, religious, gender, etc.)?

Literature review

A brief literature review of contemporary playwriting pedagogy may provide a useful rubric of suggested best practices in the college classroom. Recent scholarship suggests what should *not* be taught in the playwriting classroom. A 2016 Australian study by Paul Gardiner collected qualitative data from high school playwriting students and teachers through journals and interviews and found that many educators considered creativity in general, and playwriting in particular, an intrinsic talent. That is, many educators in the study echoed Edward Albee's claim that "Playwrighting [*sic*] can't really be taught" and is instead an innate ability, one that should be fostered and encouraged, but not tampered with through instruction in technique (Lask, 1963). This notion bears some resemblance to Wordsworth's Romantic conception of artistic creation as "the spontaneous overflow of powerful feelings," and as such Gardiner refers to this idea as a "Romantic" conception of creativity (Wordsworth and Coleridge 1963, 237). Based on reflections of students and educators during the courses and after the courses were complete, the study concluded that "the teachers' belief in the intrinsic nature of creativity and reluctance to intervene meant that they also neglected strategies, such as writing exercises that may have addressed this skill deficit before submission" (Gardiner 2016, 257). The study further suggests that, instead of immersing students solely in writing a play, "the skills of playwriting, while accessible, are specific and need to be consciously addressed" (Gardiner 2016, 259). Gardiner finally recommends a "playwriting pedagogical approach that takes account of the spectrum of theoretical approaches" from "open" experimental instruction to "closed" traditional, Aristotelian and character-driven methods.[2]

So what *should* the introductory playwriting classroom teach? The answer to this question has drawn a variety of opinions, from calls for professional training that prepares students for the future of theatre, to recommendations for a holistic, life-skill orientation. One recent consideration of playwriting pedagogy in *Howlround* ("Teaching Playwriting in the 21st Century") by professor and playwright Anne García-Romero and playwright Alice Tuan suggests that classes should prepare students for the coming challenges facing a professional playwright. They recommend playwriting be taught to (1) empower students' voices, (2) bolster intra-personal human connections in an increasingly "technologically mediated world," and (3) encourage students' ability to foster and use seemingly contradictory skills (marketplace vs. "art," solitary vs. collaborative creation, etc., [2013]). Conversely, playwright and professor Jonathan Levy's article "Why Teach Playwriting?" rejects the idea that playwriting pedagogy should focus on training students for a future as professional playwrights. In his words, "to think that playwriting is a skill that will be useful to children in their adult lives is nonsense" (2001, 13). Levy instead suggests that playwriting classes should offer students important humanistic life skills, teaching them to (1) recognize and value vivid instances and moments, (2) closely observe human behavior, (3) see through cliché "to nature," (4) develop an ability to cut or modify one's own work when working with others, (5) understand and empathize with the Other, and (6) be imaginative while working within the constraints of a given project (13–15). My own analysis will employ García-Romero and Tuan's focus on preparing students for careers in playwriting, Levy's orientation toward holistic education, and Gardiner's recommendation for a "spectrum of theoretical approaches" as a yardstick for measuring how well playwriting pedagogy is implemented in the United States. I will also examine how well playwriting students are being prepared to be "citizen/scholar/artists" who develop the potential to use critical analysis and performance to disrupt oppressive representations of humanity.

Methodology

The survey on which this analysis is based is composed of thirty syllabi for introductory, undergraduate playwriting classes from postsecondary institutions including PhD-granting research, Master's-level, BA-level, BA/ AA, and other two-year schools. Roughly two-thirds of the syllabi included in this sample were from classes listed in theatre departments, and roughly one-third were from departments of English.[3] I collected the syllabi primarily using Boolean Google searches for playwriting syllabi and secondarily from emails to individual playwriting instructors. Every attempt was made to establish a pool of syllabi representative of the general population of higher-education students in the United States. However, efforts to acquire syllabi from two-year institutions proved difficult, while playwriting syllabi from research-, Master's-, and BA-level institutions were easier to locate. The difficulty of locating playwriting syllabi from two-year institutions suggests that playwriting is more frequently taught at research- and Master's-degree-granting schools with more robust research and humanities opportunities.[4] The results from my search therefore tend to skew upward in research/ masters institutions in comparison to the national average of all students in higher education (Table 5.1). Only four syllabi in the entire sample were from departments outside of theatre or English, suggesting that the vast majority of playwriting classes in the United States are taught in theatre departments, followed secondarily by English. The thirty syllabi in this sample ranged in length from two to sixteen pages, with the average being 6.7 pages. The average course capacity is 17.5 students.

In addition to problems in the selection of syllabi, there were also inconsistencies in the data itself. Most syllabi use "objectives" or "goals" to list the primary outcomes of the course, while a few list only a course description. Still others differentiate between course and student outcomes. In these cases, I used the section of the syllabus that most clearly lay out goals for the class. Likewise, while some syllabi give detailed listings of all assignments, schedules, and readings, a few provide a skeletal outline and give the appearance of being a boilerplate list of expectations provided by the department, college, or school. Finally, data about course caps was gathered separately through phone calls and emails. Whenever information on a given variable was unavailable or unclear, it was not collected or allocated and did not weigh into averages. Given (1) the not wholly accurate representative body of collection, (2) some inconsistencies in the data, and (3) that syllabi alone can only outline what goes on in any given class during a semester,

Table 5.1 Percentages of national student body in higher education by institution, corresponding numbers of syllabi needed to represent national student body, and actual number of syllabi included from each institutional type (Carnegie Classification)

School type	Percentage of national student body	Rep. of total sample syllabi needed (out of 30)	No. of syllabi included in survey (out of 30)
Research (doctoral and high)	7%	2	5
Master's College and University	16%	5	5
All BA colleges	33%	10	9
BA/AA/other	9%	3	2
All two-year	35%	10	9

this survey should not be seen as an absolute collection of data nor a complete depiction of playwriting pedagogy. However, it does represent a large collection of recent playwriting syllabi from a wide variety of sizes and types of universities from across the United States and Canada. As such, it can provide a window on to contemporary trends in playwriting pedagogy, and perhaps alert the field to areas that are currently underrepresented.

Results

The stated, primary goals listed by the syllabi yield both consistencies and surprising differences. A word cloud of the most common words and phrases in the course objectives of all thirty syllabi points to some of the typical topics of interest listed in most playwriting classrooms: "writing," "students," "dramatic," and "plays" are the most frequently listed terms, while other popular words include "structure," "process," and "feedback" (Figure 5.1). The terms demonstrate the primary dialectical tensions in the course objectives between pedagogical approaches in the areas of reading/writing (associated with "analysis"/"writing") and so-called "open"/closed" ("process"/"structure") aesthetic sensibility.

One of the primary tensions exhibited in the course objectives is between how much the course should focus on writing, and how much of it should focus on reading or sometimes watching established plays. All classes in the sample require writing of some sort, though not all require students to write a play script of any length. Seventy-six percent of classes have a writing workshop. Classes split on the importance of feedback in the writing process, as 40 percent of syllabi describe fostering students' ability to give and receive feedback on their writing as a primary course objective. Revision, too, is generally low in the courses' priority, with 40 percent requiring students to revise scripts in some way after receiving feedback directly from the instructor or through a workshop with peers. Twenty percent of course

Figure 5.1 Word cloud of commonly listed terms from objectives section of thirty playwriting syllabi.
Note: The word cloud does not include the word "playwriting."

objectives state that students will write exercises in response to specific readings of plays or secondary texts. One Eastern BA-granting institution concentrates almost exclusively on writing plays, creating a 90–100 page writing portfolio consisting of monologues, a ten-minute play, a one-act play, and a research journal. The primary reading component of this class is to read *The New York Times* as a means of play research and prompts for finding stories to write about. This class does not require the reading of plays, but students must produce staged readings.

While the overall emphasis of the course objectives in this collection is on writing plays, there are a surprising number of objectives focused on analysis and understanding playwriting through reading, watching, and responding to established (or, as one syllabus put it, "successful") plays.

Sixty-five percent of classes require that students read published plays, while 62 percent of courses require that students attend a production of work outside of the classroom. Ninety percent of classes require either readings, or productions, or both, which suggests that instructors value student exposure to established plays. Eighty-six percent of classes require students to read secondary texts on playwriting, creative writing, or dramaturgy. One class that favors familiarizing students with established plays through reading is from a private, western-US, BA-granting institution. This course features fourteen primary and secondary readings, including six full-length established plays. The structure of the course revolves around the reading of plays, with discussions, lectures, and writing exercises stemming from specific lessons illustrated by the established plays. The primary writing responsibility of students in the class is completing writing exercises and responses to the plays, which are equally weighted. The class's playwriting requirement is ten pages of dramatic work.

The objectives also yield data on the focus of instruction between "open" and "closed" forms of dramatic creation. According to Gardiner, the "closed," traditional approach is largely based on Aristotelian dramatic structure that focuses on plot, a single protagonist, and normally includes resolved dilemmas. The "open," experimental approach often does not resolve plot or themes, sometimes adopts a cyclical structure, and rejects ultimate meaning (Gardiner 2016, 260). The data suggest that courses tend toward instruction in the "closed" dramaturgical tradition. Seventy percent of syllabi list as a course objective that students acquire (as one syllabus had it) "basic elements" of playwriting, a list that generally consists of closed components such as plot, conflict, character, and especially "dramatic structure," which was listed in 53 percent of course objectives in some shape or form. The language often used to describe structure as "basic," "traditional," "the" (as opposed to "various" forms of dramatic structure), or "the formula for writing a play" underscores the bias toward a closed or more traditional pedagogic approach.

Although 30 percent of the syllabi in the survey of introductory playwriting set a goal to familiarize students with a "variety" of "genres" of playwriting, only four syllabi in the survey clearly set out to question or problematize traditional forms of dramatic structure in what Gardiner would characterize as an open form. The latter tend to have longer objective narratives focusing on the development of personal voice, process, and an approach that draws from other art forms, such as music, film, photography, and painting. One such syllabus encourages students to discard what they think is "right," while another states that there is "no 'right' way to *wright* plays." Finally, though none of the syllabi in the survey specifically suggest that the class introduces students to devised work, or "Viewpoints" specifically, 20 percent of surveys do list as either an objective or as part of a unit that students will develop an understanding of playwriting as part of a collaborative process with others. This kind of collaboration is usually understood to be in conjunction with a director, actors, designers, and so on, and not in terms of devised work or collaborative script creation.

There is a fair amount of consistency to the primary assignments across the courses listings. All but two classes have students write either a play of some length or a sample of a play. None of the classes requires a full-length play; 55 percent of the classes require a one-act play; and 31 percent have students write a ten-minute play as the primary assignment. The courses that require a one-act generally do not have other major writing assignments, while courses that require ten-minute plays generally also require multiple ten-minute plays, revisions, or exercises. Seventeen percent require a portfolio of more than one assignment, which generally includes a short play, drafts, and writing exercises. Two classes require final exams, and one requires a research paper. Thirteen percent of classes require that students perform their work as a staged reading or a workshop production. The activities in the classes include writing workshops, lectures, discussions, writing exercises in response to readings and discussions, and play analysis.

Every course requires at least one primary or secondary text be read. The most common secondary texts in use are *Playwriting: Brief and Brilliant* by Julie Jensen and *Backwards and Forwards* by David Ball. The four most read playwrights are August Wilson (appearing in four classes), Tennessee Williams, Edward Albee, and Samuel Beckett (three classes each). The classes in the survey require students to read 3.9 full-length plays on average, with the highest number of required reading being eleven full-length plays, and eight classes requiring that no full-length plays be read. In terms of diversity of the plays read for class, 22 percent of established full-length plays read are by female playwrights, 16 percent are by domestic people of color, 15 percent are by playwrights from countries other than the United States, and 6 percent were not written in the twentieth or twenty-first centuries (Table 5.2). The established, full-length plays that are read in courses exhibit a significant underrepresentation of plays written by domestic people of color, women, international, and pre-twentieth-century writers.

Discussion and conclusion

Given the support among the sampled classes for reading or sometimes viewing established work, it is fair to speculate that, unlike the teachers in

Table 5.2 Diversity representation of published plays read in thirty playwriting syllabi

% of plays by female playwrights	% by international playwrights	% by domestic people of color	% of non-20th/ 21st century plays
22%	15%	16%	6%

Gardiner's study, the creators of these syllabi do not consider playwriting to be an intrinsic talent. Instead, by reading or watching established plays and secondary texts, these instructors hope to familiarize students with writing strategies used by playwrights, or as one syllabus has it, to "expose the students to dramatic literature that serves as an example of good playwriting." If anything, the courses surveyed here show a tendency to rely on established, "closed," Aristotelian works in the instruction of new plays. And while Beckett provides somewhat of an outlier, some of the best known works (from the survey) of Wilson (*Fences*), Williams (*Glass Menagerie*) and Albee's (*Who's Afraid of Virginia Woolf?*) generally share primary characteristics associated with Aristotelian drama: reversals, reveals, and a character who has a flaw that they attempt to overcome, but who are eventually overcome by it. More demonstrative still of this reliance on "closed" Aristotelian strategies of instruction are the ways the syllabi focus on what they term the "basic elements" of plot, dialogue, and character, which, as noted earlier, are listed as central concerns for more than two-thirds of the courses in the survey. Five of the thirty syllabi in this data set list specifically mention Aristotle's *The Poetics* as one of their secondary readings.

According to Augusto Boal's famous critique of Aristotelian drama ("Aristotle's Coercive System of Tragedy," which is listed as a secondary reading in one of the syllabi in this survey):

> Aristotle constructs the first, extremely powerful poetic-political system for intimidations of the spectator, for elimination of the 'bad' or illegal tendencies of the audience. This system is, to this day, fully utilized not only in conventional theater, but in the TV soap operas and in Western films as well: movies, theater, and television united, through a common basis in Aristotelian poetics, for repression of the people.
>
> (1985, xiv)

Not unlike the film and television work that Boal so derides, this focus tends toward mainstream, commercial work. Dolan, well aware of the commercial aspect of university programs, rejects it for a more utopian model:

> Too often, university theatres fail to use their resources to introduce their faculty and students and others to a new writer, a new performance style, a new issue or identity in the space of their stages. Rather than employing a pedagogical model of theatre production and practice, they adopt the market strategies of the industry they seek to emulate.
>
> (2006, Chapter 28)

For Dolan, this kind of focus detracts from the work of creating citizen/scholar/artists, and seems to indicate that, in that direction, playwriting classes in America still have a lot of room to grow. Dolan asks, "Shouldn't university theatres reach higher than that, and try to create performances that reach deeper, intellectually, artistically, and even spiritually?" (2006, 508). Instead of focusing merely on recreating or copying strategies that are established by mainstream plays, Dolan suggests that theatre departments instead be the site of public debate about race, class, gender, and canon through production and performance. The reliance on reading established work in the survey furthermore suggests that instructors do not generally heed García-Romero and Tuan's call for the development of authorial voice through writing. This is especially evident given that only 17 percent of syllabi called directly for developing an author's unique voice and, although some of the syllabi encourage close reading or analysis of established plays, none of the syllabi list objectives that directly observe García-Romero and Tuan's recommendation to encourage liveness in a "technologically mediated world."

The data shed light on the question of whether playwriting classrooms should focus on professionalization for future playwrights, as favored by García-Romero and Tuan or encourage humanistic life skills, as laid out by Levy. The most common primary course assignment given is the completion of a one-act play, which, while understandable as a manageable assignment for a semester-long introductory class, is not a genre of playwriting that currently seems likely to have much of a professional future. Any working playwright can contend that, while there is little "market" for new one-act plays, there is one for both ten-minute and full-lengths plays, with ten-minute play submissions widely open to playwrights without agency representation or previous publications. In a most recent call for plays from Play Submissions Helper (an online subscription service that culls calls for submissions for playwrights), for instance, only 15 percent of calls for submission are for one-act plays, while 35 percent of calls are for 10-minute plays, the remainder being a mix of full-lengths and musicals (2017). The reliance on the one-act play as the primary writing assignment of the playwriting classroom, then, raises the question: are we giving students relevant professional preparation when one-acts have so few production opportunities? Or is it worth continuing teaching the one-act because of its convenient length, one that, in my own experience, allows instructors time to have one play workshopped within a class period with enough time for student feedback. Or, in Levy's words, is it "nonsense" to even try to prepare students for lives as professional playwrights, in which case the ten-minute/one-act question is moot and instead becomes: what format best encourages humanistic personal growth? And does this lead us back to Dolan's insistence on creating citizen/scholar/artists who can effectively read the systems of power operating in their lives and respond to them through playwriting?

If, as in Levy's opinion, we should be teaching students to value particularity, closely observe human behavior, cultivate empathy, learn to be critical of our own work, and work within restraints, it would seem that the contemporary playwriting classroom, based on current syllabi, still has a long way to go. There are few instances in the syllabi collected that directly call on students to learn Levy's recommended lessons. One syllabus does list as a course objective that students will "consider idiosyncrasies of character," and another asks that students "demonstrate awareness of natural rhythms and intonations of human speech." The area of focus that appears to have the most correlation with one of Levy's recommendations is in the ability to be self-critical, to "make hard choices," and to let go if what you've created doesn't "work." This is evident in the frequent calls for students to engage in feedback for themselves and others. Nearly half of the syllabi list as a course objective the creation of an environment where feedback can be constructively given. The courses' interest in developing feedback can be seen as a way to encourage communion between both the solitary and the collaborative nature of playwriting, a seeming contradiction that is also central to one of García-Romero and Tuan's primary criteria for playwriting pedagogy.

In conclusion, the institutions represented in this survey constitute a sample that is similar to the national student body of undergraduate students at large. Survey results suggest that instructors do not view playwriting as an intrinsic aptitude but instead as something that is best taught through the example of established plays as well as writing original plays. Forty percent of classes ask students to develop an awareness of multiple forms or genres of plays, suggesting that, as is in the case of many of the metrics analyzed throughout this survey, there is still room for growth in Gardiner's recommendation that a "spectrum of theoretical approaches" be taught in the playwriting classroom (2016, 260). Playwriting pedagogy presents itself as a field of instruction still largely awaiting critical interventions that encourage the development of citizen/scholar/artists.

Notes

1 *HowlRound* originally published an earlier, abbreviated version of this chapter as "An Analysis of Undergraduate Playwriting Syllabi" on 29 November 2017.
2 According to Gardiner,

> The closed approach (heavily influenced by Aristotle's *Poetics*) focuses on the resolution of a plot, centered on a single protagonist, struggling against both their fatal flaw and an opponent/antagonist. This approach, reflecting a worldview that assumes that 'certainty' is possible and that we are agents operating with free will, normally includes 'witty and logically built up dialogue' (Esslin 1965), resolved dilemmas and consistent characters (e.g., Arthur Miller's *The Crucible* and Henrik Ibsen's *A Doll's House*). The *open* approach on the other hand is informed by the experience of twentieth-century avant-garde theatre makers (e.g., Samuel Beckett and Bertolt Brecht). These plays often choose not to resolve thematic ideas or demands of plot and may adopt a cyclical structure that rejects a reliance on 'cause and effect' and deny the existence of an 'ultimate' meaning grounded in resolution and

finality (Edgar 2009). Eco (1989) suggests that an open text is one that offers multiplicity and perhaps 'inexhaustibility' of meaning, and explores this in juxtaposition to the closed work, that contains a single meaning that reflects a belief in certainty and hierarchy.

(Gardiner, 260)

3 Institutional designations are from the Indiana University Center for Postsecondary Research, Carnegie Classification of Institutions of Higher Education. The institutions included in my survey are as follows: Austin Community College, Angelo State University, Baldwin Wallace University, Bergen Community College, Boston University, Coastal Carolina College, Colby College, College of the Pacific, Cuyahoga County Community College, Drew University, Furman University, Gordon State College, Kent State University at Stark, Laredo Community College, Macalester College, Maricopa Community College, Metropolitan Community College, Monroe Community College, Northern Arizona University, Pellissippi State Community College, Raritan Valley Community College, Texas Tech University, Towson University, University of Southern California, University of Wisconsin, Washington and Jefferson College, Walla Walla Community College, Weber State University, and Wesleyan University.

4 Percentages of all US students enrolled in postsecondary education are from *The Chronicle of Higher Education 2016 Almanac.*

References

Bial, Henry. 2016. "What Is Performance Studies?" In *The Performance Studies Reader*, edited by Henry Bial and Sara Brady. New York: Routledge.

Boal, Augusto. 1985. *Theatre of the Oppressed.* Trans. Charles A. and Maria-Odilia Leal McBride. New York: Theatre Communication Group.

"Chronicle of Higher Education 2016 Almanac." 2016. *Chronicle of Higher Education*, 14 Aug. 2016. Accessed 15 June 2017. www.chronicle.com/specialreport/The-Almanac-of-Higher/51.

Dolan, Jill. "The Polemics and Potential of Theatre Studies and Performance." 2006. In *The Sage Handbook of Performance Studies*, edited by Judith Hamera and D. Soyini Madison, Ch. 28. Thousand Oaks, CA: SAGE Publications, Inc. Ebook version. https://doi.org/10.4135/9781412976145.

García-Romero, Anne and Alice Tuan. 2013. "Teaching Playwriting in the 21st Century." *Howlround.* 2 June 2013. Accessed 10 July 2017. howlround.com/teaching-playwriting-in-the-21st-century.

Gardiner, Paul. 2016. "Playwriting Pedagogy and the Myth of Intrinsic Creativity." *Research in Drama Education: The Journal of Applied Theatre and Performance* 21 (2): 247–262.

Herrington, Joan and Brian, Crystal, eds. 2006. *Playwrights Teach Playwriting.* Hanover, NH: Smith & Kraus Pub Inc.

Hunter, Les. "An Analysis of Undergraduate Playwriting Syllabi." *Howlround.* 29 November 2017. Accessed 15 November 2018. https://howlround.com/analysis-undergraduate-playwriting-syllabi.

Koger, Alicia Kae. 1994. "Teaching Introduction to Theatre Today: An Analysis of Current Syllabi." *Theatre Topics* 4 (1): 59–63.

Lask, Thomas. 1963. "Edward Albee at Ease." *New York Times,* 27 October 1963. Accessed 15 July 2017. www.nytimes.com/books/99/08/15/specials/albee-atease.html.

Levy, Jonathan. 2001. "Why Teach Playwriting?" *Teaching Theatre* 12 (2): 13–15.

"Peterson's—The Real Guide to Colleges and Universities" *Peterson's.* n.d., Accessed 25 July, 2017.

"Plays With Deadlines, 6/22/2017" *Play Submissions Helper.* n.d., Accessed 15 July 2017. Playsubmissionshelper.com.

Schechner, Richard. 1988. "Performance Studies: The Broad Spectrum Approach." *TDR* 32 (3) 4–6.

Schechner, Richard. 2013. *Performance Studies: An Introduction,* 3rd ed. New York: Routledge.

Smith, Susan Harris. 1989. "Generic Hegemony: American Drama and the Canon." *American Quarterly* 41 (1): 112–122.

Wordsworth, William, and Samuel T. Coleridge. 1963. *Lyrical Ballads [by] Wordsworth and Coleridge: The Text of the 1798 Edition with the Additional 1800 Poems and the Prefaces.* Edited by R.L. Brett and A.R. Jones. London: Methuen.

Worthen, W. B. 1995. "Disciplines of the Text/Sites of Performance." *TDR* 39 (1): 13–28.

Part II

Classroom identities

Engaging students in theory

6 Performing blackness, ecodramaturgy, and social justice
Toward a radical pedagogy

La Donna L. Forsgren

What is "blackness"? Does blackness appertain to an individual or group? Can blackness be appropriated? How is blackness performed onstage and in everyday life? Finally, if race is simply a social construct, then why does blackness continue to matter? These complicated questions serve as the foundation for a course I teach entitled, Performing Blackness: From Othello to Jay-Z. I created the first iteration of this course while teaching at the University of Oregon prior to the formation of the Black Lives Matter movement. Reflecting on this 2012 course, I now understand that my greatest challenge was guiding my predominantly white liberal students to an understanding of how white privilege continues to operate in our society today. We were at a moment in history where many of my students expressed belief that with the presidential election of Barack Obama, we had finally advanced to a "post-racial" society. Five years later, having taught the second iteration of the course at the University of Notre Dame, I am somewhat embarrassed by my own naïve attempts to disrupt such wrong-headed thinking. Hindsight has revealed that while I may have successfully helped students understand the nature of white privilege, I neglected to fully explore blackness as a galvanizing force, nor forewarn the dangers of conservative backlash. The 2016 US presidential election taught me that the gains of the Long Civil Rights, LGBTQ+, and feminist movements are not fixed; they remain under constant threat of co-optation or outright elimination.

As scholars, teachers, and artists who study and create black performance traditions, we are in a unique position to use the classroom as a site of radical intervention. Embedded in the material we discuss are opportunities to disseminate the dangers facing US society. The activist and former editor of *The Black Panther* newspaper Judy Juanita writes:

> Black people often serve as an early warning system for the American populace; we took the hit first with heroin mid-twentieth century before drugs rushed the mainstream. We've borne the brunt of police brutality, in its myriad forms since enslavement, social media only lately exposing society's grave mistake in giving the police far greater power than we

need them to wield. ... For better and worse, the hardcore issues blacks face—guns, crime, poverty, failing schools—define the newest America.

(2016, 161)

As such, we cannot fully engage with the cultural context from which black performance traditions emerge without also revealing how African American communities disproportionately bear the brunt of societal ills. Our classrooms provide an important space wherein we can explore with our students the current state of black communities and what this might mean for the greater American populace. In other words, it is not enough to raise awareness of white privilege or even to clarify how past representations of blackness inform our present-day realities. We must also re-envision our approach to student learning and identify the ways in which blackness reveals the dangers that lie ahead if US society continues along its current path of social and ecological injustice.

Just as blackness crosses disciplinary boundaries, so too must this chapter. I interrogate the performance of blackness in theatre, film, and in everyday life, providing concrete strategies to help instructors illuminate why blackness, as a performative gesture, continues to matter. I incorporate my own experiential knowledge teaching Performing Blackness, as well as theoretical interventions from the fields of ecodramaturgy, black feminist theories, and performance studies, to argue for a more radical pedagogy; one that privileges the ambiguity and paradoxes of blackness as an essential tool for understanding past social injustices, our present ecological and societal concerns, as well as future dangers. The investigation begins with a broad overview of my pedagogical failures teaching Performing Blackness in 2012. I then share my more recent radical approach to teaching blackness as a performative gesture, which I based on the neurocognitive research of Mark Bracher and black feminist theories of bell hooks. I explain how identity-based analysis of Rachel Dolezal/Akechi Amare Diallo's public construction of "transracial identity" and an ecodramaturgical analysis of Lorraine Hansberry's *A Raisin in The Sun* (1959) help students better understand the changing contours of blackness and why the relationship between blackness and ecology remains a critical concern within social justice movements today. I then offer strategies for situating Amiri Baraka/LeRoi Jones's *Dutchman* (1964) and Jordan Peele's Academy Award winning film *Get Out* (2017) as dramatic interventions that reveal the fallacies of the American dream and "post-racial" society. I conclude with a call for cultural change within the academy; one that supports, rather than penalizes the process of working toward a more radical pedagogy.

Early errors

When I originally conceived of teaching Performing Blackness during the 2011–2012 academic year, my motives were less than altruistic. I was PhD candidate at Northwestern University, had just given birth to my third child, was directing a play, and teaching a full load of courses while struggling to find my own identity as a visiting assistant professor at the University of Oregon. With these time constraints and pressures in mind, I wanted to teach a class from within my "wheelhouse," meaning African American theatre and performance history. As I selected topics for the course, my familiarity with the material outweighed any concern I had for student learning or the material's social relevance. *I was in survival mode.*

I share my pedagogical failure because I now understand that while some of the challenges I faced were due to my individual circumstances, the "growing pains" or struggles I encountered as an inexperienced and overworked educator resonate with many. When we emerge with our graduate degrees in hand, we are often ill-prepared for the rigors of engaging students in the classroom or inspiring students to become more socially aware, life-long learners. bell hooks noted these problems more than twenty years ago in her book, *Teaching to Transgress: Education as the Practice of Freedom.* hooks writes that "there is a serious crisis in education. Students often do not want to learn and teachers do not want to teach" (1994, 12). While I did want to satisfy the teaching standards at my institution, I lacked a passion for the classroom. An attitude of survival did not foster the high level of intellectual curiosity and original critical thinking that students have now come to expect from my courses. In other words, I found our discussions stagnant, superficial, and disconnected from the socio-political realities of our time.

The theories of hooks and Mark Bracher, coupled with the formation of the Black Lives Matter movement in 2015, directly impacted my pedagogical practices. No longer could I teach about past injustices without discussing how violence against black bodies continues to permeate our society. Thus, effectively "woke," I redefined my vision of effective teaching as that which promotes a student's personal well-being and social change. This vision is not new, but rather, a fundamental principle of education. Bracher writes that "education has always been seen as a key element in social change, functioning either as a vehicle for change or an impediment to it" (2006, xii). As a double-edged sword, education can challenge or affirm deeply held beliefs; empower individuals or reaffirm the status quo. hooks writes that as educators, we are in a position to teach students how to transgress racial, sexual, and class boundaries; to envision education as the practice of freedom. Indeed, the classroom "remains the most radical space of possibility in the academy" (hooks 1994, 12).

With a deepened commitment to education as the practice of freedom, as well as five additional years of teaching experience, I revised my Performing Blackness course to include topics with stronger theoretical interventions and socio-political relevance to today. The theoretical underpinnings of the course took shape as I shifted from my "wheelhouse" of dramatic works to the inspiration found in the performance studies scholar E. Patrick

Johnson's book *Appropriating Blackness: Performance and the Politics of Authenticity* (2003). The course now situated blackness as a complex racial signifier that has been constructed and appropriated for a variety of reasons, including political galvanization (Johnson 2003, 3). Since the course now included highly theoretical reading materials, I needed to provide some familiarity and opted to continue presenting course material in a somewhat chronological order. Our exploration of blackness began with early modern England and the transatlantic slave trade, allowing us to conceptualize concepts such as "foreigner" and "Other." Using William Shakespeare's *Othello* as our guide, we discussed how fear of the "Other" permeates our society today, considering Mr. Donald's Trump's inflammatory rhetoric of "'shithole' countries" (Dawsey 2018), fear of Muslims, and increased border control in the United States. We then turned to black women's anti-lynching activism during the Harlem Renaissance and the current work of women leaders of the Black Lives Matter movement. Next, we explored the black political radicalism of Lorraine Hansberry, noting how the ecological problems addressed in *A Raisin in the Sun* continue to harm the most vulnerable within our society. Investigating Blaxploitation films and revolutionary theatre of the Black Arts Movement (1965–1976) allowed us to explore the possibilities and limitations of black political struggle within popular culture. Considering Afro Latinidad in plays such as Migdalia Cruz's *Yellow Eyes* (1999) and Chinese cultural influences in films such as *Enter the Dragon* (1973) allowed us to resist the black-white binary and consider the problematics of intercultural appropriation. Other topics of study—such as black beauty politics, black fashion, black minstrelsy and hip hopera—focused on contemporary constructions of identity through performance and how they relate to current and future societal concerns.

While selecting course content with greater care is certainly a good teaching practice; this alone does not make for radical pedagogy. If I wanted to situate the classroom as a site of radical possibilities and inspire actual life change, I had to go a step further and reconceptualize my approach to student learning. Utilizing my experience as a performer, I took an "inside" approach to student learning, meaning I began by asking students to consider their own identity formation before engaging with primary and secondary literature about blackness.

Identity formation and radical pedagogy

A more radical pedagogy appreciates how the individual identities of students impacts their learning. Bracher writes:

> The fundamental aim of education should be to support and develop students' identities, those configurations of self that provide us with vitality, agency, and meaning and give us a sense of ourselves as a force

that matters in the world. Identity development has always been a function of education, but until recently it was often more of an implicit aim or an afterthought than the primary goal of educators.

(2006, xi)

To explicitly foster the development of identity, we began our exploration of blackness as a racial signifier by considering the ways in which we, as human beings, construct racial identity. I turned to Kristen A. Renn's study *Mixed Race Students in College: The Ecology of Race, Identity, and Community on Campus* (2004). In her interview with fifty-six mixed race students across six US college campuses, Renn found that three ecological factors—physical appearance, cultural knowledge, and peer culture (or whether one experiences acceptance or rejection from peers)—greatly influenced a student's construction of racial identity (2004, 23). Renn also found that rather than view racial identity as stagnant, the college students articulated a spectrum of shifting identity formations, including: Monoracial Identity, Multiple Monoracial Identities, Multiracial Identity, Extraracial Identity (i.e., "deconstructing or opting out by refusing to identity according to US racial categories") and Situational Identity (i.e., identification shifts depending on circumstances) (2004, 67–68). I then share events that led to my own identity formation and ask students to consider how their own racial identity was formulated. While not even ten percent of my students self-identified as "mixed raced," I used Renn's study because I wanted to demonstrate to students that identity formation is a personal continual process that does not look the same for each person.

I also hoped that our analysis of Renn's study would prepare students for a thoughtful discussion of Rachel Dolezal/Akechi Amare Diallo's construction of "transracial identity." I was wrong. While students situated their own racial identity formation as deeply personal, non-static, and complicated, for whatever reason, they appeared less willing to engage with Dolezal's more public expression of identity. Dolezal, who is of white-European ancestry but identifies as black, served as president of the NAACP Spokane, Washington, chapter. However, when her ancestry was revealed in June 2015, she received media backlash and subsequently resigned from her position. As I showed her image and discussed her grassroots activism with the class, I was met with absolute silence. After prompting students to share their thoughts, I was met with seemingly nervous laughter. I continued, reading Dolezal's 2017 statement about her personal journey with blackness and "transracial" identity:

I ... encountered blackness ... for the first time ... as a response from within myself as black is beautiful, black is inspirational, from a very young child age. From there ... I just learned to repress that and suppress that because I was punished for that, and told that that was not normal. I know that my identity is still, for many, somewhat unorthodox. ...

> I'm … becoming ok with [the] level of support and rejection that's been going on for the last couple of years since my biological heritage was brought to the surface.
>
> (Roberts 2017)

This statement did illicit a verbal response from a handful of students. The body language of many students suggested anger but only a few students could articulate why (for them) Dolezal's actions represented the ultimate act of cultural appropriation.

The journalist Syreeta McFadden perhaps best explains why Dolezal's self-identified "transracial" identity provoked such outrage during our class discussion. In her article "Rachel Dolezal's Definition of 'Transracial' Isn't Just Wrong, It's Destructive," McFadden argues:

> Dolezal's messy theft and fiction of a black American identity uses the currency of a subculture of privilege that is rooted in white supremacy too. If anything, to believe that one can transfer one's identity in this way is a privilege—maybe even the highest manifestation of white privilege. … Black people are required by whiteness to transcend our race to succeed; performing blackness in order to succeed as a black person is to use existing hierarchies to your advantage.
>
> (2015)

In other words, Dolezal had the privilege to don blackness with the knowledge that she could also disavow blackness at any given point. Those who phenotypically appear of African descent do not have the luxury of situational identity. For many, Dolezal's attempts to claim black American identity, as well as create an African lineage through her name change (her new name means "gift from God" in the Igbo language, primarily spoken in Nigeria), represented an unpardonable act of cultural misappropriation (Anderson 2018). While some students were quick to condemn Dolezal's attempt to stake a claim to an African lineage, many of these same students appeared to find humor in watching Ruby Dee's portrayal of the fictional Beneatha Younger's misguided attempts to create her own vision of Africa in the 1961 film adaptation of *A Raisin in the Sun*.

Our viewing of *A Raisin in the Sun* allowed students to consider the important relationship between ecology, blackness, and social injustice. In preparation for our class discussion, students were asked to complete a one-page discussion prompt assignment that answered the following questions:

1   In what historical period was the film produced? What historical period does the film represent? What geographical location is represented in the film?

2   Why does the family want to move? Consider the dialogue as well as the environment in which the Younger family lives.
3   What do you think about the ending of the film? Is this a "happy ending"? Why or why not? What should we learn from this social drama?

It was my hope that considering these questions while watching the film would invite students to think critically about how the visual components of the film help tell the story of the Younger family's pursuit of social mobility while living within the confines of a small, dilapidated Southside Chicago apartment in segregated America.

Our analysis of why the family wanted to move from their Southside apartment and purchase a home in the whites-only neighborhood of Clybourne Park led us to a discussion of ecodramaturgy and ecoracism. First coined by the theatre historian Theresa J. May in 2010, ecodramaturgy "is theater and performance making that puts ecological reciprocity and community at the center of its theatrical and thematic intent" (Arons and May 2012, 4). In her ecodramaturgical reading of the play *A Raisin in the Sun*, May demonstrates how ecoracism, or the disproportional burden of pollutants people of color and poor communities bear, has hurt the Younger family. Lacking both the "economic means" and most basic elements of any habitat—space, water, shelter, and light, Ruth "believes she has no choice except abortion" (May 2006, 132). Systemic racism has led to the Youngers' economic disenfranchisement, forcing them to live in an uninhabitable environment that cannot sustain future generations. Since the Hollywood film does not quite capture the Youngers' abject poverty, we turn to a deleted scene in Act II from the 1959 Broadway production. I invite students—both self-identified black and non-black students—to read the roles of Ruth, her mother-in-law Lena, and ten-year-old son Travis. Listening to this omitted scene wherein Travis describes playing with rats on the streets of Southside Chicago (Hansberry [1959] 1988, 142) produced grimaces on the part of most students. I then share that in addition to an unhealthy proximity to rats, Travis is also exposed to insecticides. Stage directions in Act I Scene Two note that Beneatha sprays roach killer chemicals "with a handkerchief around her face" (Hansberry [1959] 1988, 42). She later "both viciously and playfully" sprays towards Travis, stating, "I'll cockroach you, boy" (Hansberry [1959] 1988, 43). We then discuss how the fictional Travis bears the burden of insecticide and potential disease from vermin, even while people of color and poor communities continue to bear the burden of environmental toxins in everyday life.

The point of these exercises is to help students understand how ecoracism continues to impact the health and livelihood of black and poor communities. Reading and discussing these scenes reinforces May's argument that "Hansberry foreshadows the fight for environmental justice that would embattle black communities in coming decades when Lena warns, 'Well, little boys' hides ain't as tough as Southside roaches'" (2006, 133). One needs to look no further than the water crisis in Flint, Michigan, which exposed thousands of residents to lead and other pollutants in 2014. The fact that this crisis continues unresolved does not bode well for our future. If black communities serve as an early warning system for the American populace, then perhaps Judy Juanita is correct in her assertion that "brown waters going to be everywhere!" (2018).

We continued our discussion of the past, present, and future state of black communities and America at large by exploring Baraka's 1966 film adaptation of *Dutchman* in relation to Peele's film *Get Out* (2017). *Dutchman* tells the story of the middle-class African American man named Clay (Al Freeman Jr.) and his sexual encounter with a young white woman named Lula (Shirley Knight) on a New York City subway. *Dutchman*, produced in the wake of President John F. Kennedy's 1961 Executive Order 10925 (i.e., "Affirmative Action") and just four months prior to the passage of the 1964 Civil Rights Act and Harlem riots, uses symbolism to dramatize the racial climate of the time. The Black Arts Movement theorist Larry Neal writes:

> Symbolically, and in fact, the relationship between Clay (Black America) and Lula (white America) is rooted in the historical castration of black manhood. And in the twisted psyche of white America, the Black man is both an object of love and hate. Analogous attitudes exist in most Black Americans, but for decidedly different reasons. Clay is doomed when he allows himself to participate in Lula's 'fantasy' in the first place. It is the fantasy to which Franz Fanon alludes in *The Wretched of the Earth* and *Black Skin, White Masks*: the native's belief that he can acquire the oppressor's power through acquiring his symbols, one of which is the white woman. When Clay finally digs himself it is too late.
>
> (1968, 34)

Clay represents the desire to assimilate into white America: he appears passive, speaks in standard American dialect, wears a suit and tie, and attends college. His attempts to assimilate become his undoing, as the spectre of death looms before him (i.e., overhead handles appear as nooses). By consuming Lula's apple, Clay symbolically partakes of white America's ideologies, including patriarchy and the illusion of the American dream. Only too late does Clay realize that he has been duped. Lula calmly stabs him, orders black and white passengers to toss his body out of the train, and the nightmare begins anew as an unsuspecting black passenger boards the train car. I tell students that *Dutchman* was meant as a wake-up call for black audiences. I then invite them to question the premise that succumbing to the wiles of white America will always lead to a certain death.

Together, we consider how Peele's *Get Out,* produced more than fifty years after *Dutchman*, echoes the dangers of succumbing to the illusion of racial equality. *Get Out* follows the story of Chris (Daniel Kaluuya), a young black photographer who visits the childhood home of his white girlfriend

Rose Armitage (Allison Williams). Initially concerned that Rose's parents—a doctor named Dean (Bradley Whitford) and hypnotist named Missy (Catherine Keener)—may not accept their interracial relationship. However, Dean quickly reassures Chris of his acceptance, confidentially adding that he "would have voted for Obama a third time if [he] could" (Peele 2017). During his stay Chris eventually learns that the Armitage family kidnaps, brainwashes, performs medical procedures on unwilling African Americans, and sells their bodies to wealthy whites to inhabit. Reminiscent of the auction block during enslavement, viewers watch as Dean auctions Chris's body to the highest bidder; a wealthy blind art gallery owner named Jim Hudson (Stephen Root). In contrast to the other elderly bidders who desire black bodies because of stereotypes (i.e., blacks are supposedly more athletic) or trends (i.e., blacks are "fashionable"), Hudson wants Chris's artistic talent (Peele 2017). "I want your eyes, man. I want those things you see through" (Peele 2017). Using his wealth to acquire Chris's "eyes," or the unique experiences that allow blacks to see the world as it is and how it ought to be, represents the ultimate act of appropriation. Hudson nearly succeeds because (like Clay in *Dutchman*) Chris believes the lies told by Rose. She appears as a liberal white ally when she has in fact conspired with her family to enslave countless black victims. In contrast to Clay, Chris ultimately escapes by using his intellect and physical strength to overpower the Armitages. For example, he inserts cotton (a reference to enslavement) in his ears to avoid hypnosis and uses a buck's antlers (a reference to the black buck stereotype) to defend himself against Rose's father. Chris only very narrowly escapes becoming another victim within this cycle of enslavement.

After making these connections, I then share Peele's artistic intentions with students so we can discuss the concept of a "post-racial" society. Peele originally envisioned *Get Out* as a wake-up call for those who believed in a post-racial US society. While he conceived the idea during the 2008 Democratic presidential primaries, it took several years to finance the social drama/horror film (Harris 2017). "I never thought the movie would get made. … I thought it was impossible," remembers Peele (Harris 2017). Indeed, the subject matter of the film—especially the original despondent ending—seemingly lacked commercial appeal. Peele remembers:

> I wrote this movie in the Obama era. We were in this post-racial lie. This movie was meant to call out that racism was still simmering underneath the surface. This ending felt like the gut punch that the world needed because something about it rings very true. When something rings true in your core you have to deal with it.
>
> (2017)

Peele signaled this "post-racial lie" by originally having the police, rather than Chris's friend Rod (Lil Rel Howery), arrive at the end of the film. With the Armitages dead and their home in flames, there is no extant evidence to corroborate Chris's story to authorities. The bonus features include this alternate ending, showing Chris sitting behind a glass wall wearing a prison uniform. Having spent six months in jail, he appears emotionally exhausted and accepting of his future within the criminal justice system. As he stands to return to his cell, the frame reveals countless other black men sitting behind him in prison uniforms. In his audio commentary to the film, Peele notes that "many black men are unjustly [imprisoned]" (2017). This scene forces viewers (and also students) to question if these black men might also be innocent and by extension, begin to question how racism operates within the criminal justice system. Peele ultimately changed the ending because nearly ten years after the film's conception, he felt that "people were woke and people needed a release and a hero" (2017). Indeed, while Clay's death provides a shocking wake-up call; Chris's victory against his seemingly more powerful foes offers a sobering reminder of the need to take action.

We conclude our discussion by considering how the issues raised within *Get Out* might offer an early warning signal to the American populace. The ominous premise—that wealthy, elderly whites are harvesting young black bodies to preserve their own lives—is not that far removed from reality. I ask students to consider the life of Henrietta Lacks, a poor black tobacco farmer whose cells were harvested from her cervix by doctors without her consent just months before her death in 1951 (Skloot 2010, 1). Her cells, known today as HeLa, have been reproduced and trafficked by the billions and were integral to HIV infection research and the development of the polio vaccine, gene mapping, and cloning (Skloot 2010, 215). Yet, neither Lacks nor her family received any financial compensation for such unethical treatment. Unfortunately, Lacks's story is but one of many instances—which began with "scientific" experiments during enslavement—of unethical medical treatment of black women. I tell students that *Get Out* simply provides a heightened dramatization of such unchecked medical crimes against black bodies.

While I will never fully know the long-term impact of this course, I can attest that at least one student found her own "voice" through our class discussions, one-on-one meetings, and her own creative research project. At the beginning of the course, she admitted to me that she had difficulty expressing her thoughts in a public setting. With this concern in mind, we met throughout the semester. I simply offered her encouragement, listened to her, and challenged her to share her thoughts at least once during each class meeting time. Within a few short weeks, she began to blossom before my eyes, consistently sharing her thoughts and at times, questioning the more popular opinions of her peers. In addition, rather than meet the minimum requirement for the final creative research project, she created her own documentary short that addressed what she felt were misrepresentations in the documentary *Good Hair* (2009). The student's film began with a series of photographs of the many hairstyles she has worn throughout her life, followed by a succinct explanation about why black beauty politics matter. Included in her narration was a counterargument that relaxing one's hair does not, as the comedian Chris Rock states in *Good Hair*, mean that she is in any way trying to "look white" (Stilson 2009). Rather, she believed that the styling of hair—whether relaxed, texturized, natural, braided or otherwise—afforded black women such as herself artistic expression, personal autonomy, and the right to claim their beauty. She then invited audiences to travel with her on a train ride to Chicago and witness the process of her having her hair washed, pressed, and styled by a local beautician. The documentary ended with woman-centered songs of empowerment by black artists such as Beyoncé.

This creative research project struck a chord with me because the extraordinary film exemplified a potential outcome of radical pedagogy. Her documentary invited her peers and me into her own introspection, allowing us to bear witness to her personal journey of identity formation through the lens of black beauty politics. After the conclusion of the semester, she told me that it was through my class and the process of creating this documentary— something for which she would have never done on her own—that she discovered her own voice. As educators, we are responsible for helping to facilitate these kinds of transformations.

Conclusion

I began this chapter with a personal anecdote about my own errors as an educator. I did so because I would like to differentiate *errors*, *mistakes*, and *failure*. The *New York Times* best-selling author John C. Maxwell writes that: "Errors become mistakes when we perceive them and respond to them incorrectly. Mistakes become failures when we *continually* respond to them incorrectly" (2000, 18). While I did recognize my pedagogical error, I had no idea how to properly respond. In other words, I was not committed to creating new models of effective teaching. Rather, I went through the motions, perpetuating antiquated ways of teaching; envisioning myself as the authority in the classroom who merely poured information into waiting vessels. While we now know that this style of teaching—which requires minimum introspection on the part of the instructor—does not foster actual learning, this haphazard approach is all too often rewarded.

Rather than continue this path, I suggest that we actively promote a culture of "failing forward" within the academy. Maxwell describes failing forward as the ability "to see errors or negative experiences as a regular part of life, learn from them, and then move on" (2000, 18). Building on Maxwell's work, I suggest we cultivate a culture of failing forward by first recognizing that it is only through our failures that we eventually learn how to foster radical pedagogy. A culture of failing forward does not mean that we should value ineffective teaching but rather, a much higher standard of pedagogy that requires constant self-analysis, responsive teaching, and effort to find innovative ways to promote student well-being and learning, as well as social change.

Unfortunately, failing forward is rarely (if ever) rewarded within the academy. In fact, experimentations that lead to errors are most often penalized. For example, consider how teaching effectiveness is often evaluated for promotion and tenure purposes. If an instructor attempts an innovative approach to student learning, experiences resistance from reluctant students who favor traditional models, they will likely receive poor teaching evaluations. These scores then become one piece of a larger conversation about whether an instructor is an effective teacher. With their job on the line, there are few incentives to innovate teaching practices. In addition to the very real threat of losing one's employment, failing forward to promote a more radical pedagogy also proves ontologically dangerous, inasmuch that doing so can potentially undermine the status quo. If we are to bring about social change through education, we cannot continue to merely "survive" or repeat the same ineffective practices of the past. New teaching models that speak to the concerns of the 21st century are needed. If we don't create them, who will?

References

Anderson, Tre'vell. April 27, 2018. "Four Takeaways From 'The Rachel Divide,'" Netflix's New Documentary About Rachel Dolezal," *Los Angeles Times*. Accessed September 15, 2018. www.latimes.com/entertainment/movies/la-et-mn-rachel-dolezal-netflix-documentary-20180427-story.html.

Arons, Wendy and Theresa J. May. 2012. "Introduction." In *Readings in Performance and Ecology*, edited by Wendy Arons and Theresa J. May. New York: Palgrave Macmillan, 3–10.

Baraka, Amiri. 1977. *Dutchman: A Play*. London: Faber.

Bracher, Mark. 2006. *Radical Pedagogy: Identity, Generativity, and Social Transformation*. London: Palgrave Macmillan.

Dawsey, Josh. 2018. "Trump Derides Protections for Immigrants from 'shithole' Countries." *Washington Post*. Accessed August 15, 2018. www.washingtonpost.com/politics/trump-attacks-protections-for-immigrants-from-shithole-countries-in-oval-office-meeting/2018/01/11/bfc0725c-f711-11e7-91af-31ac729add94_story.html?utm_term=.32dd9ee54865.

Hansberry, Lorraine. (1959) 1988. *A Raisin in the Sun*. Thirtieth Anniversary Edition (Revised). New York: Samuel French.

Harris, Brandon. 2017. The Giant Leap Forward of Jordan Peele's Get Out. New Yorker. 4 March 2017.

hooks, bell. 1994. *Teaching to Transgress: Education as the Practice of Freedom*. New York and London: Routledge.

Johnson, E. Patrick. 2003. *Appropriating Blackness: Performance and the Politics of Authenticity*. Durham, NC: Duke University Press.

Juanita, Judy. 2016. *DeFacto Feminism: Essays Straight Outta Oakland*. Oakland: EquiDistance Press.

Juanita, Judy. August 14, 2018. Interview with La Donna L. Forsgren.

Maxwell, John C. 2000. *Failing Forward: Turning Mistakes into Stepping Stones for Success*. New York: HarperCollins Leadership.

May, Theresa J. 2006. "'Consequences unforeseen …' in *A Raisin in the Sun* and *Caroline, or Change*." *Journal of Dramatic Theory and Criticism* 20 no. 2: 127–144.

McFadden, Syreeta. June 16, 2015. "Rachel Dolezal's Definition of 'Transracial' Isn't Just Wrong, It's Destructive." *Guardian*. Accessed September 12, 2018. www.theguardian.com/commentisfree/2015/jun/16/transracial-definition-destructive-rachel-dolezal-spokane-naacp.

Neal, Larry. 1968. "The Black Arts Movement." *Drama Review* 12 no. 4 (Summer) 28–39.

Peele, Jordan, director, 2017. *Get Out*. Los Angeles: Blumhouse Productions, DVD.

Renn, Kristen A. 2004. *Mixed Race Students in College: The Ecology of Race, Identity, and Community on Campus*. Albany: State University of New York Press.

Roberts, Sophie. July 26, 2017. "Who Is Rachel Dolezal? The White Woman Who Pretended to be Black Claiming She Is 'Transracial'" *Sun*. Last modified July 26, 2017. www.thesun.co.uk/living/3195364/rachel-dolezal-white-woman-pretended-black-changed-name/.

Skloot, Rebecca. 2010. *The Immortal Life of Henrietta Lacks*. New York: Broadway Paperbacks.

Stilson, Jeff, director. 2009. *Good Hair*. New York: HBO Films, DVD.

7 Casting Christopher

Disability pedagogy in *The Curious Incident of the Dog in the Night-Time*

Samuel Yates

By any measure, Christopher John Francis Boone is not your average protagonist. As the narrator of *The Curious Incident of the Dog in the Night-Time*, he is committed to discovering who killed Wellington, his neighbor's dog. The text of Mark Haddon's 2004 bestseller is structured as a novel-within-a-novel and Simon Stephens's 2012 stage adaptation is a play-within-a-play; the narrative is penned from Christopher's perspective as an autistic person. Christopher's account of solving the murder mystery, however, does not only contain the requisite information and plot devices for the book to function within the murder mystery genre. Christopher's writing, featuring a mixture first-person narrative, illustrations, math equations, charts, and prime-numbered chapters, challenges the ontological status of a "proper novel" as he navigates issues of truth-telling, linear development of plot, and authentic representation of the self. And yet, both Haddon and Stephens allow readers to encounter Christopher without a diagnosis of autism.

In this chapter, I use Haddon's novel *The Curious Incident of the Dog in the Night-time* and Stephens's stage adaptation to discuss approaches to disability in theatre and performance studies classrooms. Using the novel, Stephens's playscript, webpages for the UK West End Production and the New York Broadway Production, and key readings, students learn key disability studies concepts that prepare them to examine issues of disability representation in commercial theatre, such as: casting able-bodied actors to play disabled characters; marketing disability; audience education and engagement; and how disability impacts elements of stage design.

"Nearly 1 in 5 People Have a Disability," the United States Census Bureau claims, suggesting that nearly 20 percent of the American public lives with a visible or non-visible disability (2012). The World Bank estimates the global number of disabled persons at approximately 15 percent, but you are unlikely to understand the cultural prevalence of disability by visiting the theatre. As a live art form, most commercial theatre is built on the expectation of nondisabled actors, relying on the capacities of nondisabled performers who perform the physical labor of a live play production up to nine times a week. Despite these performance expectations—or perhaps because of them—theatre is obsessed with disability. Popular plays like

Tennessee Williams's *The Glass Menagerie* (1944), William Gibson's *The Miracle Worker* (1959), and Bernard Pomerance's *The Elephant Man* (1977) are awards vehicles for nondisabled actors because they test the limits of skilled representation. As disability moves to center stage in contemporary productions it takes value as an identity and embodied experience in its own right rather than being used as an indicator of character flaw or moral judgement. Deaf West's production of *Spring Awakening* (2015), Martyna Majok's Pulitzer-winning *The Cost of Living* (2016) and the 2019 Broadway revival of *Oklahoma!* featuring Ali Stroker, a wheelchair-user, as Ado Annie exemplify this shift. If 15 percent of people are disabled, then we can safely assume disabled artists are working in our field, disabled spectators are in our audiences, disabled students are in our classrooms. How are we preparing student artists to thoughtfully engage with disability and represent disabled embodiment on stage with sensitivity and accuracy?

Much ink has been spilled over the portrayal—or lack thereof—of autism in the novel and stage adaptation of *The Curious Incident of the Dog in the Night-Time*. From Elizabeth Bartmess's critical review of autism in the novel, to Petra Kuppers's 2008 article in *Text and Performance Quarterly* that takes *Curious Incident* as a "site at which autism is under construction," the responses to Christopher's influence on representational and performance practices widely vary (Bartmess 2015; Kuppers 2008, 192). Stiofán MacAmhalghaidh Âû's well-circulated *HowlRound* essay critiquing the choice to cast a non-autistic Christopher in *Curious Incident*, MacAmhalghaidh Âû reminds us that autism is a physical condition, one based on neurological difference, that is "something distinct, it is something which at a very fundamental level, is indescribably Other" (MacAmhalghaidh Âû 2015). As the play and its twin websites on either side of the Atlantic make plain, there is an apparent tension between the need to provide an interpretative or pedagogical framework for the theatrical production and the aim to promote an immersive experience of the medium (theatre) itself.

I teach Stephens's play as a case study for staging disability, although I also consider how both Stephens's play and Haddon's novel engage with "proper" or normative modes of storytelling. Concerns about discriminatory casting and disability representation are deeply entwined in the West End and Broadway production histories, as are questions about theatre's duty to mimetic representations of "reality" as such. Even beyond this, there is a consideration of the ethics of marketing: how does the promotion of a play set the public's horizon of expectations for the transformative work of the play itself? To help students establish the stakes of this conversation, each of the following sections is organized around readings and exercises that emphasize keywords and concepts to support engagement over multiple sessions in the classroom. In each section I take as a given that students have already read both Haddon and Stephens; you may use any of the suggested readings to supplement discussion of these primary texts with undergraduates or as instructor resources to guide conversation when time is limited.

Casting Christopher: cripping up, disability drag, and faithful representation

Keywords: Casting, Cripping Up, Disability Drag

Reading: Komporály, Jozefina, "'Cripping Up is the Twenty-First Century's Answer to Blacking Up': Conversation with Katie O'Reilly on Theatre, Feminism, and Disability—6 June, 2005, British Library, London," pp. 58–67; MacAmhalghaidh Âû, Stiofán, "Casting a Non-Autistic Christopher in *The Curious Incident of the Dog in the Night-Time* on Broadway"; Siebers, Tobin, "Disability Masquerade" from *Disability Theory*, pp. 96–119.

Begin discussion by opening up Katie O'Reilly's definition, "cripping up" and Tobin Siebers's "disability drag." How are they similar? Where do they diverge? Students might be more sensitive to conversations about color-conscious or "non-traditional" mixed-gender casting but may not yet have developed a language for discussing casting practices with regards to disability. Given that both O'Reilly and Siebers draw upon blackface minstrelsy traditions to characterize nondisabled actors playing disabled characters, ask students; Why do you think disability drag persists in an era when blackface is widely understood to be offensive and impolitic? MacAmhalghaidh Âû advances a politics of fair artistic representation for disabled actors (or at least a practice of casting disabled characters with disabled actors instead of able-bodied actors "cripping up" or performing what Tobin Siebers calls "disability drag")—and rightly so (Siebers 2008, 114–15).[1] As a deaf/hard-of-hearing artist and scholar invested in disability performance, I use my own experience during professional and educational theatre productions to advocate for the equitable casting of disabled actors across a wide variety of roles; in particular, a disabled character should be portrayed by a similarly-bodied actor whenever possible. In the absence of disability narratives within the class, you might invite students to think about the material particularity of living with a disability. What kind of knowledges about navigating the world are unique to disabled persons?

You can support conversations about these questions through a twenty-minute in-class discovery session, during which student groups are directed to briefly research answers using different apparent physical and invisible disabilities. Be sure to place an emphasis on discovering personal narratives in newspaper and magazine op-eds, academic articles, and social media feeds. Students should be able to quickly generate a list of material considerations of everyday life using anecdotal evidence. After groupwork is complete, use these lists to emphasize the broad range of ways to be in the world as a disabled person.

In Stephens's adaptation of *The Curious Incident of the Dog in the Night-Time*, however, Christopher does not explicitly identify as autisitic. The focus on contextualizing Christopher within a schema of biocertificative legibility is a misplaced errand as no material evidence in either the novel or the play proffers a diagnosis validating Christopher's verifiable, biological identity status as an autistic. If, as Mark Haddon has stated on multiple occasions, Christopher does not have Asperger's or Autism Spectrum Disorder (ASD), then is Christopher's cultural determination as such a fantasy of identification? Such a fantasy, as Ellen Samuels writes, is a "thing we not only imagine, but desire to be true" (Samuels 2016, 6). In our haste to locate Christopher within a cohesive, legible group identification, we forget that the frame of both the novel and play versions of *Curious Incident* are wrought by able-bodied artists with no specific investment in the autistic community.

Haddon shies away from positioning himself as an expert on autism; he writes on his blog that, "if anything, [*Curious Incident*] is a novel about difference, about being an outsider, about seeing the world in a surprising and revealing way. it's [*sic*] as much a novel about us as it is about Christopher" (Haddon 2009). Continuing further, we can see that by his own admission, Haddon only read "oliver sacks's essay about temple grandin and a handful of newspaper and magazine articles about, or by, people with asperger's and autism [*sic*]," before working purely from his own imagination (Haddon 2009).[2] Given Haddon's artist statement that "imagination always trumps research," is it fair to hold Christopher up as a fair representation of autism when that was never the artistic intent? I do not believe we should divest artists from political concerns or an ethic of care in their work. *Curious Incident* is a case in which the circulation of material moved afield of Haddon's intent. That we still demand diagnostic veracity from Christopher speaks to the broader cultural problem of disabled persons who are repeatedly denied opportunities to see themselves represented in popular culture. In this light, it is easy to understand why the role of Christopher is a touchstone for activism and scholarship concerning disability casting and mainstream representations of autism. One cannot help but wonder if the close proximity between Christopher and ASD might be a disability version of queer-baiting—hinting at Christopher's autistic tendencies to appeal to a disability-invested market, then denying his medical status or critical assumptions about his behavior. Even if so, requiring a specific biology to portray an autistic character onstage seems antithetical to MacAmhalghaidh Âû's artistic claim that we are dealing with a play that is "fiction, not an instructional video" and the purpose of art is to "explore possibilities and truths" (MacAmhalghaidh Âû 2015).

Divide students into small groups to examine the following two casting notices for the character of Christopher:

> Christopher Boone, Male, 18+: to play teens; an English teenager who is an outsider due to his unique perception of the world, which he sees in surprising and revealing ways. He notices things in minute detail yet has difficulty understanding social and emotional cues and

difficulty empathizing with others. This lack of understanding often makes the world seem frustrating and frightening to him, and he can become agitated and even violent when he has to deal with too many overwhelming external stimuli. Incredibly intelligent but shy and mistrusting of strangers, Christopher feels things deeply but doesn't know how to express or articulate them. He has a brilliant mind, can be fixated on certain topics, and thinks in a highly logical way, which makes him excel in math and science, but because he perceives language literally, he does not understand sarcasm or metaphors. From a diagnostic point of view, he is probably on the autism spectrum and exhibits some behavior that might be characterized as having Aspergers Syndrome, though what is most important is that he is different; must be physically very fit and agile and must weigh less than 150 lbs; English accent. Ethnicity: All Ethnicities.

(Backstage 2015)

Christopher John Francis Boone (Lead): Male, 14–17. A unique, charming, brilliant, and socially awkward teenager who is on the autism spectrum; he is a very gifted mathematician and curious with a capital "C"; he should feel like a boy becoming a man; when Christopher discovers his next-door neighbor's dog Wellington with a garden fork in his chest, dead on the lawn, he sets out to discover who killed Wellington; his search takes him out of his comfort zone in his small suburban neighborhood to the big city by bus; besides solving the mystery of the dog's murder, Christopher goes on an emotional journey that would rock the world of any 15 year old; he uncovers truths about his parents, fidelity, love, and betrayal; and in the process, he learns how to deal with his emotions, dig deep in his heart for forgiveness, and understand the world, even when he discovers that the world we live in is sometimes one without logic or fairness. Ethnicity: All Ethnicities.

(Backstage 2019)

The 2015 casting notice for Christopher is a *Backstage* advertisement for the Broadway production of *Curious Incident*; the second is the 2019 casting notice for the film adaptation in the same publication. Ask students to compile a list of characteristics they feel are important for casting Christopher, based on the language of the casting call. Have each group of "Casting Agents" present their desirable qualities to the remainder of the class. How are they similar? Different? Would the same actor be desirable based on the casting needs of every group? Why or why not? How does the language about athleticism and disability in the respective casting calls shape students' perception of who is suitable for the role? Does the transition from stage to screen matter here? Why or why not? Do we expect more or less authenticity on stage when we are in the room with a live actor?

These questions tend to get students into an ethical conundrum, so how do you lead them out of this bind of "truthful" representation when it comes to a disabled character or an actor? Is there a way to read Haddon and Stephens's work more generously? Remind students about Siebers and O'Reilly's ethical and political imperative: until there are equitable representations of disability by disabled actors, any form of cripping up and disability drag is damaging to an already-marginalized community. A crip-centered approach suggests we cannot sacrifice ethical commitments based on aesthetic assumptions about disability.

By abandoning the search for a diagnostic truth in the script or the casting of Christopher, we open space for what Haddon and Stephens *did* curate: a conversation about artistic creation. I present the stage adaptation as attempting to resolve diagnostic over-determinations of Christopher in two ways. First, throughout the play Christopher's teacher Siobhan is positioned as the editor of Christopher's writing, generating tension between Christopher's alternative cognition and the neurotypical ways of looking that Christopher calls lazy "glancing" (Haddon 2004, 140). Second, the digital footprints for the West End and Broadway productions took opposite approaches to presenting Christopher as Autistic. The West End production's online media featured robust dramaturgical support for spectators to learn about autism, while autism was never explicitly mentioned in the Broadway transfer's marketing materials. Cumulatively, the commercial stage adaptation is a useful case study for teaching Disability Studies concepts in theatrical contexts; it explicitly takes up the question of how to represent and strategically manage disability on stage. This lesson is designed to help students gain purchase with disability as a social construction—that is, understanding that we must approach stage disability with as much thoughtfulness as we do race, gender, and sexuality, if not more so because of the comparative dearth of representation. I also use *Curious Incident* as a case study for students to think critically about plays as pedagogical tools and about the art form of theatre-making.[3]

Siobhan's pedagogical work

Keywords: Narrative Prosthesis

Reading: Mitchell, David and Sharon Snyder, "Introduction: Disability as Narrative Supplement," pp. 1–15, and "Performing Deformity: The Making and Unmaking of Richard III," pp. 95–118, from *Narrative Prosthesis: Disability and the Dependencies of Discourse*.

In Haddon's book, Siobhan instructs Christopher on how to write a "proper novel" (Haddon 2004, 19). As he begins, she offers framing advice typical of normative cognition: "Siobhan said that *the book should begin with something to grab people's attention*. That is why I started with the dog. I also started with the dog because it happened to me and I find it hard to imagine things which did not happen to me" (Haddon, 5, emphasis mine). Christopher takes up his instructor's advice by beginning with a gripping event—in this case, the death of his neighbor's dog. The novel features several short citations of Siobhan's lessons. Although they remain in Christopher's voice, indicating that he has absorbed and "learned" them, the reader comes to understand Siobhan as a book editor for her student writer. In Stephens's stage play, Siobhan educates Christopher on how to write a book, which she later decides to adapt into a play. Her initial suggestion for Christopher to write his personal experience becomes a more massive project of community building through her artistic vision, proposed at the beginning of the second act:

> Siobhan: Christopher, I want to ask you something. Mrs Gascoyne has asked if we would like to do a play this year. She asked me to ask every-body if we'd like to make some kind of performance for the school. Everybody could join in and play a part in it. [...] I was wondering if you'd like to make a play out of your book. [...] I think a lot of people would be interested in what would happen if people took your book and started acting bits out of it.
>
> (Stephens 2013, 53)

If Haddon is concerned with the project of the "proper novel," Stephens's play pedagogically relays the components for an excellent playscript through the character Siobhan. The community-driven task of "making" together rhetorically works to explain the stage devices for the audience members, who take either the role of (presumably neurotypical) family members or schoolmates watching the school play.

   The West End and Broadway productions eschewed theatrical conventions in favor of a disability-centered worldmaking: the stage, a four-dimensional "blue box" with all-projection-available surfaces, is an extension of Christopher's mind, and various cast members besides the actor playing Christopher took extended monologues from the perspective of Christopher himself. The use of technology in the theatre space aids spectators in understanding Christopher; it also generates every location in and between Swindon and London, as well as imagined sites for Christopher's own musings. This experience is bounded by the play's explicit acknowledgement of the dramatic frame:

CHRISTOPHER: And I wrote a book.
SIOBHAN: I know. I read it. We turned it into a play.

> (Stephens 2013, 102)

Ask students to closely attend Christopher and Siobhan's final exchange. Not only is this interaction a distillation of the production's two projects—dramatic immersion and aesthetic didacticism—but it also stresses Siobhan's curatorial hand in the final product. Siobhan's use of "we" when discussing the artistic work emphasizes at the play's close that while the stage traffic audiences witness are Christopher's experiences, the play is artistically arranged by herself. How should we view Siobhan? As a presumably neurotypical character who is a not-so-subtle proxy for Haddon and Stephens, do the stakes of representation change if we cast a disabled woman in the role? Her response reiterates the community-oriented aspect of the play's conceit: actors, technicians, and audiences all have to invest in the world of the play for the "truth" of the performance to be made accessible. What is the pedagogical duty for a production of *Curious Incident*? How might a production fulfill MacAmhalghaidh Âû's call for a theatre that "enriches [audience] understanding of the human experience in all its diversity" without demanding an unfair burden of representation (MacAmhalghaidh Âû 2015)?

These dramaturgical investigations lay the groundwork for you to introduce a key Disability Studies concept: *narrative prosthesis*. Developed by disability scholars David Mitchell and Sharon Snyder, narrative prosthesis is the deployment of disability within a narrative that ultimately serves to reinforce forms of normative comportment by reining in excess. Using close readings of passages and production stills, how does the stage adaptation simultaneously rely on and strategically manage Christopher's disability? Siobhan's shaping of Christopher's narrative gives students some clues, as well as the very concept of creating an iterable theatrical representation of alternative cognition patterns for individuals on the autistic spectrum. Much like an actual prosthetic device visually approximates normalcy, despite having functional differences for the disabled user, Mitchell and Snyder demonstrate how "disability inaugurates narrative, but narrative inevitably punishes its own prurient interests by overseeing the extermination of the object of its fascination" (Mitchell and Snyder 2000, 56–57). In other words, the plot relies on disability for its forward momentum but it cannot be grounded *too* much in the deviant forms of embodiment lest it lose any sense of normative cohesion or universality.

Are there recuperative ways of casting and staging Christopher that might curtail prescriptive ideals of normative embodiment or autistic cognition patterns? In *The Biopolitics of Disability*, Mitchell and Snyder (2018) discuss Christopher's "excessive diversity" as a positive form of consciousness rather than negative way of being in the world—"a form of knowing perhaps best described as ways of not knowing" (200). Organize students into small "companies," with each student speaking from the role of director, dramaturg, casting agent, and various designers. Invite them to create "dream designs" or conceptual frameworks for a new production of *Curious Incident* that builds upon the concept of narrative prosthesis to resist the commodification of disability. How can we ensure that disability remains at the fore for audiences in a production built upon the rejection of diagnosis?

Curious online: a "site at which autism is under construction"

It should not be lost on us that debates over Christopher's casting invoking a need for "truth" are far more prominent in America than in the United

Kingdom, where the production originated. To think through why this is, I guide students through the websites for the respective West End and Broadway productions, where the tensions between immersion and frame are spectacularly coded. Guiding students through the UK production's online presence is an object lesson in modes of practicing audience education, marketing, and digital engagement. The difference between the two websites is simple: the West End website sets up a pedagogical framework for interpreting or engaging with the production, while the Broadway production's web page marketed the show as an immersive theatrical experience.

It is a curious thing indeed when the "Purchase Tickets" option on a website designed to sell seats for theatrical performances is only one of several prominent features on a production's digital counterpart. However, such is the case with the online presence for the West End production of *Curious Incident* (CuriousOnStage.com). Arriving on the homepage one had to scroll through a banner of reviews, production stills, videos of interviews, and a contest invitation for young stage designers to receive professional commentary on their work, before one reaches the invitation to "Book Tickets." Visitors scrolling down the short landing page could listen to the score composed for the show as they are invited to "Join the Conversation" on Instagram and Twitter with the hashtag #CuriousIncident. The site banner directs the visitor to other pages—"About," "Gallery," and "Learning." Each page is designed with a menu breakdown featuring a minimalist, high-contrast background and no images; the website is more easily navigable through text-readers used by low-vision persons, and for those with other sensory- or information-processing disabilities. Unlike Christopher's experience in the train station during the play, the navigational aids on the page mitigate the potential for information or sensory overload.

Visitors to the "Learning" hub navigate to individual pages that discuss adapting the novel "From Page to Stage," as well as various aspects of the text as an example of "English" (Literature), "Drama," and "Design." Most pages present text descriptions of how the play graphs into teaching curricula designed by the National Association of Teachers of English (NATE) or videos produced in-house with cast members performing from the show. These two elements converge in download-capable printable resources at the bottom of each page. The performance of a commitment to scholarship itself mirrors the narrative arc of the novel and play, which focus on an institutional education of storytelling and Christopher's social maturation.

By presenting materials on drama pitched towards both teachers and parents, CuriousOnStage.com imagines its audiences as guardian figures like Siobhan or Christopher's father rather than Christopher himself. This gesture is problematic not only in its echoing the frameworks of capital necessary to attend and participate in the cultural production of theatre but also in that it renders its audience as enterprising visitors who have engaged with digital education. The knowledgeable audience member may not, in fact, be present in the theatre. Finally, in a stark shift from both novel and playscript, which purposefully and pointedly do *not* call Christopher autistic or mention autism by name, the "Learning" section closes with a brief "Autism Resources" section. For a play publicly working as a cultural touchstone for autism, its digital counterpart surprisingly serves as little more than a gateway linking to other information. In many disability narratives, able-bodied/neurotypical writers editorialize disabled persons to maximize the intended audience's understanding of life with a specific physical condition. Commentators usually perform this editorial control through forewords, interviews, and footnotes to the narrative, and I see similar work here. Gérard Genette calls these editorial notes "paratext," defining surrounding textual apparatus as "the means by which a text makes a book of itself and proposes itself as such to its readers, and more generally to the public" (Genette 1991, 261). It is worth discussing with students how the website casts audiences as a Siobhan or Father-type (that is, an able-bodied proxy who vouches for the veracity of Christopher's narratives in almost every instance). Put another way; one might say the paratexts suggest modes of identification with the story's other characters, not the protagonist Christopher. Even as this paratextual space facilitates a medical model of disability, it also holds possibilities for resisting this framework.

One such form of resistance is the open-source coding of the widgets embedded in the homepage, which accumulates audience-generated social media posts using the hashtag #CuriousIncident. Some autistic persons and their allies disidentified with the portrayal of Christopher and ASD, subverting the positively-framed #CuriousIncident hashtag to open an honest dialogue problematizing autism being "Curious On Stage." José Esteban Muñoz's *Disidentifications* (1999) examines minoritarian subjects seizing social agency through artistic performances. Muñoz's work, which takes the performance of queers and people of color as a serious object in inquiry, positions disidentification as a strategy of resistance practiced "to negotiate a phobic majoritarian public sphere that continuously elides or punishes the existence of subjects who do not conform to the phantasm of normative citizenship" (Muñoz 1999, 4). The widgets embedded on the site pick up both positive and negative critiques of *Curious Incident* through the hashtag; in this way, the material archive has the potential to radically change based on user involvement. Invite students to compare examples of production-generated social media content against posts created by production visitors. Do they curtail the particularity of disability experience, thereby reifying Siobhan's normative perspective? Or does the multimodal digital material actually bring us closer to the ways in which Christopher experiences the world?

The lack of original content demonstrates the hard line of expertise CuriousOnStage curates as a digital archive; it proffers arts education but shies away from an authoritative position regarding disability education and politics. It is perhaps this caveat that stymies creative concerns over the casting of Christopher in the United Kingdom—by acknowledging that the play is *not*, nor strives to be, an official source about ASD, it moves the play away from the nebulous realm of 'truthiness' or a presumption of authenticity. But by marketing the play through social media posts and educational materials *about* the production, CuriousOnStage transforms what might otherwise be a ticketing portal into a digital humanities project that compels user participation, insofar as it (1) creates a digital archive of resources and (2) implicitly calls together a community of users (Stommel 2015). CuriousOnStage, then, offers a model of digital pedagogy as a public performance: one that foregrounds learning through a performative engagement with digital tools before reinforcing lessons with an "analog" performance by actors in the theatre. The UK website is markedly different from its Broadway sibling on this point.

The now-defunct "CuriousOnBroadway" forwent an access-friendly UDL design for a text-light and media-heavy scrolling page, a visual echo of the realized stage design that sells the immersive theatrical experience. There is substantial evidence to suggest this tactic was not unconscious. Haddon and Stephens developed *Curious Incident* with a creative team at the Royal National Theatre, a company that receives the majority of its funding from Arts Council England, which invests money from the government and the National Lottery in arts and cultural projects across the United Kingdom. The Council's mission is to champion, develop, and invest in enriching cultural experiences; the play's stage and online presence in the United Kingdom were direct recipients of a portion of an estimated £1.1 billion invested in the arts between 2010 and 2013 (Naylor et al., 2016 12–15). Broadway's production, by contrast, existed as a privately funded venture whereby theatre producers hoped to replicate the success of the West End production for significant financial gain. Thus, the promotion of the play in the States abandoned the educative apparatuses of the UK site in favor of setting up an immersive, hyper-mediated, "real" experience in the theatre. Visitors scrolling through the CuriousOnBroadway page could not manipulate themselves outside of the continuous loop of media-heavy materials. The UK site gives its visitors tools to intellectually engage with the play, whereas the US site leads its users through a multi-sensory experience without a critical apparatus. Following the UK production's success, the Broadway production's producers presumably knew how Christopher circulates in pop culture as an example of autism. This lack of an acknowledgement of ASD similar to the one on CuriousOnStage—or otherwise— underscores the ethical questions set by MacAmhalghaidh Âû. How much "truth" do we demand of our art? Is it negligent to not acknowledge Christopher's autism when the show all but calls itself authentic?

Although the play adaptation recalls the work's prior incarnation as a novel, the production reworks conventions of education and development that underlie novelistic genres, too. Considering how the West End and Broadway productions scaffolded their online presence, the UK site constructed a community of teachers/adults while the US site failed to articulate its imagined audience clearly. As a case study, artists and students alike can look to *CuriousOnLine* and *CuriousOnBroadway* to see divergent executions of digital identity, audience engagement and education, and web-accessibility for iterations of the same production. Inviting your students to comparatively read the "page to stage" media transformation in the production design against these web pages—or considering how other commercial productions translate their artwork online—might produce fruitful close readings about the world of the play, and challenge students to determine the essential components of a given production's identity. In arts management and producing courses, *Curious Incident* presents an opportunity to articulate exactly what the materials promoting your work online should achieve: paratextual framing or an experiential immersion?

Concluding concerns: theatre's commitments to the "real"

Following MacAmhalghaidh Âû's charge to productively challenge the doubt that inevitably accompanies our differing frames of reference, in my own teaching I attempt to make the case that while it is preferable to have an autistic play Christopher, I fear that a demand for an artistic "truth" stemming from diagnosis is a repackaged form of the medical model of disability masquerading as social model activism. MacAmhalghaidh Âû's position that "trueness cannot be achieved by anyone who has not directly experienced it" is well placed, and indeed, we must ensure that there is room on our stages for actors all-too-frequently Othered (MacAmhalghaidh Âû 2015). A performance by an actor who can draw from his or her specific embodied experience will inevitably texture their work in rich, generative ways. If we can put ableism (and racism, sexism, ageism, or any other ungenerous modes of relation) aside, however, what does the fixity on certain embodied truths mean for theatre artists who learn and share by exploring other lives, other worlds, other ways of relating? Who gets to verify these truths? I share my worries about what precedents policing embodied experiences might set for future imaginative means of artistic collaboration. But, mostly, I caution taking *Curious Incident*, or the casting of an autistic Christopher, as the panacea for neurodiversity and disability inclusion in commercial theatre. Neither play nor character was created to be representative and diagnostically viable, or to withstand the weight of a community long in need of plays more hospitable for self-representation.

Notes

1 Siebers describes disability drag is a constitutive form of disability masquerades because able-bodied actors playing disabled are "usually as bombastic as drag performance" (115).

2 The essay to which Haddon refers is Oliver Sacks's profile of Temple Grandin in the December 27, 1993, issue of *The New Yorker*, "An Anthropologist on Mars." In Christopher, Haddon echoes Sacks's framing of animal scientist and autism rights activist Grandin as someone who "[cares] deeply about science and animal life … [but feels] absolutely alienated from even the simplest of human emotions and interactions."

3 For this chapter, I only consider the original West End and Broadway productions of *Curious Incident*. A 2017 regional theatre co-production between Indiana Repertory Theatre and Syracuse Stage cast Mickey Rowe, an autistic actor, as Christopher. For a profile about Rowe's work in this later production, see Collins-Hughes (2017).

References

Backstage. 2019. "'The Curious Incident of the Dog in the Night-Time'." Accessed July 30, 2019. www.backstage.com/casting/the-curious-incident-of-the-dog-in-the-night-time-306575/?role_id=943554.

Backstage. 2015. "'Curious Incident of the Dog in the Night-Time', B'way." Accessed July 30, 2019. www.backstage.com/casting/curious-incident-of-the-dog-in-the-night-time-bway-68437/.

Bartmess, Elizabeth. 2015. "Review: The *Curious Incident of the Dog in the Night-Time* by Mark Haddon." *Disability in Kidlit*. Last modified April 4, 2015. http://disabilityinkidlit.com/2015/04/04/review-the-curious-incident-of-the-dog-in-the-night-time-by-mark-haddon/.

Collins-Hughes, Laura. 2017. "The World Really Is a Stage, Scripts and All, to an Actor With Autism." *New York Times*. Last modified November 6, 2017. www.nytimes.com/2017/11/06/theater/actor-with-autism-curious-incident-of-the-dog-in-the-night-time.html.

Genette, Gérard. 1991. "Introduction to the Paratext." *New Literary History* 22, no. 2 (Spring): 261–72.

Sacks, Oliver. 2006. "Introduction." In *Thinking in Pictures: And Other Reports from My Life with Autism*, by Temple Grandin, xiii–xviii. Vintage Books, 2006.

Haddon, Mark. 2004. *The Curious Incident of the Dog in the Night-Time*. New York: Vintage Books.

Haddon, Mark. 2009. "Asperger's & Autism." Mark Haddon Blog. Last modified July 16, 2009. http://markhaddon.com/aspergers-and-autism.

Komporály, Jozefina. 2005. "'Cripping Up Is the Twenty-First Century's Answer to Blacking Up': Conversation with Katie O'Reilly on Theatre, Feminism, and Disability—6 June, 2005, British Library, London," *Gender Forum: Illuminating Gender*, Vol. 12: 58–67.

Kuppers, Petra. 2008. "Dancing Autism: *The Curious Incident of the Dog in the Night-Time* and *Bedlam*." *Text and Performance Quarterly* 28, nos. 1–2: 192–205.

MacAmhalghaidh Âû, Stiofán. 2015. "Casting a Non-Autistic Christopher in *The Curious Incident of the Dog in the Night-Time* on Broadway." *HowlRound*. Last modified April 4, 2015. https://howlround.com/casting-non-autistic-christopher-curious-incident-dog-night-time-broadway.

Mitchell, David and Sharon Synder. 2000. *Narrative Prosthesis: Disability and the Dependencies of Discourse*. Ann Arbor: University of Michigan Press.

Mitchell, David T., with Sharon L. Snyder, 2018. *The Biopolitics of Disability: Neoliberalism, Ablenationalism, and Peripheral Embodiment*. Ann Arbor: University of Michigan Press.

Muñoz, José Esteban. 1999. *Disidentifications: Queers of Color and the Performance of Politics*. Minneapolis: University of Minnesota Press.

Naylor, Naylor, Bethany Lewis, Caterina Branzanti, Graham Devlin, and Alix Dix. 2016. *"Arts Council England Analysis of Theatre in England."* London: BOP Consulting. www.artscouncil.org.uk/sites/default/files/download-file/ACE_Theatre_Analysis_BOP_FINAL_REPORT_Feb_2017.pdf

Samuels, Ellen. 2016. *Fantasies of Identification*. New York: New York University Press.

Siebers, Tobin. 2008. *Disability Theory*. Ann Arbor: University of Michigan Press.

Stephens, Simon, Playscript. 2013. *The Curious Incident of the Dog in the Night-Time*. London: Bloomsbury.

Stommel, Jesse. 2015. "Stand and Unfold Yourself: MOOCs, Networked Learning, and the Digital Humanities." Last modified January 30, 2015. www.slideshare.net/jessestommel/stand-and-unfold-yourself-moocs-networked-learning-and-the-digital-humanities.

United States Census Bureau. 2012. "Nearly 1 in 5 People Have a Disability in the U.S., Census Bureau Reports." Last modified July 12, 2012. www.census.gov/newsroom/releases/archives/miscellaneous/cb12-134.html.

The World Bank. 2019. "Disability Inclusion." Last modified April 4, 2019. www.worldbank.org/en/topic/disability#1.

8   Greening the curriculum
Introducing ecocriticism and ecodrama to students in the classroom and rehearsal studio

Miriam Kammer

What was attempted? What was accomplished? Was it worthwhile? Theatre and drama educators may recognize these questions as prompts we might assign students tasked to review a play, or of student actors and designers critiquing their work after the close of a production. Activists in many fields may recognize these questions, too, as parameters by which they measure their own work; perhaps environmental activists would use these questions to reflect on a recent climate change resistance event.

This is just one illustration that demonstrates the multiple similarities between acts of theatre and acts of activism. At its most basic, the tools of the theatre are space and time, often some sort of text, and usually, people. Theatre juxtaposes highlighted bodies within and against framed, defined spaces, and as such, is an exceptional way to both illustrate and practice ecocritical theory, for at its core, ecocriticism does very similar work—it interrogates the relationship between human beings and the natural world, a type of space, how one affects and is affected by the other, and to what result. This chapter outlines guidelines for introducing principles of ecocriticism and ecodrama to students with and without backgrounds in theatre and performance. It will focus on pedagogical and dramaturgical strategies developed through programming for both the classroom and rehearsal hall, drawing on experiences in directing undergraduate students for mainstage production, teaching theatre history, theatre and social change (a class framed as a basic introduction to critical theory), and a liberal arts seminar in the first-year experience program. Although my examples will be drawn largely from my experiences at my current academic home—a small, liberal arts college near a Midwestern city with a primarily Caucasian student body, about half of whom lean politically left (moderate-liberal, progressive) and half lean right (moderate-conservative, regressive[1]—my writing is intended to be helpful to all professors at varied institutions.

Introducing ecocriticism

Understanding that ecocriticism is not familiar to everyone, I will begin by shaping the parameters of the field. For a definition of ecocriticism that my students have found particularly helpful, I look to the piece "What Is Ecocriticism?" by Cheryl Glotfelty, Professor of Literature and Environment at the University of Reno. She states:

> Simply defined, ecocriticism is the study of the relationship between literature and the physical environment. Just as feminist criticism examines language and literature from a gender-conscious perspective, and Marxist criticism brings an awareness of modes of production and economic class to its reading of texts, ecocriticism takes an earth-centered approach to literary studies.
>
> (Glotfelty 2015)

For a working definition of ecodrama, we look to Theresa May of the University of Oregon, who states:

> Ecodrama stages the *reciprocal connection between humans and the more-than-human world*. It encompasses not only works that take environmental issues as their topic, hoping to raise consciousness or press for change, but also work that explores the relation of a "sense of place" to identity and community.
>
> (May 2007, "What Is Ecodrama?")

Ecocriticism presents a host of opportunities for reading (and re-reading) canonical and non-canonical texts. It welcomes intersectional inquiry, producing rich conversations in fields such as Indigenous and Traditional Ecological Knowledge, Solastalgia Research,[2] Critical Animal Studies, Environmental Justice, Ecosocialism, Queer Ecologies, and Ecofeminism, to name a few. It calls to account and rallies against oppression and exploitation. Ecocritics speak for the people, but they also "speak for the trees," rejecting Cartesian binaries of culture and nature, and viewing the ecosystem as a network of connections, not distances, between people, flora and fauna. Many reject the Enlightenment models of nature and the universe outright, finding them too fragmentary, mechanistic, or as some would put it, patriarchal.

In our own era of compounding ecological crises, it would seem that the stakes for teaching ecocriticism and its cognates ecodrama, environmental arts, and environmental literature could not be higher, particularly as ecocriticism holds value as a critical lens and practical theatrical tool. However, not all students may be able—or willing—to absorb a message of environmental conservation. In my experience, some have not wanted to; some have not cared. A few have objected to it, sometimes rather vehemently, often on political or religious grounds. In order not to lose students such as these and risk shutting out their fellow classmates along with them, I try not to begin our semester together with a "heavy hand," so to speak. For instance, I do not begin with an admonition to "do your part" about climate change, for inevitably, not all students will believe that (a) it exists, or (b) it's anthropogenic, even when presented with scientific data. Similarly, I do not start by talking about our damaged waterways or industrial pollution practices, as a number of students go to college to study business and entrepreneurship or descend from farming families.[3] These students may become offended and shut down. Therefore, I begin the semester discussing a principle that we can generally all agree on—caretaking.

Caretaking is a key component of ecocritic Greg Garrard's concept of dwelling (2011), which examines the deep, long-term relationship between humans, their histories, and the land upon which they live. On paper, caretaking, or the good stewardship of land, air and water, is so basic a principle of environmentalism one would imagine it to be uncontested. In action, however, it becomes far more complicated: How far, how deep, or how long should our caretaking go? Until an ecosystem is destroyed? Until it is damaged? Until it is restored? Or until profits dry up? Herein lie the arguments, controversies, and gradations of "Green" movements. While these conversations are indeed vital to spaces such as ecocritical seminar rooms and environmental arts studios, I have found that they can be overwhelming for younger undergraduate students and those who are newer to critical thinking. Therefore, I start off small. For instance, though I make no calls for them to become vegan vegetarians, I ask them to appreciate what many vegans do, that is, make a personal commitment to steward the land and protect its creatures through choices in food consumption. I do not ask them to initiate any resistance actions, but I do show videos of performance-protest pieces, such as those of Reverend Billy and the Stop Shopping Choir, individuals who use their vocal talents to raise alarms about a range of climate change and environmental justice issues. In sum, I do not ask students to reconsider who they align themselves with culturally and politically, but present arguments that engender empathy for these "dirty hippies" (or, as ecocriticism would term them, "deep ecologists") they may have been warned about. Though there is nothing "sexy" in it, even a recognition of the campus recycling bins and low-flow toilets can be a step in the right direction toward a regular practice of caretaking. From these humble foundations, deeper and more intricate work can begin. And in these sessions, students already interested or invested in environmental protection can expand their knowledge and skills by gaining a refresher course in pertinent topics, participating in peer-sharing and peer-teaching opportunities, and learning new approaches in framing eco-issues.

Another stumbling block to greening the curriculum, however, is that not all professors, artists, or humanists yet accept ecology and the environment as valid categories for critical investigation. I would urge them to consider, for one, theatre critic Charles McNulty's 2014 statement: "The humanities cannot turn a blind eye [to] scientific concerns and stay relevant." In his piece for the *L.A. Times*, he presents a call to action:

[I]t is artists and storytellers, not scientists, who can potentially reconcile the viewpoints of the priest with those of the entomologist, who can
expose shortcomings in both perspectives and complicate deterministic
philosophies. ... The arts and humanities aren't the place to look for
solutions to the climate change crisis, but in taking up [the] challenge
to join hands with science, they may be our best hope of shifting public
consciousness substantially enough to give our descendants a fighting
chance.

This fight continues to grow more urgent as new reports and statistics come
to light. For instance, due to anthropogenic interference, animal extinction
and biodiversity loss is accelerating[4] (Plumer 2019), the number of deaths
from water, soil, and air pollution are rising[5] (Santhanam), and heat waves
are becoming so intense and so frequent that by 2050 hundreds of locations
throughout the country may endure "an entire month each year with heat
index temperatures above 100 degrees if nothing is done to rein in global
warming"[6] (Rice 2019). Students (and teachers) of sciences, arts, humanities, and all fields can appreciate these emergencies.

Greening the curriculum: from the rehearsal studio to the undergraduate stage

It is in this spirit that I have adopted an ecocriticism of/and/for performance as a touchstone of my scholarly, directing, and classroom work, all of
which for me are interconnected, as they are for so many of us working in
academia today. In each of these settings, I take a two-pronged approach
to sharing this field with students and artists: on one hand, as a school of
critical theory and user-friendly lens for analysis, and on the other, as a
launchpad for social and environmental activism, but not always in that
order, depending on the needs of the particular situation. One situation is
directing undergraduate students.

As a professor at my college, I am contracted to direct one show each
year, and I am fortunate to have a large say in which shows I direct; therefore, almost inevitably my directorships become opportunities for my theatrical practice and scholarly interests in critical theory to connect. For
instance, in 2015 I directed a production of *Pericles* inspired by my research
in Shakespearean staging and ecofeminist dramaturgy. Our production,
which was a mainstage play of our college's theatre season, also served
as an embodied, performance-as-research testing ground for my critical
eco-theory work.

Questions that inspire my theatre scholarship include, what are the keys to
ecocritical reading, and what makes or has made for a producible ecocritical
interpretation? How can classical or mainstream theatre respond to socio-
ecological crises? In what ways can it foreground for its audiences real world
ecological and cultural imperatives?[7] In partial answer to the first question

on "greening" script analysis, I often turn to May's "Green Questions to Ask a Play," published in the September 2007 edition of *Theatre Topics*. These twelve questions are useful in a number of ways, from discussion starters to share with fellow actors, designers, dramaturgs and director(s) on production teams to essay prompts for students in classroom settings. I employed these questions myself as I began editing and adapting our production's text of Shakespeare's play. For *Pericles*, I found May's following three questions resonated most strongly:

- How are place and person permeable? How does the performance blur the boundaries of individual and ecological community?
- How does the body as signifier and medium function as the borderland where ecological identity is negotiated?
- What are the clues to the ecological conditions of the "world of the play"? How do those conditions intersect with representations of race, class, and gender (May 2007, 105)?

The story of *Pericles, Prince of Tyre* progresses along a rather expansive plot: Pericles, a young prince, has lost his father and sets out to find a new one through marriage to the princess of Antioch. This does not come to pass, and in the ensuing years Pericles crosses the Mediterranean region via a series of sea voyages. During his travels, he saves the kingdom of Tarsus from famine, finds a wife, Thaisa, the Princess of Pentapolis in another, and loses her and their daughter Marina on a voyage to his home kingdom of Tyre. Thaisa makes a home of her own on Ephesus as a priestess of Diana, and Marina, who had been given over to the King and Queen of Tarsus to be raised, is kidnapped and transported to Myteline, a port city on the island of Lesbos where she is sold to a brothel. Finally, after years of separation, Pericles, Thaisa, and Marina all discover each other again in Ephesus and are reunited.

Unsurprisingly, critics have traditionally sought unity in the play by centering their commentary solely on Pericles, the title character and "first wanderer" of the story. Understanding the play in this way, however, can lead to a disregard for the richness and complexity of the play's setting, themes, and ensemble cast of characters. When viewed ecocritically, however, *Pericles* is a poly-vocal, multi-faceted story that centers upon the unifying force of the Mediterranean Sea. A true ecodrama—it even has two tempests and a shipwreck—*Pericles* narrativizes ecofeminist theorist Charlene Spretnak's concept of radical nonduality which undermines hegemonic notions of self versus other, human versus nature, and by extension, human *over* nature, which ecocritics and environmentalists seek to critique and undo. *Pericles* is a cyclical story in which complementary characters, conflicts, landscapes, and tropes appear and reappear with only minor situational adjustments. To emphasize this, I challenged the actors (and costume designer) with double, triple, and quadruple casting of roles. Two young men played eight characters; even the actor playing Pericles took on more than one role.

Most notably, I altered the presence of the character of Gower, the narrator who appears throughout the play. Traditionally portrayed as a man, I cast a woman, and, through doubling and tripling of roles, I expanded the presence of the character of Diana—deity of the moon, the woodlands, wild animals, and childbirth—by doubling her with the same actress playing Gower, the narrator. The combination seemed quite logical, as narrators tend to be omniscient and godlike in their storytelling duties already, and mythologies are full of instances where gods disguise themselves as mortal humans or animals. Through this expanded presence of Diana-as-Gower, an omnipresent, natural force appeared regularly on stage, visibly exerting influence over the characters, the environment, and the story. In this version of *Pericles*, if there is a "main" character, it's Diana-as-Gower. This actress also took on the role of Servant to Cerimon, the man who revives Thaisa, Pericles' wife who appears to have perished in a shipwreck, and delivers the play's final speech, usually given by Gower, as the goddess Diana instead. The actress was present in twelve of the play's twenty-two scenes, the same number of scenes in which Pericles appears, balancing their presences in the play.

In additional to textual preparation, I sought to keep ecocritical principles in mind throughout the production process, from scenic, lighting, sound, and costume design to executing blocking choices that would manifest the ecological entanglements that undergird the play. For instance, the names of the cities where Pericles takes place—Antioch, Tyre, Tarsus, Pentapolis, Ephesus, and Mytilene—are collectively mentioned in the text more than seventy times, and as the play roams so much across geographic space that it moves the very idea of setting from the background to the fore, table work for actors began with a study in mapping the Mediterranean Sea and its contemporary coastal cultures. We set our production in a simulacrum of the ancient world, as Shakespeare intended, but noted that this human need to roam, cross, and conjoin with one another through physical space that motivated Pericles still drives people today. To emphasize this, I presented to the designers a student image from a recent interdisciplinary, mathematics based competition. (Bruett, McIntosh, O'Conner). We imagined this graphic—a data map taken from a 2014 analysis of American transportation trends—to represent a geographical "map" of the Mediterranean Sea and surrounding areas. The graphic's dense webs of lines and circles of varying sizes visually captured the essence of the play—the affective entanglement(s), large and small, of people and situations across and through a broad but specific geographic area. This interconnectedness stood in stark contrast to other scenographic interpretations that I have researched, such as Tony Richardson's 1958 staging at the Shakespeare Memorial Theatre at Stratford-Upon-Avon. This production took a less than ecological approach to the piece: Richardson's designer,

Figure 8.1 "Moon Arch." Used for almost all interiors on set of *Pericles*. Design by
Rick Goetz. Photo by Luke Behaunek.

Timothy O'Brien, framed the space with tall, blank walls which tilted inward,
and set at the front of the stage an enormous curtain with a drawing reminiscent of Da Vinci's naked "Vitruvian Man." A large dodecahedron hung near
the ceiling opposite the stage floor. For spectator and critic Peter Wright, the
chamber-like shape of the set resembled "the inside of Pericles' mind" (Skeele
1998, 113), a motif which would speak to the singularity, if not supremacy,
of man. For our *Pericles*, designer Rick Goetz framed the area with a "moon
arch," a large semi-circular opening that extended across the back of stage,
just in front of the scrim as seen in Figure 8.1. We created this dominant set
piece so that it would both reflect the shape of the moon and echo the semi-
circular curve of the stage floor which extended far into the audience seating.
Stage dressing included bundles of wood, tangles of nets, and crisscrossing
layers of ropes, all intended to add to a sense of connection and inclusion
between the stage and the audience, and the play and *each* of the players, not
just the lone Pericles.

For my student actors, assistant designers, and dramaturg who brought
this four-hundred-year-old play to life, ecocriticism was a significantly new
way of thinking that generated new invigorating ways of processing and creating theatre. Our process yielded a strong result, but it was still inherently
risky. At all times we needed to keep a delicate balance between an application
of the eco lens (aka, "the concept") and an adherence to and fundamental

understanding of the action of the play. I cannot stress this enough. It was and is so tempting to get lost in the world of "concept," where one exciting revelation discovered through a critical lens can lead to the exhilarating next, but these "a-ha!" moments do not always translate into the best choices for the audience. I do not mean that we should pander to our patrons or students by any means, but as we teach in our most fundamental classes, the first step in creating good theatre is to make strong, clear choices that best serve the play and do not obfuscate meaning. For example, our decision to make lunar imagery a recurring motif in the scenery, costuming, and lighting emphasized multiple elements inherent in the script, such as the moon's gravitational force on the Mediterranean tides, its totemic power for Thaisa and the priestesses of Ephesus, and the influence of the moon goddess Diana (again, present throughout our production as the narrator Gower) as she steers Pericles on his life path, *without* jarring the audience visually or causing them confusion. A moon motif was (pardon the pun) a "natural" choice.

When working with classical texts, I find that ecocriticism can be a strong lens to discover interpretations that are faithful to the play and to the times in which they were first produced and produced now. Still, I am not quite so naive as to think that everyone "got" the ecodramatical subtexts and contexts in our staging of *Pericles*. For instance, doubling roles in Shakespearean plays is nothing new; due to the high number of characters called for in most of his scripts, it is actually rather common. I did, however, seek to double, triple, and quadruple the characters as meaningfully as the frequency of actors' entrances and exits would allow. For instance, with the exception of Gower/Diana, I sought to assign roles in accord with Spretnak's ecofeminist concept of nonduality, combining contrasting characters into a slate of personas that would blur the lines upon which we usually delineate binaries such as masculine and feminine, passive and aggressive, and agential and inert. In the case of *Pericles* characters, we troubled the delineations of good and evil. The actor who played Pericles, the protagonist and hero, also played a pirate in a human trafficking gang that kidnaps Pericles' daughter and sells her into slavery. The actress who played Lychordia, life-long nurse to Pericles' wife and later his daughter, also played Bawd, the female brothel owner who forces Pericles' daughter into prostitution. The incestuous King of Antioch who slaughtered his daughter's suitors doubled with Cerimon, a kindly physician renowned for his healing powers. In the end, I realize that those who just saw actors "doubling" just saw actors "doubling," while those who picked up on something more had a much deeper experience for it, perhaps beginning to ponder the ideas of false binaries and non-dualistic thinking that ecocritics advocate for, though of course not in so many words. I know the students involved with the show experienced the play quite broadly and deeply; they gained skills in reading the cannon diversely and realized the need for the artists to be able to operate ecoconsciously.

Greening the curriculum: within undergraduate classrooms

Engaging with ecocriticism and ecodrama inside the classroom tends to become much more political than in the rehearsal hall and therefore much more intriguing, energizing, rewarding, frustrating, disturbing, time-consuming, and yet overall worthwhile. In sum, depending on the demographics of students and one's personal inclinations, greening the curriculum may not be for the faint of heart. The overall student mindset of the course sections in which I have taught at least one unit of ecocriticism and/or ecodrama have ranged from very ecocritically liberal to more conservative. I will begin with my class that tends to draw the most progressive students, even though the course matter is the most canonical—my bi-annual sections of Plays and Performance I: Ancients through 18th Century, and Plays and Performance II: 18th Century through the Contemporary Era. These courses survey theatre history and literature within their time periods, and as they are degree requirements, are almost always populated with theatre majors and minors who tend to be rather left-leaning in their politics.

In Plays I, the department's prescribed anthology offers Shakespeare's *The Tempest* as a selection of an Early Modern drama, and I highlight the play for students beneath ecocritical as well as post-colonial lenses by assigning essays on colonialism and post-colonialism alongside ecocritical discussions on the pathos of the sea and sublimity in the Renaissance mindset. For instance, I regularly use excerpts of Steve Mentz's article, "Shipwreck and Ecology," which states that in Shakespeare's time the appearance of a sunken ship in a work of art was often no accident, but was by and large a "powerful symbol of mortality adrift in a hostile universe" or a sign of "disharmony in the human experience of the world" (2006, 166). We have also addressed some broader cultural and environmental contexts of Shakespeare's time, a good source for which is Gabriel Egan's study *Green Shakespeare*. His chapter on "Supernature and the Weather" examines the early moderns' and American colonialists' burgeoning interests in meteorology via the discovery of a thermoscope in Jamestown (2006, 153) that students find interesting.[8] In Plays and Performance II, we read *Mud*, a 1983 play by Maria Irene Fornes. The play appears simple to students at first, as it has only three characters and is set in one room, but soon reveals itself to be quite complex. *Mud* centers around Mae, a young woman living with two men and the household pig (whom we hear about, but never see) in a small, impoverished home in rural America. Situations of violence, incestuousness, misogyny, and disease motor the play, and layered within this is a constant stream of nature imagery, particularly invocations of water and the sea. We discuss the imbrication of these motifs and take time to imagine what indoor and outdoor stagings might look like. In particular, we look to Marlboro College's 1996 environmental "experiment" ("*Mud* ..." 2008) as a case study. For this production, audiences were led on a seven-minute walk through the woods of rural, southern Vermont to a rough-hewn platform stage and seated on bales of hay to watch the play.

My Theatre and Social Change class tends to attract students from both the theatre and general education programs who hold a range of political views. I have crafted this class as a primer on critical theory where we cover a few different areas (Marxism, critical race theory, gender studies, etc.). For green studies, we start with readings on ecocriticism and ecodrama, and then work through the play *Salmon Is Everything*, a collaboration between theatre artists, Native American tribal members, and nontribal residents of northern California and southern Oregon. The play recalls and illuminates events surrounding the 2002 fish kill along the Lower Klamath River that left over thirty thousand salmon rotting along the banks of the watershed (Bettles 2014, xiv). It is an activist piece of ecodrama that we analyze as a literary response to an environmental justice issue, a site of social change activism, and as a case study in devising community-based theatre that students can adapt to implement in their own work.

My first-year experience seminar, titled Simpson College Colloquium: Eco-Arts and Media, is designed with majors and non-majors in mind. I cover a range of fields, including narrative film, documentary film, short story, visual art, environmental sculpture, and also, theatre. Plays we have read in this class include Henrik Ibsen's often revived and re-translated *Enemy of the People*, a play about water pollution, corporatism, and local politics (although this play is over 130 years old and set in Norway, students spend a fair bit of time remarking on the similarities they see between Ibsen's world and ours); José Rivera's, *Marisol*, a play with a young Latinx heroine which imagines a world on the verge of environmental apocalypse; and the Pulitzer Prize-Winning *Kentucky Cycle* by Robert Schenkkan, a series of nine one-acts chronicling two hundred years of history of a plot of land on the Cumberland Plateau which pairs very well with discussions of dwelling and caretaking. A popular unit that the class is known for is "Hitchcock Week" where we discuss Edmund Burke's treatise, *A Philosophical Enquiry into the Origin of Our Ideas of the Sublime and Beautiful*, while viewing the film *The Birds*. In these class periods, ecocritical theory and artistic observation combine to illuminate meaning in a lasting way, as students take in the sweeping vistas of the California hills in nearly the same moments as they encounter the silent yet mysterious masses of black birds. Nature becomes both wonderful and frightening, delightful and dangerous.

Of each of my courses where I introduce ecocritical thinking or assign ecodramatic plays, this first-year, interdisciplinary seminar usually attracts the highest number of politically and religiously conservative students. Of course, ecocriticism is not necessarily incompatible with conservative values. However, there are moments of disconnect between my pro-environment views and those that are less eco-friendly, and between my reflex to personally engage and my need to remain steady and focused, that I do need to regularly keep in mind and be ready to address. For handling difficult situations in the eco-political and cultural classroom, I find we must meet students where they are. Though we may personally disagree vehemently, as long as neither I nor my other students are in immediate danger, I must set personal feelings and beliefs aside momentarily. Studies in psychology and educational environments repeatedly point to a need for an atmosphere of "safety and inclusion" (Lain 2018, 786) for learners to do their best. As Erin Lain writes in her work on racialized interactions and diversity in the classroom:

> Feeling safe goes beyond physical aspects; safety also refers to the emotional and psychological security of the student. ... Psychological safety allows students to be open to learning without a sense of vulnerability. When safety is lacking, students evoke defense mechanisms that monopolize the students' cognitive energy.
>
> (2018, 786)

As I see it, if I can make *all* of my students feel safe and welcomed in my "green" classroom, then even climate-deniers can open up to "new" ideas and evidences, such as the data behind anthropogenic climate change or reports on toxic chemical wastes. The imperative of comfort is not a wholly new concept to theatre instructors. Often we are assigned general education classes that attract students from outside the arts, some who may be scared to death at the prospect of having to speak in public or act. For these students, we often work to build a supportive classroom environment. As Lain points out, a key component of educational safety is "free[dom] from humiliation," where "being humbled is acceptable but being humiliated is not." A student may own up to an error but should not find themselves "questioning her worth or whether she belongs" or suffering from "unreasonably hurt feelings" (Lain 2018, 787).

Looking back, I am pleased that my more conservative students felt comfortable enough to raise contradictory concerns in class. At times, they might push back against climate science statistics ("but not *all* scientists believe that climate change is real"), naysay plans to curb carbon emissions ("but all our factories will close and the economy will crash"), argue against land preservation ("Profit is what's important—*drill, baby, drill!*"), etc. These comments not only demonstrated that these students were engaging with the material, they became the bases from which we started classroom conversation and debate, and a little at a time, we chipped away at poor logic with critical thinking, reconsidering old ideas with fresh knowledge doled out as critical theory reading assignments, playreadings and discussions, and film viewings, asking students not so much to abandon old beliefs (who wants to feel threatened?) but to consider new ones. For most students that I have encountered in my classes, this approach works.

Whether we invoke ecocriticism in the classroom, the rehearsal hall, or in everyday discussion, at its core lies the fact that nature exists as an active (not passive), dynamic (not static), material entity in and of itself. As Rebecca Salazar writes in her work on performing outdoor Shakespeares, "Ecologies do not exist simply to be strip-mined for metaphors" (461). The natural world is extensive, indispensable, and holds its own intrinsic value beyond the aesthetic or commercial. It is also in a critical state. What I've written here are some pages of what could fill a series of books, and I will end this brief essay with a request: Please consider exploring ecocriticism and ecodrama it in your own teaching and creative work. Life may depend on it.

Notes

1 These are my own estimations.
2 Solastalgia may be defined as a sense of distress that "exists when there is recognition that the beloved place in which one resides is under assault" (Albrecht 2006, 35).
3 In the region where I teach, pollution from factory farming is a growing environmental hazard.
4 According to an assessment conducted by the Intergovernmental Science-Policy Platform on Biodiversity and Ecosystem Services and summarized in a May 2019 report to the United Nations.
5 According to a 2017 report by The Lancet Commission on Pollution and Health.
6 According to a 2019 report by the Union of Concerned Scientists.
7 I address several of May's questions in two of my essays: "Eco-Epic Theatre: Materiality, Ecology, and the Mainstream," published in *Journal of American Drama and Theatre*, and "Breaking the Bounds of Domesticity: Women in Nature-Space in *Love's Labor's Lost*," in *Shakespeare Bulletin*. In "Eco-Epic Theatre," I examine the production of two, late-twentieth century ecodramas (*The Water Engine* by David Mamet and *Girl Science* by Larry Loebell), while "Breaking the Bounds" discusses strategies for staging classical plays ecocritically, taking a 2009 Globe Theatre production of *Love's Labour's Lost* as an example.
8 As time allows, readings in environmental ethics, environmental justice, and a reading of Aimé Césaire's 1969 play *A Tempest* would complete a stronger unit.

References

Albrecht, Glenn. 2006. "Solastalgia." *Alternatives Journal* 32 (4–5): 34–36.
Bettles, Gordon. 2014. "Foreword." *Salmon Is Everything: Community-Based Theatre in the Klamath Watershed*. Corvallis: Oregon State University Press.
Bchaunek, Luke. 2015. "'Moon Arch' in *Pericles*." Design by Rick Goetz. Photo.
Bruett, Kelly, Alec McIntosh, and Addison O'Conner. "Research Image/Visual Metaphor for *Pericles*—'Using Measures of Impact and Centrality to Identify Influential Nodes within Research Networks and Traffic Networks.'" Submission to COMAP Interdisciplinary Modeling Contest at Simpson College. February 10, 2014. Diagram.
Burke, Edmund. 1844. *A Philosophical Enquiry into the Origin of Our Ideas of the Sublime and Beautiful: With an Introductory Discourse Concerning Taste*. Adapted by Abraham Mills. New York: Harper & Brothers.

Egan, Gabriel. 2006. *Green Shakespeare: From Ecopolitics to Ecocriticism.* London: Routledge.

Fornes, Maria Irene. 1986. *Mud.* In *Plays: Maria Irene Fornes.* New York: PAJ Publications, 13–40.

Garrard, Greg. 2011. *Ecocriticism.* 2nd ed. London: Routledge.

Glotfelty, Cheryll. 2015. "What Is Ecocriticism?" *Association for the Study of Literature and Environment (ASLE).* www.asle.org/wp-content/uploads/ASLE_Primer_DefiningEcocrit.pdf. Accessed 1 August.

Hitchcock, Alfred, dir. *The Birds.* 1963. Hollywood, CA: Universal Studios Home Entertainment, 2000. DVD.

Ibsen, Henrik. *An Enemy of the People.* 2011. Translated by Richard Nelson. New York: Broadway Publishing.

Kammer, Miriam. 2018. "Breaking the Bounds of Domesticity: Women in Nature-Space in *Love's Labor's Lost.*" *Shakespeare Bulletin* 36 (3): 467–483.

Kammer, Miriam. 2009. "Eco-Epic Theatre: Materiality, Ecology, and the Mainstream." *Journal of American Drama and Theatre* 21 (1): 49–64.

Lain, Erin C. 2018. "Racialized Interactions in the Law School Classroom: Pedagogical Approaches to Creating a Safe Learning Environment." *Journal of Legal Education* 67 (3): 780–801.

May, Theresa J. 2007. "Beyond Bambi: Toward a Dangerous Ecocriticism in Theatre Studies." *Theatre Topics* 17 (2): 95–110.

May, Theresa J. 2014. *Salmon Is Everything: Community-Based Theatre in the Klamath Watershed.* Corvallis: Oregon State University Press.

May, Theresa J. 2007. "What Is Ecodrama?" *Earth Matters On Stage Ecodrama Festival.* https://pages.uoregon.edu/ecodrama/whatis/. Accessed 23 May 2019.

McNulty, Charles. 2014. "The Arts Become Earth-Aware: Dawning Age of What Are Known as Eco-Arts." *Los Angeles Times.* www.latimes.com/entertainment/arts/theater/la-et-cm-ca-mcnulty-essay-20141228-column.html. Accessed 23 May 2019.

Mentz, Steve. 2006. "Shipwreck and Ecology: Toward a Structural Theory of Shakespeare and Romance." *The Shakespearean International Yearbook*, 8, edited by Graham Bradshaw, T G. Bishop, and Peter Holbrook, 165–182. Aldershot: Ashgate.

"*Mud* … Is Dirt and Water." 2008. *Laboratory for Enthusiastic Collaboration.* www.l4ec.org/productions/Mud/index.html. Accessed 2 Sept. 2018.

"*Mud*, Scene 1." YouTube video by Aaron Kahn, 6:56. 6 Nov. 2013. www.youtube.com/watch?v=PkTMtvBudVg. Accessed 3 Sept. 2018.

Plumer, Brad. 2019. "Humans Are Speeding Extinction and Altering the Natural World at an 'Unprecedented' Pace." *New York Times.* 6 May. Accessed 23 July 2019.

Reverend Billy and the Stop Shopping Choir. www.revbilly.com. Accessed 1 Sept. 2018.

Rice, Doyle. 2019. "'Breaking' the Heat Index: US Heat Waves to Skyrocket as Globe Warms, Study Suggests." *USA Today.* 16 July. www.usatoday.com/story/news/nation/2019/07/16/heat-waves-worsen-because-global-warming-study-says/1734127001/. Accessed 23 July 2019.

Rivera, José. 1992. *Marisol.* New York: Dramatists Play Service.

Salazar, Rebecca. 2018. "A Rogue and Pleasant Stage: Adaptive Adaptation in Outdoor Shakespeare Performance." *Shakespeare Bulletin* 36 (3): 449–466.

Santhanam, Laura. "One Out of Six Deaths Worldwide Were Pollution-Related in 2015." *PBS News Hour*. 20 October 2017. www.pbs.org/newshour/health/one-out-of-six-deaths-worldwide-were-pollution-related-in-2015. Accessed 23 July 2019.

Schenkkan, Robert. 2016. *The Kentucky Cycle*. New York: Grove Press.

Shakespeare, William. 2005. *Pericles*. Edited by Barbara A. Mowat and Paul Werstine. New York: Washington Square Press.

Shakespeare, William. 2015. *The Tempest*. Edited by Barbara A. Mowat and Paul Werstine. New York: Simon & Schuster.

Skeele, David. 1998. *Thwarting the Wayward Seas: A Critical and Theatrical History of Shakespeare's* Pericles *in the Nineteenth and Twentieth Centuries*. Newark: University of Delaware Press.

Spretnak, Charlene. 1997. "Radical Nonduality in Ecofeminist Philosophy." *Ecofeminism: Women, Culture, Nature*, edited by Karen J. Warren, 425–436. Bloomington: Indiana University Press.

9 Teaching African American plays as "reality checks"; or, why theatre still matters

Isaiah Matthew Wooden

In 2015, British newspaper *The Guardian* launched a series of columns aimed at grappling with "some of the most common queries" that people ask the search engine Google.[1] Titled "The autocomplete questions," the series invited a diverse range of writers to venture thoughtful, nuanced responses to the inquiries that seemingly seize people's attentions with some frequency—among them, What if I fail? Why do humans kiss? Am I a good person? What does grief feel like? Should I get a tattoo? After many months of covering topics big and small, existential and mundane, the series turned attention to one of the world's most enduring art forms: theatre. The specific query that London-based writer and arts administrator Lauren Mooney tackled in her March 2017 column was: Does theatre matter? (Mooney 2017).

For those pursuing theatre professionally, Mooney observed in the essay, this question likely bubbles up often, especially when doubt creeps in, stirring uncertainty about career paths and life choices. Others, she surmised, likely turn to Google to satisfy their curiosity about why, given the advancements and proliferations of new entertainment forms, we still need theatre. Mooney offered up theatre's unique capacity to create shared experiences of storytelling as one of the more potent reasons the art form continues to command our attentions. "[H]umans love to share stories, and each new way of doing that gives us more opportunities for, respectively, escapism from and better understanding of the world around us," she explained.

> In a culture that demands you continually remain in reach of your emails and accessible to your boss, spending time sat in the dark being told a story, obstinately suspending your disbelief with people you don't know, can be as defiant an act of self-care as any other.

Mooney concluded the column by declaring, "At its best, theatre brings things—people, stories, places—to life" (Mooney 2017). Accordingly, she insisted, there will never be a time when theatre isn't important or doesn't matter.

While my own experiences teaching university courses have led me to similar conclusions about the significance and relevance of theatre, they have also required that I give thoughtful attention to the query animating Mooney's column: Does theatre matter? This question takes on even greater urgency in the classes that I teach that fulfill university general education and/or core requirements. Such courses, which tend to privilege breadth over depth, draw students from a broad array of departments and disciplines who usually have little, if any prior knowledge about theatre history or dramatic literature and, in many cases, have yet to attend or have only seen one or two live theatre events. Teaching such a diverse range of students is certainly not without its advantages; the fresh perspectives they bring to course materials and class discussions, for example, often open up new lines of inquiry for both their peers and for me. It does mean, however, that I can never take for granted that those who have joined me in the classroom share my convictions about why and how theatre matters. Indeed, even as many of the students that I teach demonstrate an interest in learning more about the history, theory, and practice of theatre, they also reveal a healthy skepticism about the relevance of the art form—a likely effect of having to negotiate a world that increasingly expresses contempt for the important work and contributions of the arts and humanities. Given this, I often find it productive to incorporate lessons and activities in my teaching that help concretize for students any demonstrative claims that I make about theatre's value.

In this chapter, I detail and reflect on some of the pedagogical strategies I deploy to demonstrate for students in my general education/core courses why and how theatre still matters. More specifically, I explicate how I engage work by African American playwrights—Lorraine Hansberry and Robert O'Hara, in particular—to examine the ways plays and performances can serve as "reality checks" that invite audiences to interrogate certain assumptions and, indeed, to imagine fresh possibilities for effecting change. Broadly speaking, "reality checks" refer to those instances in which an encounter with a set of facts leads to a more truthful awareness and/or appreciation of a situation. "Reality checks" can also refer to those occasions in which the state of things is illuminated with greater clarity. For the purposes of this chapter on theatre pedagogy, I further consider "reality checks" to be what Harry J. Elam Jr. theorizes as those moments that "brusquely rub the real up against representation in ways that disrupt the spectators and produce new meanings" (Elam 2007, 173). Such "reality checks," Elam asserts, not only compel audiences to freshly reconsider the distinctions drawn between the real and the representational but also have the capacity to excite social action. Providing several examples from African American history, including the funeral that Mamie Till-Mobley held for her teenage son, Emmet Till, on September 4, 1955 in their hometown of Chicago, Elam elaborates a definition of "reality checks" that is much narrower than the one I ultimately mobilize in my teaching.[2] Nevertheless, I find it essential to assign his writing on the topic to students. In addition to enhancing their critical and theoretical vocabularies, doing so gets the class collectively thinking about ways we might analyze and measure the efficacy of "reality checks." I also like to use one or two of the plays on my syllabi to explore what "reality checks" are and to consider their potential impact. Among the questions I invite students to think about: Might this play—on the page or in performance—serve as a "reality check"? If so, what are some of the formal and/or dramaturgical strategies that the playwright employs to bolster the force of the "check" the work provides? And, how might we assess the impact of the play as "reality check"?

To be sure, there are some texts that prove more generative for investigating these questions than others. Given the deep, consistent commitments that many African American playwrights have maintained in using their writing to call attention to and intervene in various histories, realities, inequities, and injustices, I generally turn to that body of work for objects that my students and I can closely read and analyze together. African American artists, Harvey Young writes, have often "employed the theatre not only to comment upon the events and concerns of their present but also to record and preserve their experiences and everyday realities for future consideration" (2013, 3). Correspondingly, much of the work that emerges from the African American theatrical tradition is ripe for getting students to reckon with pressing and vexing social, cultural, and political issues. In what follows, I demonstrate how I explore two plays from this tradition with students—Hansberry's canonical 1959 family drama, *A Raisin in the Sun*, and O'Hara's cheeky 2016 domestic comedy, *Barbecue*. (Hansberry 1994; O'Hara 2016). I also share the vital insights that this pedagogical approach has yielded about the significant role that theatre continues to play in shaping how we come to understand and respond to social and cultural events and phenomena.

Exploring *A Raisin in the Sun* as "reality check"

As one of the most studied and produced plays in the American theatrical canon, *A Raisin in the Sun* might seem like a predictable choice to include on a syllabus for a general education theatre course. For decades, it has served as the go-to text for introducing students to the genre of African American drama (there are, no doubt, some who continue to believe and teach that the drama marks the *beginning* of the genre, despite the many plays by and about African Americans that precede it). I only began assigning the text regularly in my courses a few years ago after discovering how few of my students had even heard of its title. In addition to tracing the storied journey the play took to become the first work by an African American woman playwright staged on Broadway, I was initially interested in teaching the text as one of the finest examples of realistic family drama, a genre that proved wildly popular on the American stage in the mid-twentieth century and that no doubt continues to resonate with contemporary audiences. The more I delved into Hansberry's background and the play's socio-historical context with students, the more it became apparent that the work could also prove a worthwhile object for asking larger questions about how playwrights use theatre to engage in important debate about pressing matters and to bring greater awareness to issues that require addressing. I decided to alter my approach to teaching the text accordingly. Along with asking students to think specifically and critically about what, if any, "reality checks" the play might offer on the page or in performance, I also began encouraging them to consider why Hansberry's dramaturgy—that is, the formal, stylistic, and thematic characteristics of her dramatic composition—has continued to captivate audiences in the decades since its original Broadway run.

Among the things that students are frequently surprised to learn is that Hansberry turned to her own family's history for inspiration to craft the play. When the playwright was a child, her father, Carl Hansberry, purchased a house in the Washington Park subdivision of Chicago's Woodlawn neighborhood. Much like the fictional Clybourne Park community that the Younger family moves into at the end of *A Raisin in the Sun*, the neighborhood had adopted a racially restrictive covenant in the 1920s that prohibited white homeowners from selling or renting their property to non-whites—African Americans, in particular. The number of whites seeking housing in Washington Park and other neighborhoods like it in Chicago decreased exponentially during and in the aftermath of the Great Depression. As such, some white homeowners opted to disregard the covenant (the homeowner who sold his property to the Hansberrys, James Burke, did so, in part, because of financial reasons but also because of a vendetta he had against some of his neighbors). This led to a series of lawsuits. Members of the Woodlawn Property Owners Association sued to have their neighborhood's racially restrictive covenant enforced. While they were successful in the Illinois Supreme Court, the elder Hansberry, with the support of the National Association for the Advancement of Colored People (NAACP), petitioned to have the nation's highest court hear the case. Carl Hansberry ultimately secured a victory, but it was on procedural grounds.[3] (Kamp 1987) The Supreme Court avoided the argument his attorneys made about the unconstitutionality of racially restrictive covenants, choosing to focus instead on the rules governing class actions.

As Imani Perry points out "The case that resulted from Carl's bold move sits somewhat dully in constitutional law textbooks today" (Perry 2018, 13). Nevertheless, it had a significant impact on the Hansberry family, who, Perry explains, lived "under siege" while occupying their Washington Park home. Outside the Hansberry door, Perry writes, "a howling white mob lay in wait. [Lorraine Hansberry] and her siblings were hit, spat upon, and cursed out as they walked to school. In the evenings, her mother protected the home with a German Luger pistol while Carl was often out of town working with a team of lawyers fighting for their right to be there" (2018, 13). The resistance that the Younger family anticipates being met with in Clybourne Park—"Well—well—'course I ain't one never been 'fraid of no crackers, mind you," Ruth, for example, exclaims, before asking, "but—well, wasn't there no other houses nowhere?" (Hansberry 1994, 93)—was no fiction or abstraction for the playwright who rendered them. Hansberry and her family had experienced firsthand the racist backlash that often follows efforts by African Americans to claim a piece of the "American Dream."

Inevitably, upon deepening their knowledge about the personal and social circumstances that motivated Hansberry to write her groundbreaking work, students begin to percolate with myriad ideas about the "reality checks" it invites and stages. One of the first things they often highlight is how the drama disabuses its audiences of any notion that white racial hatred of blacks was somehow less prevalent or severe in northern cities like Chicago or New York during the Jim Crow era. They point to the Younger family's awkward confrontation with Karl Lindner, the representative from the Clybourne Park Improvement Association. What starts out as a seemingly friendly exchange, with Karl stating that he is visiting the family in his capacity as the chair of the neighborhood's "Welcoming Committee" (Hansberry 1994, 115), ultimately takes a more threatening turn. The real motivations for Lindner's visit become clearer to the Youngers once the former begins outlining the purpose of the committee: "I mean they, we— I'm the chairman of the committee—go around and see the new people who move into the neighborhood and sort of give them the lowdown on the way we do things out in Clybourne Park," Lindner explains (Hansberry 1994, 115). In short, Lindner adds, Clybourne Park is a place

> made up of people who've worked hard as the dickens for years to build up that community. They're not rich and fancy people; just hard-working, honest people who don't really have much but those little homes and a dream of the kind of community they want to raise their children in.
>
> (Hansberry 1994, 117)

And, although he insists that "race prejudice simply doesn't enter it," still, he believes that it is "for the happiness of all concerned that our Negro families are happier when they live in their *own* communities" (Hansberry 1994, 118).

For Walter Lee, Ruth, and Beneatha, Lindner's intentions are unambiguous. It is not surprising to them, then, that when Walter rebuffs the Association's offer to buy back the property from the family, Lindner's demeaner shifts dramatically:

> Well—I don't understand why you people are reacting this way. What do you think you are going to gain by moving into a neighborhood where you just aren't wanted and where some elements—well—people can get awful worked up when they feel that their whole way of life and everything they've ever worked for is threatened.
>
> (Hansberry 1994, 119)

As these attempts to prevent the Youngers from occupying the home intimate, a different set of tactics may have been used to ensure and enforce segregation; many whites in the north shared similar beliefs as their southern counterparts about white supremacy and black inferiority. To be sure, the men who murdered Emmett Till were not without doubles in the hometown the youth shared with the Youngers and Hansberrys.

Another idea that students routinely remark upon is how Hansberry's dramaturgy subtly calls into question investments in an abstract idea of citizenship, one that grants everyone equal rights and protections under the law. In casting a spotlight on the various forms of discrimination the Youngers face while negotiating their everyday lives, the play prompts considerations of the ways that African Americans have long experienced what we might call, following Salamishah Tillet, a "crisis of citizenship" (Tillet 2012). Often spurring this crisis, Tillet writes, is the sense of "civic estrangement" that many African Americans feel "because they have been marginalized or underrepresented in the civic myths, monuments, narratives, icons, creeds, and images of the past that constitute, reproduce, and promote an American national identity" (Tillet 2012, 3). Further spurring it is the keen awareness that many African Americans have about the exclusionary qualities of US citizenship. With these assertions in mind, I encourage students to consider the ways that, through the Youngers confrontation with Lindner, Hansberry perhaps provides a "reality check" on how the strict regulation of who can own and inhabit particular spaces has long served as a way to deny groups of people—African Americans, especially—access to the full rights and benefits of citizenship. I also invite them to think about how *A Raisin in the Sun* might be read as an effort to re-center African Americans within the narrative of American national identity and, indeed, as a call to interrogate the civic myths that we continue to cling to and reproduce.

To supplement my teaching of the play—and to enhance students' engagement with Hansberry's rich dramaturgy—I assign additional readings to spark further discussion. While in the past I have focused on supplemental texts that have spoken to some of the play's central themes and formal qualities, in recent years, I have assigned essays that get at some of the questions that I pose about the play's relevance and resonance in a twenty-first century context. One text that has proven especially fruitful for expanding students' thinking and our classroom conversations is Ta-Nehisi Coates's provocative essay, "The Case for Reparations" (Coates 2014). Published in the June 2014 issue of *The Atlantic*, where until 2018 Coates served as a national correspondent, the essay lays out in careful detail some of the ways that both official governmental policies and unofficial discriminatory practices have aided and abetted the systemic plunder of black life and resources throughout US history.

Of particular interest to students' considerations of the urgency of Hansberry's plotting is the focus Coates sharpens on the federally-sanctioned efforts to thwart African Americans from enjoying the benefits of home ownership in the aftermath of World War II, a period in which, historian Thomas J. Sugrue writes, "home ownership became an emblem of American citizenship" (Qtd. in Coates 2014). African Americans, Coates argues, were categorically denied access to that emblem:

> The American real-estate industry believed segregation to be a moral principle. As late as 1950, the National Association of Real Estate Board's code of ethics warned that "a Realtor should never be instrumental in introducing into a neighborhood ... any race or nationality, or any individuals whose presence will clearly be detrimental to property values."
>
> The federal government concurred. It was the Home Owners' Loan Corporation, not a private trade association, that pioneered the practice of redlining, selectively granting loans and insisting that any property it insured be covered by a restrictive covenant—a clause in the deed forbidding the sale of the property to anyone other than whites. Millions of dollars flowed from tax coffers into segregated white neighborhoods.
>
> (Coates 2014)

What Coates's essay encourages students to contemplate is how cultural artifacts like *A Raisin in the Sun* help us better engage in ongoing conversations about knotty topics such as the persistence of social inequality and the racial wealth gap. One of my goals in teaching it is to open up space for students to consider how Hansberry's play also shrewdly invites its audiences to reflect on how, despite the Fourteenth Amendment purportedly granting African Americans equal protection under the law, the state and private industry continued to conspire to inhibit African Americans from accessing the "emblems of American citizenship" well into the twentieth century. This, I hope, will compel them to interrogate the ways those conspiring efforts remain in progress. And, for those students continuing to struggle with questions about theatre's value, I also hope it will make clear how the art form connects to their everyday lives.

The success of *A Raisin in the Sun*, Margaret Wilkerson explains, led many critics, including several notable figures in the Black Arts Movement, to dismiss the work as "integrationist and accommodationist" (Wilkerson 2001, 40). In their haste to rail against the play, Wilkerson notes, many of these critics failed to recognize the radical views that Hansberry embedded throughout her script. Exploring how the play engenders or enables "reality checks" about the legacy of housing discrimination in the United States and white racist backlash against black social mobility undoubtedly nets fresh insights about many of those views for students. Powerfully, it also affords them opportunities to come to some conclusions about why the play and, more broadly, theatre continue to resonate with new generations of audiences. There is no doubt that *A Raisin in the Sun* continues to reveal much about the costs and consequences of race and racism.

Interrogating the real and representational in *Barbecue*

Whereas *A Raisin in the Sun* likely strikes many as an obvious text to teach in a general education theatre course, Robert O'Hara's *Barbecue* probably registers as a curious one. Premiering at the Public Theatre in 2015, O'Hara's profoundly irreverent play diverges significantly from *Hansberry's* domestic drama in form, style, and tone. It does, however, share thematic resonances with the earlier work—resonances that make it an especially fecund object for exploring "reality checks" with students. Of course, for those who have been following O'Hara's career since he made his professional debut as a playwright with *Insurrection: Holding History* in 1996, Hansberry's influence on his dramaturgy is unmistakable. Much like Hansberry, O'Hara has demonstrated a flair for using the complex dynamics within families as a springboard to probe larger existential questions and themes. His appreciation for Hansberry's dramaturgical imagination is perhaps most explicitly reflected in the 2010 drama *The Etiquette of Vigilance*, which leaps forward in time some fifty years after the end of *A Raisin in the Sun* to imagine and dramatize what happens to the Younger family in the aftermath of their move to Clybourne Park.[4] Other plays in O'Hara's ever-growing body of work, which includes *Antebellum* (2009), *Bootycandy* (2011), and *Mankind* (2018), among others, also bear traces of Hansberry's influence (even if it manifests somewhat less conspicuously). They also evince the playwright's keen interest in "checking" dominant narratives and representations of black people by staging and providing incisive commentary on the conditions of black life across geographies and temporalities.

O'Hara does this, in part, by shrewdly deploying what I have called elsewhere "defamiliarizing dramaturgical strategies" (Wooden 2018). Indeed, rendering the familiar strange to provoke critical thinking and to unsettle the hegemony of particular perceptions, perspectives, and ideologies has become one of the hallmarks of his *oeuvre*. In a 2016 interview with fellow playwright-director Michael Van Duzer, O'Hara suggests that what often motivates him to create a new work is his desire to pose and grapple with "provocative questions" (Van Duzer 2016). "While I never know everything that is going to happen in my work before I start creating it, there are always a cavalcade of questions that I'm exploring as I write," he explains (Van Duzer 2016). "I'm not interested in answers. I'm interested in asking provocative questions. What's the most exciting versions of why, who, what, and where that I can find, and have all those questions bumping up against each other in a story" (Van Duzer 2016). Given O'Hara's penchant for orchestrating probing clashes, collisions, and juxtapositions in his writing, I have found his plays useful for further exploring questions about the significance of theatre and its capacity to provide and provoke "reality checks" with students. Although not as well known or critically regarded as some of his other work, *Barbecue's* unconventional plotting affords students vital space to contend with some of the ways that, in a world increasingly marked by simulation and hypermediation, the lines between truth and illusion are becoming indistinguishable. Furthermore, the formal inventiveness O'Hara displays in the play compels students to interrogate how dramatists mobilize form and style to stage important interventions and critiques.

The wild journey that *Barbecue* takes its audiences on as it spins the tale of four siblings—James T, Lillie Anne, Aldean, and Marie O'Mallery—who gather in a nondescript park in Middle America to host a barbecue for their crack-addicted sister, Zippity Boom (also known as Barbara), tends to win students over fairly quickly through its bold use of humor. It also prompts them to give careful attention to the unexpected twists and turns O'Hara embeds throughout the script. I encourage them to sharpen their focus on the play's stage directions. While, for example, the stage directions for the first two scenes in Act One call for a group of actors who appear racially white to portray the siblings who convene to convince Zippity Boom to attend a drug treatment facility in Alaska ("*James T, a forty/fifty-ish white man, stands speaking on a cell phone*"; "*Soon, Lillie Anne comes onstage. She is fifty/sixty-ish and white*"; "*Two forty/fifty-ish white women enter. They are Aldean, who carries a carton of menthol cigarettes, and Marie, who carries a large bottle of Jack Daniels*" [O'Hara 2016, 7–11]), the next scene directs that actors who appear racially black embody the roles ("*James T, Lillie Anne, Aldean, and Marie are all now played by black actors. They are in the same costumes as the white actors from the last scene. It is VERY IMPORTANT that there be no attempt to make either cast look (physically) like the other, besides wearing the same costume.*" (O'Hara 2016, 17)). The stage directions that follow instruct that the two casts should rotate until it is revealed at the end of the act that the black performers are not, in fact, siblings but instead a group of actors shooting a scene for a forthcoming movie. This revelation infuses an already convoluted story with an even greater sense of risk and unpredictability. Significantly, it also opens space to investigate questions about the politics of race and representation.

I ask students to reflect on the ways O'Hara uses this formal strategy provide a "reality check" about our diminishing capacities to differentiate fact from fantasy in the age of social media and reality television. Like I do with *A Raisin in the Sun*, I assign a supplemental text that complicates their perspectives on the topic. Kelefa Sennah's 2011 *New Yorker* essay, "The Reality Principle," has proven an especially valuable teaching tool in recent years (Sennah 2011). Sennah traces the rise of reality television as a genre—from its origins in the 1970s to its explosion at the turn of the twenty-first century. He draws attention to the various tropes that producers and peddlers of the genre frequently use to worry the lines between the real and representational, thereby reinforcing stereotypes and, indeed, hegemonic social norms. Citing the work of journalist and activist Jennifer L. Pozner and gender studies scholar Brenda R. Weber, Sennah describes how make-over shows such as *The Swan* and *What Not to Wear* serve to discipline women's sartorial choices and, more generally, to police their behaviors.[5] I bid students to consider the ways that the shifts in the racial makeup of the casting that O'Hara scripts in *Barbecue* invite audiences to confront and renegotiate some of the ideas that reality television helps fortify and proliferate about race.

Interestingly, O'Hara credits A&E's reality series *Intervention* with inspiring him to write *Barbecue*. He notes that he was struck by the number of white people featured on the show:

> I wondered why it was more acceptable to see white folks getting a chance at recovery than people of color. It's common knowledge that there's a lot of drug abuse in all parts of our culture, and yet we seem to surround our "reality" shows with nothing but white people.
>
> (Van Duzer 2016)

In grappling with this assertion, students quickly discover that part of what is at stake in *Barbecue* is an honest reckoning with some of the racial ills that continue to structure our everyday lives. This point is brought into even greater focus when we turn attention to the play's second act.

O'Hara centers the act on a conversation between the black and white performers who portray Zippity Boom about the former's desires to option the latter's popular memoir detailing her struggles with addiction and recovery. The conversation, which takes place a year prior to the events of the first act, features the pair discussing what aspects of "White Barbara's" life story will have to be altered so that "Black Movie Star Barbara's" performance will register as believable to movie-going audiences. "Black Movie Star Barbara" expresses some concerns about several of the memoir's details:

BLACK MOVIE STAR BARBARA. Sooo.
WHITE BARBARA. Where would you like to begin—
BLACK MOVIE STAR BARBARA. When was the last time you smoked crack?
    Beat.
WHITE BARBARA. I never smoked...crack, I smoked meth.
BLACK MOVIE STAR BARBARA. Oh, we have to change that to crack for the movie.
WHITE BARBARA. But that's not—
BLACK MOVIE STAR BARBARA. You have to be a crackhead. Black folks don't smoke meth.
WHITE BARBARA. Uh... Well actually...
BLACK MOVIE STAR BARBARA. Black folks in movies don't smoke meth. Black folks in movies smoke weed. And crack.
WHITE BARBARA. ...Okay.
BLACK MOVIE STAR BARBARA. So...when was the last time you smoked crack?
    Beat.
WHITE BARBARA. As I wrote in my memoir, there were a couple of relapses but for the most part I don't happen to smoke "crack" anymore."
    (O'Hara 2016, 79–80)

Black Movie Star Barbara's suggestion that on-screen Barbara's drug of choice should be changed from methamphetamines to crack cocaine—because, as she puts it, "Black folks in movies don't smoke meth. Black folks in movies smoke weed. And crack." (O'Hara 2016, 80)—calls into question a number of the bigoted assumptions proliferated by media representations of race. To be sure, the scene's ludic engagements with harmful racial stereotypes proves challenging for some students. However, it also provides an opportunity to reflect on the potency of the dramaturgical techniques that the play uses to "check" certain dominant racial narratives and representational strategies, thereby affirming students' engagements with the play as "reality check."

Conclusion

What I have come to value most about exploring both *A Raisin in the Sun* and *Barbecue* as "reality checks" with students in my general education/core courses are the ways in which this approach boosts our conversations about the capacity of theatre to, as Elam might put it, produce new meanings societally. While there are inevitably some students who, perhaps because they oppose the idea of fulfilling general education/core curricular requirements, continue to question theatre's relevance, most will acknowledge that the stage has a vital role to play in promoting new ways of knowing and understanding and, concomitantly, inspiring and effecting meaningful change. Among the crucial lessons that I hope to reinforce for students by engaging the pedagogical strategies I outline in this chapter is that the "reality checks" that a work stages can find fresh resonances in times, spaces, and contexts that far exceed what their creators might have imagined or intended. This, at least to my mind, is one of the most notable reasons why theatre still matters.

Notes

1 The tagline for the full series reads: "Every day, millions of internet users ask Google some of life's most difficult questions, big and small. Our writers answer some of the most common queries" (Mooney 2017).
2 Till-Mobley, upon learning of her son's killing in Mississippi by Roy Bryant and J. W. Milam, relatives of a white store clerk who accused the youth of whistling at and harassing her, insisted that his disfigured corpse be returned to her in Chicago. She then had an open-casket funeral so that the world could see what anti-black racism had done to her only child.

> The reality of [Till's] badly beaten, mutilated face (he was killed … for the audacity of looking at a white woman) stood in stark contrast to the picture of the smiling, handsome, light-eyed, young black boy of fourteen that hung inside the lining of the casket. … This performative moment—performative in how it impacted the viewing and doings of its audience—orchestrated by his mother intentionally induced a discomfort, a restless dissatisfaction on

the part of its audience and, in so doing, catalyzed the anger of the spectators, which enabled them to translate long-held frustrations over racial injustices into social resistance.

(Elam 2007, 173)

Importantly, by refusing to hide what had been done to her son, Till-Mobley helped galvanize the freedom struggles that would radically alter the social, cultural, political, and racial landscapes of the United States in the mid-twentieth century. Elam explains, it was not just Till-Mobley's choice to place her son's maimed and decomposed body on view for the public that provided observers a "reality check." It was also her decision to juxtapose the consequences of her son's brutalization with a picture of her son that at once served as a reminder of his humanity and called into question his attacker's false accounts of him as a lascivious predator. Till-Mobley, Elam argues, made it so that the

> viewing audience could not avoid or ignore the dissonance between the reality of the faceless body and the image of a serene, boyish, bodiless face. … Till's schoolboy portrait in its serenity screams out, counterposed to the violence that is now written on his body.
>
> (Elam 2007, 175)

The clashes between the real and the representational that the scene staged compelled all that witnessed it not only to take stock of the racial violence regularly committed against black people in the United States, but also to begin pondering and plotting ways to upend the laws and customs designed to sanction and perpetuate it.

3 For a fuller accounting of the history of the Hansberry family's legal case, see Kamp (1987).
4 It is fitting that *The Etiquette of Vigilance* is featured in *Reimagining A Raisin in the Sun: Four New Plays*, an anthology that includes four plays that directly grapple with Hansberry's drama (Rugg and Young 2012)
5 Senna engages extensively with Pozner's *Reality Bites Back: The Troubling Truth About Guilty Pleasure TV* and Weber's *Makeover TV: Selfhood, Citizenship and Celebrity* in the essay.

References

Coates, Ta-Nehisi. 2014. "The Case for Reparations." *The Atlantic*, June 2014. www.theatlantic.com/magazine/archive/2014/06/the-case-for-reparations/361631/. Accessed 3 November 2019.

Elam, Harry J. "Reality ✓." 2007. In *Critical Theory and Performance Studies (Revised and Enlarged Edition)*, edited by Janelle G. Reinelt and Joseph Roach, 173–190. Ann Arbor: University of Michigan Press.

Hansberry, Lorraine. 1994. *A Raisin in the Sun*. New York: Vintage Books.

Kamp, Allen R. 1987. "The History Behind *Hansberry v. Lee*," *20 U.C. Davis Law Review* 481 (1987).

Mooney, Lauren. 2017. "Does Theatre Matter? You Asked Google—Here's the Answer." *The Guardian*, March 15, 2017. www.theguardian.com/commentisfree/2017/mar/15/does-theatre-matter-google. Accessed 3 November 2019.

O'Hara, Robert. 2016. *Barbecue/Bootycandy*. New York: Theatre Communications Group.

Perry, Imani. 2018. *Looking for Lorraine: The Radiant and Radical Life of Lorraine Hansberry*. Boston: Beacon Press.

Pozner, Jennifer L. 2010. *Reality Bites Back: The Troubling Truth About Guilty Pleasure TV*. Berkeley, CA: Seal Press.

Rugg, Rebecca Ann and Harvey Young, editors. 2012. *Reimagining A Raisin in the Sun: Four New Plays*. Evanston: Northwestern University Press.

Sennah, Kelefa. 2011. "The Reality Principle," *The New Yorker*, May 9, 2011. www.newyorker.com/magazine/2011/05/09/the-reality-principle. Accessed 3 November 2019.

Tillet, Salamishah. 2012. *Sites of Slavery: Citizenship and Racial Democracy in the Post-Civil Rights Imagination*. Durham, NC: Duke University Press.

Van Duzer, Michael. 2016. "Choking on Satire: Playwright Robert O'Hara Talks *Barbecue* at the Geffen." *@This Stage Magazine*, October 6, 2016. https://thisstage.la/2016/10/choking-on-satire-playwright-robert-ohara-talks-barbecue-at-the-geffen/. Accessed 3 November 2019.

Weber, Brenda R. 2009. *Makeover TV: Selfhood, Citizenship, and Celebrity*. Durham, NC: Duke University Press.

Wilkerson, Margaret B. 2001. "Political Radicalism and Artistic Innovation in the Works of Lorraine Hansberry." In *African American Performance and Theater History: A Critical Reader*, edited by Harry J. Elam Jr. and David Krasner, 40–55. Oxford: Oxford University Press.

Wooden, Isaiah Matthew. 2018. "Robert O'Hara's Defamiliarizing Dramaturgy." In *The Routledge Companion to African American Theatre and Performance*, edited by Kathy A. Perkins, Sandra L. Richards, Renee Alexander Craft, and Thomas F. DeFrantz, 287–290. New York: Routledge.

Young, Harvey. 2013. "Introduction." In *The Cambridge Companion to African American Theatre*, edited by Harvey Young, 1–14. Cambridge: Cambridge University Press.

Part III
Studio
Theorizing praxis

10 Deep thought

Teaching critical theory to designers

Jeanmarie Higgins and Michael Schweikardt

The graduate program in Theatre at the Pennsylvania State University—
which offers the MFA degree in scenic design, costume design, costume technology, musical theatre directing, and music direction—requires students
to take four theatre history, theory, and criticism seminars in addition to
studio courses, shop hours, mainstage production jobs, and assignments as
teaching assistants for undergraduate courses. Jeanmarie and Michael met as
instructor and student in the first course of this sequence, Research Methods,
a course that contains a module of intensive critical theory instruction.[1] This
chapter advocates for teaching critical theory to design students not only
to enhance their artistic work, but also to encourage their awareness of
how structures of power organize academic and professional theatre, and
to show how emerging artists can produce satisfying work despite the time
pressures that come with a life in professional theatre production.

Research methods revisited (Jeanmarie)

When I first arrived at Penn State in Fall 2017 I had never taught MFA
students. Having only my own graduate student experience as a guide—
and having never taken a research methods course in my MFA or PhD
studies—I began by engaging students in a lackluster survey of, well,
research methods. The first classes involved library orientation: here's how
to find a journal article; here's how to request a book through interlibrary
loan. I soon realized that my course syllabus had no argument other than
"research is important," or worse, "all research should be modeled on how
I do research." It was only when I asked students to introduce their own
approaches that I learned how to teach them. From cosplay websites, costume technologist, Heather, showed us how to build period-specific armor;
Mark, a music director, showed us where to find orchestrations for musicals
online; Michael showed us the American Theatre Wing's Downstage Center
podcast, which features interviews with creatives and actors. I added to the
conversation by showing students how to find evidence of 1930s concert
dance in the unindexed publications that I consulted as the dramaturg for a
modern dance reconstruction (Higgins 2015).

That class session underlined that MFA students are chiefly concerned with finding the materials they need to make their artistic work, and that this work must be made on a schedule over which they have little control. This time constraint mirrors production timelines in professional settings. Furthermore, the sources the grads presented were what I now call "found;" like found objects, in the language of classical semiotic theory, found sources signify as research within codes known to certain practitioners. The singularity of each of the grad's research archives inspired me to switch gears. They already had sound research methods.

Instead of introducing them to research, I condensed an upper level undergraduate seminar in theory into a four-week module, introducing semiotics, phenomenology, psychoanalytic theory, feminism, queer theory, and postcolonial theory using Mark Fortier's textbook, *Theory/Theatre*. We read Bertolt Brecht's "The Modern Theater is the Epic Theater" and Antonin Artaud's *The Theater and Its Double*, Jill Dolan's *The Feminist Spectator as Critic* and Charles McNulty's essay, "The Queer as Drama Critic." My hunch was that teaching the grads to theorize their own work within the structures of our own School of Theatre (and beyond) would prove more valuable than introducing them to sources that primarily serve scholars. My contribution to my graduate students' constant task of creating under time constraints became to develop their relationships to their materials as thinkers, collaborators, and in some cases—as this chapter's writing collaboration shows—writers of scholarship in theatre pedagogy and practice. Although we explored many critical lenses, this chapter describes Michael's iteration of our class dramaturgy "pitch" project (which we have come to call simply "The Assignment") and brief outlines of two students' (Bekah and Tania's) approaches to design presentations for the Mid-America Theatre Conference Practice Symposium.

The class's practical inquiry into materialist theory starts with an in-class exercise to prompt discussion about labor and power structures in the theatre. Students are asked to imagine the program from the last show they designed, directed, or built. I ask: where does your name appear? Designers whose names are listed on the title page are asked, where do the names of those who drafted, cut, built, and painted your creation (assuming they are not also you) appear? The directors are asked to list the kinds of labor they perform versus the kinds of labor their designers and music directors perform. They then imagine that those who perform more physical labor have a more prominent place in the program; following this imaginary rule, the master electrician, the carpenters, and the drapers are now listed on the front page in large type, and the designers are relegated to a list on the back page, their names in alphabetical order in small print. What is the audience asked to notice in *this* production, then? As one student replied, "They'd look very carefully at how the floor is painted." This exercise convenes a discussion of how so-called intellectual labor is privileged over physical labor in the theatre.[2]

The Assignment (Michael)

After spending twenty-four years as a freelance scenic designer, I enrolled as a graduate student at the Pennsylvania State University. The last time I had seen the inside of a school, Bill Clinton was president—the year was 1993. I approached the idea of being a student again with some trepidation. The Penn State School of Theatre is not a conservatory. As Jeanmarie notes above, the course of study for all graduate students includes theatre history and literary criticism with a heavy emphasis on theatre theory. I was skeptical of this. Design, for me, had been about the given circumstances of action and environment, not concept, or theory. Nevertheless, I entered my first class and met Jeanmarie. I read, I studied, I wrote. I was interested but saw little use for putting theory into practice as a scenic designer. That is, until The Assignment.

As a course project, students were asked to choose a play or musical and to imagine for it a production that views the show through a particular theoretical lens. Students were prompted to mock-pitch this theory-driven production to a particular theatre company of their choosing. I worked for a while hypothesizing a feminist production of John Colton and Clemence Randolph's 1922 stage adaptation of Somerset Maugham's short story, *Rain*, but I could not get an idea to take root. At the same time, in my professional life, I was actively designing a production of *Oliver!*, Lionel Bart's 1963 musical adaptation of the Charles Dickens novel *Oliver Twist*, for Goodspeed Musicals in East Haddam, Connecticut. And I was struggling with how to get under the plucky facade of the piece.

I felt compelled to free *Oliver!* from the cloying trappings of musical comedy and uncover the politics that I believe are in its DNA. I started with the script analysis methods I had used throughout my career as a set designer: Whose play is this? "Oliver's" seemed like the logical answer. After all, he sets the plot in motion when he says, "please sir, I want some more." Do you know the setup? The government in England in the mid-nineteenth century has decided that they are sick and tired of paying to take care of the poor. They want out of the welfare business, so they pass laws that compel communities to organize and run their own workhouses—essentially big dormitories where the poor live and work. Oliver is in such a workhouse when—having finished his meal—he asks for more food. From that moment, the rest of the story happens *to* Oliver. He passively walks from one situation into the next. This is hardly the quality of a good protagonist, and I couldn't make sense of it.

With two projects stalled, I asked a critical question: what would happen if I overlapped my theory assignment with my professional duties—what if, when imagining my physical production for Goodspeed Musicals's *Oliver!*, I were to apply a Marxist materialist lens? Materialist theory, particularly Marxism, argues that economic forces determine and define all political, social, cultural, and intellectual aspects of a society. As Fortier puts it, "All materialist theory ... rejects the belief that we are independent agents who are free to impress our ideas on the world. Rather, the world impresses itself upon us"[3] (Fortier 2002, 153).

I reviewed the story of how Oliver became an orphan, this time through the lens of economic class. Oliver's mother was a young woman of high class. She was having an affair with her father's best friend and business associate. When her lover dies, she discovers that she is pregnant, and rather than disgrace her family's good name, she runs away, wanders into a workhouse, gives birth to Oliver, and promptly dies. Nine years later, Oliver gets caught picking the pocket of a wealthy man, Mr. Brownlow, who takes pity on him and gives him a home. In a twist of fate, Mr. Brownlow turns out to be Oliver's grandfather. Suddenly it hit me. *Oliver!* is not *Little Orphan Annie*, which is to say, it is not a story about a plucky orphan who breaches his class. *Oliver!* is, in fact, the story of a boy of high birth who is accidentally displaced into a class that is lower than his birthright. He then unwittingly goes on a journey whereby the universe restores him to his proper place. Applying a Marxist lens to *Oliver!* explains the main character's passivity as a protagonist—the driving force in the story is not Oliver's desire to achieve a better life for himself, it is society's insistence on maintaining a fixed class system in which he has no free will to move about.

I proposed to begin *Oliver!* by introducing the notion of a cooperative to the audience. The storytellers—in this case, the actors, musicians, and crew—present themselves to the audience as equals, a picture of a society where no class system exists. The storytellers then divide and start to acquire elements of the character they are going to become—maybe Brownlow puts on a beaver-fur top hat, maybe an orphan takes off his shoes and puts on a smock—exposing the apparatus of the theatre, as Brecht would have it, in order to show class as a construction (Brecht 2003, 446–9). As each storyteller dons a symbol of his or her character, he or she is assigned to a social class, and with this, they behave differently toward one another. The point is two-fold: (1) it shows that the class system is an applied construct, and (2) it shows that class, not free will, determines who we are and how we treat one another.

A Marxist lens changes the nature of the famous line "I want more." A poor boy does not ask for more, but a boy of a higher class like Oliver does. "I want more" transforms from a meek plea into a demand. "I want *more!*" Quite possibly it becomes a battle cry that causes a riot. Maybe one of the orphans writes the phrase on a wall and it lives there for the rest of the show. Maybe the entire media campaign for the show gets built upon the demand "I want *more!*" What if we cast two dozen orphans in this production and what if those kids, instead of being precocious "child actors" are actually kids from the community? What if we go to the most underserved parts of the community and invite those kids to be in our show? We'd be doing two things: (1) forcing the audience to confront the poverty that exists in their own community and (2) doing something good for these children by making them a part of our cooperative; we build their confidence; we teach them life skills; we feed them; and most importantly we pay them for their labor. There could be a third unintended result: some of these kids might internalize this Marxist "thing" we are doing, and they may come to think more like activists in the future.

Oliver! turned out to be the perfect text to explore Marxist theory. But while my class assignment was well satisfied, my Marxist-inspired production of *Oliver!* was never going to happen at The Goodspeed. The audience for Goodspeed Musicals is largely composed of upper-middle- to upper-class white people who tend to be older, heterosexual, and cisgender. They have a lot of disposable income, consume a lot of products, and may or may not be aware of the power and privilege they carry in the world. They might benefit from a Marxist *Oliver!* But, unfortunately, conservatism in commercial entertainment rules. This vision for *Oliver!* was never going to make it onto that stage.

So, why do it? Why put the effort into applying theory to production and imagining the potential result? Is it an academic exercise in futility? No. The Marxist lens revealed that *Oliver!* exists in a world of a fixed, unbreachable class system and this became the guiding principle for the actual Goodspeed production.

While I grant that what I ultimately designed for *Oliver!* came nowhere near the production I imagined for my class assignment, I am certain that the journey had a profound effect on my work. The design that was later realized on the Goodspeed stage was not a charming diorama of Victorian London, but a brutal environment where economic forces determine and define all political, social, cultural, and intellectual aspects of society. It was not a spectacle that sat within a frame, it was a stripped down and intimate setting that made the audience feel like they were in the story; it forced them to engage. Despite the conservatism of the theatre company and the audience's demand to be entertained, Marxism still worked its way subversively on to their stage (Figure 10.1).

As an artist I have to work within a financial system. In this sense, it is not a system of free will. I must work in order to survive, and so I take the work I am offered. However, on any given show I get to decide how I am going to approach the material. Therein lies the territory where I have free will and I get be an artist.

Three spins on *A Doll's House* (Jeanmarie)

Another of the assignments for the Research Methods course is for students—who are MFA practitioners, not scholars—to write an abstract they might submit for an academic conference. Two of the students in this course submitted their abstracts to the Practice and Production Symposium of the 2018 Mid-America Theatre Conference; their proposals were accepted. Rebekah Unsworth presented a paper about her design idea for *The Sins of Sor Juana*, the 1998 Kate Zcarías play about a sixteenth century Mexican nun. Using

Figure 10.1 Scenic design for *Oliver!*. Scenic Design and Photo by Michael Schweikardt. Rob Ruggiero, director. Goodspeed Musicals, 2018.

a postcolonial lens, the materials Rebekah chose for this hypothetical production incorporated Aztec and Mayan relief sculpture and elements of Spanish Baroque, implicating the disruption of conquest and colonialism in the repressive society Juana must navigate.

Using each of the types of feminism Dolan describes in her foundational book, *The Feminist Spectator as Critic*, another student, Tania Barrenechea, made three set drawings for Henrik Ibsen's 1879 play, *A Doll's House*, each of which proceeded from a different feminist argument. Her design sketch for a liberal feminist production made clear through her choice of color and material that the Helmers' parlor "belonged" to husband, Torvald, following Dolan's point that liberal feminists do not seek to change the system but to succeed within it (Dolan 2012, 3). Her cultural feminist sketch embraced a cultural feminist lens, as Tania arranged the audience in a circle, echoing the consciousness raising sessions emblematic of 1970s feminist gatherings. Particularly illustrative of materialist feminism as Dolan defines it, an idea that "look(s) at women as a class oppressed by material conditions and social relations" (Dolan 2012, 10), in her third drawing, Tania exposed the set's construction, drawing attention to the constructed quality of Nora's circumstances (Figure 10.2). Tania's drawings are schematic, they are not practical set designs, but that is the point. This starting point allows the designer to dream the big idea before dealing with the details of production as other artists on the team dictate.

Figure 10.2 Drawing by Tania Barrenechea. Presentation at 2018 Mid-America Theatre Conference, "Three Spins on *A Doll's House.*"

Conclusion

Theatre artists work within an economic system (as do we all). It can seem at best luxurious and at worst superfluous to teach theory to theatre practitioners, but this "luxurious whimsy" became precisely the point of the Penn State graduate cohort's class in research methods, underscoring what both students and the professoriate know all too well—that we need some relief from a schedule that requires us to produce our artistic and scholarly work in shorter and shorter periods of time. All of the graduate students at Penn State think deeply about their work, and they meet their deadlines. Theory gives them tools to separate those two sets of skills. It also gives them a way to integrate them; Michael's dream of a Marxist *Oliver!* is just such a respite that can have tangible results in production. Current discourses on the relationship between speed and stress in scholarly work, as outlined by humanities scholars Maggie Berg and Barbara Karolina Seeber offer: "Research shows that periods of escape from time are actually essential to deep thought, creativity, and problem solving" (Berg and Seeber 2017, 26).

The neoliberal university structure, with its increasing demand for measurable results, points to an intervention needed in our pedagogy for those students whose job it is to labor in the service of art. As Seeber and Berg point out (but that they didn't need to tell us): "the problems of time stress will not be solved by better work habits" (25). I would challenge anyone to offer up a harder working cohort than graduate students. For MFA candidate theatre artists, material, work, and creative production are so intricately woven together that it is worth pointing out their tangle. Our students' economic power and ability to create on the time schedules of others while honoring the fruits of their own deep thought depends on their acquiring the necessary tools to talk about this very issue.

Notes

1   The authors wish to thank their student/colleague collaborators from Fall 2017 Research Methods class: Tania Barrenechea, Rebekah Unsworth, Heather Hirvela, William Young, Jordon Cunningham, Mark Galinovsky, Wes Drummond, and Phillip Fazio.
2   It is also worth noting that arguably the most "intellectual" of theatre practices, dramaturgy, is rarely remunerated.
3   Of course, new Marxist theory finds a place for art in relationship to—but outside of—economics (Williams 1977).

References

Artaud, Antonin. 2003. *The Theater and Its Double*. Translated by Mary Caroline Richards. New York: Grove Press.
Berg, Maggie, and Barbara Karolina Seeber. 2017. *The Slow Professor: Challenging the Culture of Speed in the Academy*. Toronto: University of Toronto Press.
Brecht, Bertolt. 2003. "The Modern Theater is the Epic Theatre." In *Theatre/Theory/Theatre: The Major Critical Texts from Aristotle and Zeami to Soyinka and Havel*. Edited by Daniel Gerould. New York: Applause. 446–53.
Dolan, Jill. 2012. *The Feminist Spectator as Critic*. Ann Arbor: University of Michigan Press. ProQuest Ebook Central, https://ebookcentral.proquest.com/lib/pensu/detail.action?docID=3415102. Accessed 11 November 2019.
Fortier, Mark. 2002. *Theory/Theatre: An Introduction*. London: Routledge.
Higgins, Jeanmarie. 2015. "Iconicity and the Archive: Martha Graham's *Imperial Gesture* 1935/2013." *Review: Journal of Dramaturgy* 24 (1): 8–18.
McNulty, Charles. 1993. "The Queer as Drama Critic." *Theater* 24 (2): 12–20.
Unsworth, Rebekah. 2018. "Set Design and Syncretism: A Post-Colonial Spin on *The Sins of Sor Juana*." Mid-America Theatre Conference, 16 March 2018.
Williams, Raymond. 1977. "Dominant, Residual, Emergent." *In Marxism and Literature*. Oxford: Oxford University Press.

11 Reimagining the actor's presence through contemporary neuroscience

Andrew Belser

When we teach performance, what we mean when we speak of "being present" or "finding the moment" is full of assumptions about our experiences of presence. Who defines these things for our students? Are we teachers and leaders of acting studios the esteemed guardians of the now? We owe our actors expanded associations for language around objectives, impulse, actions, learning, and for common phrases like "living truthfully in the present."

The foundations of Western contemporary performance training are rooted in the late nineteenth century in the infancy of psychology being known as a field. Our current conundrum is that we live in a frontier time in which frameworks of conceiving of the brain/body interaction with the world are being taken up by revolutionary research at a crossroads between philosophy, cognitive neuroscience, computational sciences, ecological psychology, to name but a few disciplines. These new understandings are commonly viewed as vast field of inquiry for which I will use the umbrella term *neuroscience* (a term that has specific meaning within scientific communities and is not a comprehensive term).

I propose that practices and language of performance training need to be updated through the lens of contemporary neuroscience research. In this chapter, I re-imagine what presence means, to more fully recognize dimensions that may be at play as an actor constructs a present moment. How might we prepare ourselves as teachers to be more articulate guides for actors to sense the depth and width of resonant presence? Our students need more than our personal reflections on their work. As we speak of presence, we owe them the ability to sense for themselves when they are not working before our eyes and ears. We owe them the belief in their own sensations and ability to construct a layered daily practice of knowing when the work is hitting the mark and when it is not. Emerging contemporary understandings of memory, prediction, and embodiment can fundamentally help us as we train actors. Intending to join with and inspire existing teaching, in this article I sketch tracelines toward understanding presence, and suggest a few ways to pass along this learning in digestible language and practices.

I offer two initial prompts to expand and locate our imaginations. The first is a research paradigm, 4EA, that is a useful catalyst for exploding past notions of human thought, emotion and action. 4EA is also a digestible thumbnail of an influential contemporary research stream known as Embodied Cognition (EC). 4EA suggests that cognition, or our ability to meaningfully interact with the world, can be understood as:

Enactive: existing through active engagement with the world

Embodied: critically dependent on and shaped by the linked body/brain to responses to the world

Embedded: thinking, feeling, sensing, and doing as multi-directionally connected with a constantly changing series of environments, whether actual or simulated

Extended: our brain/bodies have developed extended systems of memory, perception, and culture

Affective: meaningful action connected and driven by affect, or emotion
(Stapleton and Ward 2012)

I offer 4EA not as a structure for this article, but as something akin to a workshop-opening exercise, a way to open the space for new understanding.

Second, I offer an acting parable to locate our discussion for how presence is sought and interrupted in contexts of specific performance practices:

Tom is an undergraduate student in a well-recognized actor training program. At his audition for the program, teachers comment on his athleticism and sensitivity. A movement teacher speaks of Tom's need to release his "muscular bearing," suggesting that movement training may be an easy point of entry for Tom's learning given his years of athletic training. A voice teacher adds that Tom's voice is forced, but that she could work with the movement teacher to release his breath into a softer belly and a more flexible and productive vocal column. Acting teachers view Tom's "emotional availability" as a plus, recalling moments when Tom seemed on the edge of tears.

At the end of his second year of training the same faculty are disappointed in Tom's progress, commenting that his impulses are switched either "on" or "off" with little in between, and noting that when Tom is "on" he seems present. When he is "off" he seems to career from one wild impulse to another. They sense Tom's increasing frustration and reluctance to fully engage in some exercises. Though he has done little research on such a condition, one teacher wonders whether Tom might have an attention disorder. Teachers comment that Tom's reluctance to risk more in exercises hinders his ability to fully invest in scene work. Tom spends hours learning lines, but when he comes to class he suddenly forgets them. As he heads toward an uncertain future in the program, Tom believes he has disappointed his beloved teachers; this disappointment gives him flashes of hot shame in his skin and a queasy feeling in his stomach. Tom simply doesn't know how to try harder or be a better learner.

We all know many versions of Tom in our work. Reflect on an image of Tom floundering; imagine how you might help him. Depending on our particular area of expertise, each of our interactions with helping the Toms of the world to inhabit a fuller present take different paths like movement, voice, or acting strategies like intention, listening, or shaping action trajectories. I propose that all approaches can gain from reconsidering the natural aspects of the human presence using a lens of contemporary neuroscience.

While we devote ourselves to the fervent pursuit of presence, if pressed, we may be challenged to articulate what it is. Consider that our individual notions of presence are only approximations that could be sharpened through focused seeing through the lens of contemporary neuro-research. Consider our assumptions about presence as products of old·thinking framed by colloquial language passed through studio practice. Our devotion to these assumptions may be blinding us to the need to expand our own understanding, and teaching methods, in ways that can help students like Tom.

One assumption is that actors should take direct aim at the "now." For a moment, re-imagine presence not as a "thing" by itself, but as a *spiraling woven threefold thread* made of memory, now, and predictions of future. Pulling forcefully on one of the strands—memory, now, future—may momentarily obscure the other two. This happens regularly as we foreground a memory or future hope in a temporary moment … and then … the threefold weave falls back into a flexible dance. As you read, perhaps you are here now, but only partly here. And you may momentarily feel less present as your "presence weave" is focused now on a memory strand of a recent conversation and now on a future strand of today's plans.

This simple image of a *spiraling woven threefold thread* offers useful space into which our students can grow and dance. Rather than training a hard focus on taxonomies of character history and on goal-oriented objectives, we might offer presence as an active and flexible happening that always includes three strands of this woven reality. Rather than a devotion to the "now," we might teach actors how to gently return again and again back to "now" from memory or future possibilities. These fluid, soft, and continuous returns are the skills of being present. If we want our actors to take aim at something, perhaps it can be creating thin, permeable, and delicate veils between past, present, and future. When an actor says "I wasn't in the moment" perhaps we can help her reframe self-critique by asking "Where were you, and how did you return?"

As become specific in our understanding, first of memory and then of prediction, we guide actors toward a more resonant or "thick" presence. We can articulate the human nervous system that quite naturally relies on presence as a weave of past, now, and future. Much of the language of western actor training is built on behaviorist sequences of action in which the present is a reaction or response to a stimulus. "Listen and react," a common trope in actor training, is only a partly accurate sequence that can be reconsidered in light of contemporary research. I propose that updating the language and practices of actor training to work with rather than against the innate tendencies of our nervous systems will equip actors with powerful tools to live more fluidly in the present and also to address the inevitable life stresses and insecurities that inevitably impact actors throughout their careers.

I will constrain our investigation to two emergent areas of understanding in the nervous system—memory and prediction— then discuss how they are entwined with the present to shape our actor training methods and studios in ways that potentiate learning.

Memory

Deepening our understanding of memory is a first step toward a more robust, and ultimately helpful, definition of presence for actors. Memory is not the past at all but is an active and embodied present composed from layers of experiences, emotions, thoughts, sensations, places, and more. The EC revolution of the past twenty-five years, and sketched through 4EA, offers compelling and influential understanding for how humans have developed complex brain, body, and environment interactions to hold and extend personal and collective memory. Each performer is, at any moment in the studio, acting through a complex web constructed of personal, familial, and cultural learning (memory).

Contemporary research suggests complex memory storage and retrieval processes far beyond prevalent metaphors of the brain as a static "hard-drive" holding memory in an anatomical location like the hippocampus, from where it can be retrieved in "whole cloth" form. These place/location-driven notions of memory storage and retrieval serve to fix our imaginations in old notions of the brain as separate parts, each having one function rather than the complex web of networks that we now understand it to be.

Western actor training methodologies as practiced through the past one hundred years tend to obscure crucial aspects of memory as a fundamental element of presence and of meaning-making. Consider that when asked to share a memory, most will offer a plot-driven, biographical story of their past built from the *what happened* story details that can be explicitly retrieved with some amount of conscious effort. Those *what happened* details are often not the reason the story continues to hold meaning; they are not important *newsworthy* bits that are why the memory has been stored for so long. Often, the *news* of a memory is held in forms of unsayable, or even irretrievable, bits of experience. For actors and the characters they materialize, a great deal of life force is held in largely irretrievable forms of memory. The *retrievable* forms of memory are commonly known as *explicit memory*, while the *irretrievable* forms of memory are commonly known as *implicit memory*. As cognitive psychologist Peter Levine notes in his book *Trauma and Memory*:

> The most salient of our memories are imbued with sensations and feelings, whether good or bad, joyful or sad, angry or content. It is, in fact, the emotional impact associated with a memory that is largely responsible for initiating and strengthening learning.
>
> (Levine 2015, 6)

In part, memories hold us so powerfully *because* we cannot easily retrieve, or diminish, their potency. The imagination of humans as equipped with memory-retrieval hard drives that can be accessed or cleaned is an inaccurate metaphor for living or acting.

It is far more useful to consider implicit and explicit memory patterns as personal learning, an interconnected web of habits (of mind, action, sensation, emotion) that the nervous system has acquired to make meaningful action responses to the world. Memory forms signature patterns that are core features of identity, such as: movement qualities and relationship with space; breath, vocal tone, inflections, et cetera; speed and contours of thought. Memory shapes not only responses to situations, but also changes how we perceive a situation, or how we take the world into conscious selves. All perceptions are biased from our individual experiences (memories); what I perceive is different than what you perceive. My embodied response to this moment of writing emerges through a different web of learning (memory) than you or any other writer. As I meet the demands of writing, my past experiences (and future hopes, as we will soon discuss) with writing are present with me through a learned web of responses that include such things as sensation, emotion, mood, mind states, and movement patterns. Automatic, or autonomic, parts of my system—patterns of breathing, heart rate, skin changing temperature, and biochemical responses, all of which are largely beyond my conscious control—ready me for today's writing action in signature ways based on my learned life experiences. All of this learning/memory biases my ability to materialize my thoughts in writing.

The same is true for any action. Each performer's abilities and perceptions are shaped by learning/memory in every present moment of acting. Performers show us not only *what* they see, but *how* that vision is filtered through past memory. Akin to wine aged in old, memory-infused wooden barrels, the filtering of life experience through memory is an important flavor that audiences can sense with accuracy.

We must begin to see our students as beings who bring memory into their present moment, and their capacity to embody the present is wholly shaped by learnings from the past. This requires reshaping our ideas of presence to include the learned response patterns that, without conscious thought, influence the quality of their presence. Some students like Tom will struggle because the web of nervous system response patterns has become fixed and obligate in ways that will override studio learning. We needn't know what in Tom's life fixed his responses. The contemporary flinch toward diagnoses naturally pulls our attention toward some physiological "dis-ease." But it is likely that, for many of our students as for us, living has brought us to this place, this quality of presence filled variously with tension and ease. And now, patterns of memory hold us here.

It is useful to further distinguish between explicit retrievable memories and implicit memories that our whole system encodes long term learning in many ways that cannot be consciously retrieved.[1] Western (Stanislavski-based) actor training has long incorporated the human body's capacity to experience the world through sensation as a form of memory (sense memory). However, those same methodologies do little to help us understand the complex and submerged parts of memory that actually animate much of human behavior. Those parts are often languaged as either: held in a pool of the subconscious—an *inner* world that is only partly knowable; or enacted in a pscyho-physical gestural life. Read that sentence again to experience language straining to name ineffable parts of humanity as inner life (*unconscious*) or to hybridize our categorization of inner and outer worlds (*psycho-physical*).

New paradigms underpinning contemporary memory research posit the distribution of memory far beyond the images conjured by long-standing inner/outer conversations around acting process. Psychiatrist and philosopher Thomas Fuchs questions the constructs and limits of memory as an "inner" happening:

> What is the locus of this embodied knowledge or body memory? Is this only a metaphorical term, and do we in fact have to locate it in the brain? ... if "memory" means not some kind of static inner depository, but *the capacity of a living being to actualize its dispositions acquired in earlier learning processes*, then this capacity is bound to the ongoing dynamic coupling between body and the environment.
>
> (2017, 336–337)

Like many others working in the pioneering space of reconceiving human memory, Fuchs points to a need to update the language of applied practices (e.g., actor training). As we train to create the cultural systems we have come to call a *play*, Fuchs explores memory as a question of the body/brain in relationship with the world of places, social systems, and cultures:

> The intimate connection between culture and embodiment is bound to a specific kind of memory, which usually escapes our conscious recollection or deliberate actualization—a system of embodied habits and skills acquired by the individual, which may also be termed body memory.

This memory is of a kind quite different from the episodic memory by which we recollect and represent the past.

(2017, 333)

These new threads of understanding explode earlier conceptions of memory as retrievable bits of data encoded by the brain and retrieved through mental processes.

We are tipped into salient memories not just by an inner life, but also by cues in space and environment. For actors, understanding that memories happen in relationship with the world, and not only in an interior brain landscape, offer actors new paths toward materializing inner life in relationship with space and time. Working from the space/time rootedness of memory brings other environments into the acting rehearsal and performance space. Why do we travel to old cities or ruins, or to familiar places in our own past, if not to evoke the deep layers of presence those places hold for us? Expand and extend your understanding of how we connect with the world through memory and you can begin to re-imagine how presence works.

Consider Tom's plight through the first two years. For Tom, the thread of implicit memory has become his way of knowing the world, shaping all of his perceptions and actions, and his identity. And yet, his very natural ways of knowing the world are now problematic in the acting studio. The ever-tightening thread of memory will not easily release in him to allow a three-fold dance of presence to emerge fluidly. If he could release it, he would. But he doesn't know how, and now these experiences of not being present in his acting are forming his identity as a jangle of disparate pieces. For students like Tom, increasing the intensity of our suggestion sets up an inner battle to overcome things that seem out of reach.

The interwoven memory patterns that hold Tom back are the same patterns of memory encoded into the life of a character where some memories are also available for recall and some are not. How might our approach to character analysis change if we were to reframe a character's actions through the lens of learned patterns of implicit and explicit memory? We might begin to see how memory potentiates a character's action rather than seeking linear cause/effect action sequences drawn from character history. Honoring the submerged, implicit memory landscape of a character offers possibilities to engage with qualities of a character's personal memory, as well as the extended and culturally embodied memories of the familial and cultural heritage of the character.

Prediction

Our larger imagination of the present through an expanded understanding of memory can grow further through understanding how future predictions are vital to the present. This may seem heretical to some; after all, in aiming performers at presence, we are often explicitly directing them to let the future take care of itself. Increasingly, many areas of neuroscience research highlight prediction as a crucial aspect of the nervous system, including: how neurons process massive amounts of data flowing through perception; planning for efficient, quick, and conservative energy expenditure; trajectories of motor actions and balance; and how emotions are entwined with meaningful action. Further, predictive processing offers ways to expand notions of presence for the actor's nervous system, and for shaping approaches to inhabiting a character in ways that potentiate meaningful future action.

While guiding students toward "staying in the present" is useful in learning to act, prediction of future events is a natural and necessary part of that presence. In facing this time-based paradox, it may be tempting to ignore compelling research about the nervous system as a prediction engine. Cognitive scientist and educational theorist Guy Claxton sums up a human neuro-reality:

> Basically, the brain is constantly generating its best guess about what's out there, and then feeding predictions, based on that guess, out to sensory receptors to create a downward tide of centrally generated sensory expectations meeting an incoming tide of sensory information.
>
> (2015, 74).

As I walk down the street looking for a restaurant I see a pizza place. Immediately and largely unconsciously, well-formed categories of good and bad pizza lead me to compare past images of perfect pizza slices (for me, crispy thin New York style pizza with cheese that is slightly golden). The satisfying mouthfeel I get from the crunch, the slightly sweet sauce binding with the cheese, animate my gaze at a pizza place. Now I am measuring past sensations of pizza against predictions of future pizza and predicting how this pizza might match with what I have learned to love.

Lawrence Barsalou illustrates the binding of past memory with future goal pursuit. As he points out,

> Glenberg ... argued that traditional accounts of memory focus too much on the passive storage of information and too little on the importance of situated action. Glenberg proposed that memory primarily serves to control situated action, and that the patterns stored in memory reflect the nature of bodily actions and their ability to mesh with situations during goal pursuit.
>
> (2008, 623)

Consider Barsalou's phrase *situated action* as a call to regard action as bound with environment alongside time-based goal pursuit. Barsalou is suggesting that actions emerging from our awareness of the present is composed not of discreet *now* moments, but of relational past/future oscillations.

The binding of memory with future predictions is a critical part of the cycle of action and perception that we need to reassess in actor training. Categorizing our experiences and matching them with prediction starts at birth and continues through our lives; past/future oscillation forms a vital processing stream underlying and creating meaning while keeping us safe as we move through the world. The past/future oscillation process measures risk, guiding us toward decisions of a future that might be worth leaving the learned or stable past aside to explore new and potentially chaotic possibilities. As we ask them to change and grow, our students are constantly performing an embodied dance composed from lifetime patterns of learning (body/brain memory) so well known that they scarcely can imagine changing it in their efforts to imagine, predict, and build new future acting patterns.

Additionally, research suggests that perception itself is already engaging in future action in our brain/bodies. Because the world presents us with vast amounts of information, we select our attention. These selections, guided by past experience and future predictions, shape or bias our perception. Guy Claxton notes "Perception is not neutral: it is already weighted with no conscious thought or awareness" (2015, 68). As noted above, contemporary neuroscience research repeatedly demonstrates that, far from being objective, perception is biased by our learning; we are each prepared to act differently in the future based on our memory.

The good news is that this selection and learning process never stops and we can relearn perceptual biases. One path toward this learning can be to use simulation of images to organize and engage our whole selves differently in preparation for action. Sports psychologists routinely use mental imagery to train athletes like professional golfers to prepare for each shot by imagining parts of the action sequence or the resulting action. Athletes are trained to employ images that match past experience with future events to clarify and facilitate powerful action. While this image work appears to be mental activity, it actually actively engages many parts of the nervous system to organize perception, motor control, sensation, emotion, and more. Myriad research studies point to imagination not as a mental activity, but as an integrated action process. Barsalou crystalizes findings from diverse research studies confirming that image simulation activates the body's motor control planning very early in the imagination process, "As people perceive visual objects, simulations of potential actions become active in preparation for situated action." (2008, 624) It is not an exaggeration to say that when we image-ine (or simulate an image) our brain/bodies are already engaged in action. We talk a lot about the imagination in actor training, but do we really understand how deeply connected it is with aspects of action or prediction, or how dynamically it is engaged with meaningful action? The simulation of images is a steady and streaming part of daily life that offer imagination as an important process for actors and their training.

We can use this research as an opportunity to also reconsider how prediction of the future may offer a resonant architecture of presence constructed from diversity of materials and engagements. Our predictions of our future happen in a narrow band of imagery drawn from fixed responses drawn from memory/learning. This ongoing past/future oscillation bonds onto the present through unseen and largely unconscious obligate patterns of responses that inhibit our readiness for action. Relearning these responses is possible, but it takes time and delicate guidance on the teacher's part. For Tom, prediction is a such critical aspect of his implicit strategies to stay safe in threatening environments that teaching exercises or strategies have not yet broken into his system. Can we fault Tom's aptitude or will? Or might the answer lie in reconsidering the way we offer Tom a path of relearning the hard fusion of past/future that is driving his present?

Contemporary research here offers reconceiving our strategies to help Tom through a novel time-based approach. Researchers Peter Payne and Mardi A. Crane-Godreau's 2015 article "The Preparatory Set: A Novel Approach to Understanding Stress, Trauma, and Bodymind Therapies" proposes a Preparatory Set (PS) model that shifts common conceptions of stress, and interventions to mitigate it, by targeting the time before the stressful moment arrives as the most fertile place for learning:

> Here we use the term (preparatory set) to refer to the rapid, largely sub-cortical preparation of the organism for response to the environment. We suggest that this preparation involves an organization of core features of the organism in readiness: physical posture and muscle tone, visceral state, affective or motivation state, arousal and orientation of attention, and (subcortical) cognitive expectations.
>
> (2015, 178)

The PS model suggests that we can prepare the nervous system for a more flexible relationship with future events by offering mindfully intended physical learning.

The PS model also illustrates how implicit memory plays a significant role in preparing for future actions. Echoing Barsalou's reference to Glenberg's important work in reframing memory, Payne and Crane-Godreau write:

> Implicit and procedural memories are quickly activated and are accessed at a subcortical level. They activate a set of expectations about the situation. Glenberg suggests that the main function of memory is to guide appropriate action (and therefore preparation for action) in the present moment.
>
> (2015, 178)

Through the PS model, we begin to understand memory and prediction (past and future) as deeply entwined in present meaningful action in the world. Furthermore, we can begin to understand how responses to threat driven by a taut strand of implicit memory push a nervous system up against the threshold of overloaded response, prompting inflexible action closely tied to survival responses. Living at that threshold of stress takes a toll on one's ability to act meaningfully in nuanced ways.

When Tom came to the program, he imagined success through studio learning. He has no understanding of the implicit or body memory dominating his work. Tom's imagination of his future as an actor has become fraught with dire images of failure, born largely from his learned self-critical nature. Knowing that he senses disappointment from his teachers must inform teaching strategies. First, teachers can help Tom sense relationships between excessively active physical patterns and things like his strain for short-term memory, his jagged attentional abilities, and his lurching emotional outbursts. Then, they can shine some gentle awareness on those relationships and offer time-based learning strategies in place of momentary solutions.

The key is to help Tom to slowly gain adaptability and flexibility in his awareness of himself, as he senses, thinks, feels, and acts in the world. Through personal writing, body-mindfulness work, and encouragement Tom can be guided to understand and sense changes in the flexibility of his past/future thinking. Slowly, he can shift his preparatory state so that in the minutes or hours before a performance he is practicing the return to settled breath and a deep sense of the ground. He can be helped to practice a fluid awareness that the past and future are always here with him and the return to the present is always just a breath away. Tom must learn that he has the capacity to foreground one element of the threefold strand over another with lightness and flexibility, and that learning can only happen in small steps over time. Slowly and compassionately, his teachers can envision the learning that formed Tom into this person and performer. Tom's teachers are fully capable of offering him ways to relearn his patterns, but the work with him must be framed in the *how* of the exercises as much as the *what* he should be doing.

Body-mindful practices really have begun to offer Tom some help, at least on some days in the studio. But that practice seems to rarely transfer in performance situations, when his nervous system seems to escape to some wild state. So, for example, Tom spends many hours learning his lines, then repeatedly forgets them in stressful situations when the web of his implicit memory responses overwhelms him. While that may frustrate his scene partners and his teachers, it is not a question of Tom's desire or effort. In fact, more effort in learning lines will not help him. Tom is struggling with the activation of patterns held largely by implicit memory and therefore out of reach of his conscious self. These patterns are now bound in a tight embrace with prediction that can be changed through the repeated practice of body-mindfulness, but only if Tom's nervous system can begin to assess safety within the context of stressful performance moments. Celebrated psychophysiologist Stephen Porges notes: "Only in a safe environment is it adaptive and appropriate to simultaneously inhibit defense systems and exhibit positive social engagement behavior" (2004, 20). Following Porges's idea, we might imagine that we teachers are constructing the performance training studio and stage as a "socialization" zone.

Body-mindful practices like yoga, Tai Chi, Feldenkrais, and Alexander Technique usefully encourage increased attention to the sensory information available at any given moment, increasing actors' ability to interact with the world in safe and sensitive ways. These practices have long been important elements of actor training, merging with the myriad lessons encoded in generations of post-Stanislavski studio teaching to help actors learn to focus and shift attention. However, through these practices, actors can also begin to unhelpfully intuit that the goal is to remain glued to a notion of presence that is only about what is "right here and right now." Again, the awareness of what is happening in the present is an undeniable core of artistic expression, but we must profoundly change the sense and quality of "now" in light of interdisciplinary neuroscience research. Our training practices should reflect the oscillating past/future qualities of presence, offering actors clear image-based metaphors for that oscillation, and helping them to skillfully return from past/future excursions as a natural feature of presence.

We can extrapolate from the PS model's suggestion that body-mindful practices can change a person's *preparatory state*, or readiness for action. It is not enough to simply teach body-mindful practices; instead, we must help students to understand the dynamics of how to "practice these practices" to shape their whole being in ways that afford easy readiness for action. The real value of body-mindful practices may lie in teaching our students a way to accumulate practice so that their nervous systems become adept at linking action with perception and desire, and in preparing for action with more nuance and awareness.

In the United States, it has long been customary to suggest that we are teaching actors a "toolbox." While true and always meant with the best intent, it also may be a bit of a cop-out. Give me a toolbox of jeweler's tools and I will have a toolbox, but no understanding for what these tools allow me to do, nor the sequence or combinations in which they might be useful. I would be just as likely to bang on the back of watch with a small hammer, when there is a tool for opening the watch. The tools our performance students need may be less about which practice or another will help to build resonant presence than about how we help them link practice with the rich complexities of human body-brain engagement with the world. Building a robust toolbox requires us to re-imagine memory and to sense its essential coupling with prediction, especially in the midst of deep presence.

Images like the threefold woven thread can guide our students through the boundaries between memory, present, and future as permeable layers that can be crossed with flexibility and trust. For example, such flexibility may be the entryway for an actress feeling her way into playing Hedda Gabler whose present, just returned from a honeymoon, is overwhelmed by strands of memory and future that are further amplified when past love arrives. Allowing light to shine out of Hedda's presence requires deft and flexible ability to interweave past, present, and future in ways that move beyond language. Therein lies the challenge and beauty of resonating a Hedda sufficiently rooted in a thick present powerful enough for audience members to leave their seats and float with her through their own memories and future hopes.

To help students like Tom, we must offer compelling metaphors for understanding how presence contains the past and future. The language and imagery that we use to render such potent metaphors must actively propel our actors toward natural understandings for how nervous systems build consciousness in present moments. I have offered one metaphor in the threefold strand of past, now, future. With increased understanding you can mine your own life experience, poetry, and visual art for other metaphors. The goal must be to offer images of how past, presence, and future enrich our lives, and then to fold those images into our acting methodologies.

We may want to believe that we are only teaching performers but, in truth, our students will be a next generation of teachers as well. We are passing along a tradition not only of the craft and art of acting, but ways of learning that potentiate performances that reverberate through culture. Our students' acting will mentor other actors and many will teach their own students. Instead of attachment to teachers, better that we equip our students to understand and mentor their own nervous systems, affording a complete possession of their work that they can pass forward to their students.

Note

1 See Levine (2015).

References

Barsalou, Lawrence W. 2008. "Grounded Cognition." *Annual Review of Psychology* doi:10.1146/annurev.psych.59.103006.093639.

Claxton, Guy. 2015. *Intelligence in the Flesh*. New Haven, CT: Yale University Press.

Fuchs, Thomas. 2017. "Collective Body Memories." In *Embodiment, Enaction, and Culture: Investigating the Constitution of the Shared World*. Cambridge, MA: MIT Press.

Levine, Peter. 2015. *Trauma and Memory*. Berkeley, CA: North Atlantic Books.

Payne, Peter, and Crane-Godreau, Mardi A. 2015. "The Preparatory Set: A Novel Approach to Understanding Stress, Trauma, and Bodymind Therapies." *Frontiers in Human Neuroscience*. https://doi.org/10.3389/fnhum.2015.00178.

Porges, Stephen W. 2004. "Neuroception: A Subconscious System for Detecting Threats and Safety." *Zero to Three* 24 (5): 19–24.

Stapleton, Mog and Dave Ward. 2012. "Es Are Good: Cognition as Enacted, Embodied, Embedded, Affective and Extended." *Consciousness in Interaction*. 86–89.

12 Drag evolution

Re-imaging gender through theory and practice

Jean O'Hara

I want to first situate myself both as a researcher and a professor who is an Irish-American genderqueer dyke[1] who currently lives on Treaty 6 territory, traditional meeting grounds and home for many Indigenous people, including Cree, Saulteaux, Blackfoot, Dene, Métis, and Nakota Sioux. As a theatre artist, I research and write about gender performance both on and off the stage. I have been interested in some of the following questions: How do we perform or not perform our assigned gender in our everyday lives? Can theatre allow for a wider range of gender expression? How does gender intersect with race, class, (dis)ability, sexuality, and sovereignty? As the Gender Studies field continues to grow and as our incoming students' genders fall within and outside of the binary of women and men, I wondered, how could theatre address these changes? I started to imagine a drag course that could integrate both theory and practice. I wanted to support students as they interrogate, study, and create (drag) performances that could trouble the gender binary. I was equally interested to investigate if drag could possibly have a liberatory effect on participants.

In 2006 I began to devise a Multicultural Queer Theatre course at Humboldt State University as a way of acknowledging all the Two-Spirit/LGBTIQ+ theatre artists whose queerness was erased in my theatre literature education including but not limited to: Maria Irene Fornes, Lorraine Hansberry, Tomson Highway, George Wolfe, and Edward Albee. I was also interested in less well-established or known queer playwrights. As I began reading these queer plays, I quickly recognized I wanted to stage them. Playing off the anthology title *O Solo Homo: The New Queer Performance* (Bornstein 1991), I titled the evening of LGBTIQ+ plays as *Homo Expo: A Queer Theatre Extravaganza* and staged in the fall of 2007. The first act was a mix of excerpts from solo performances that also included a staged adaptation of the book *Butch is a Noun* by S. Bear Bergman. The second act was a circus adaptation of Kate Bornstein's play *Hidden: A Gender* (1995).

Interesting questions about power and gender norms arose in the process of costuming and performance of drag. Craig Hickman's piece, *Skin and Ornaments,* was performed by a Black cis man, while a white queer cis man performed Bornstein's transition process (Bornstein 1995). We were far into the rehearsal process when the first man came to the costume shop to try on outfits for his drag queen role. As is often the case, the college costume shop was filled with women. After trying out multiple dresses and wigs, the costume designers found the perfect fit. The actor had a small build and was easily read as a woman. The actor looked beautiful and all the women verbally shared this with him with enthusiasm. To my surprise the actor started performing this hypermasculinity. His voice got lower, he started to flex his arm muscles, and spread his legs out wide (despite being in a short dress). I had never seen him act this way in any of the rehearsals nor when I saw him perform drag at a local club, so I was left confused. An hour later, the other cis man came to try on clothing/costumes for when his character transitions to wearing "women's clothes." Again, many dresses and wigs were tried on until the perfect costume was found. This actor also had a small build and again could easily be read as a woman just by changing his hair and clothes. The women in the costume shop were pleased and stated how beautiful this actor looked. To my amazement, this second actor started to mimic a hypermasculinity as well. His actions were almost identical to the last actor's actions and voice modulation. I wanted to have a conversation with both performers but knew there was no time to dive into this likely unconscious reaction.

Later upon reflection, I recognized that once these cis men were read as women they immediately lost power politically, intellectually, economically, *et cetera*. From a gender theory perspective, it appeared that they were trying to regain their power by asserting through how they positioned their bodies and actions that despite looking like women they were indeed men. I think they also experienced what most women experience in North America; that our bodies are consistently objectified and sexualized by the dominant heteropatriarchy. Also, we are told very early on in our lives that our greatest assets are our beauty and our sexual appeal, the standards of which are rigidly defined and unattainable. It was after the production that I started imagining a drag class that would allow us to have these conversations. I had delved into drag kinging and had experienced the gender hierarchy from a different place. By just darkening my eyebrows and changing my clothes, I could easily be read as a young man (this would happen off the stage later as well). This gave me access to white male power; I could take up more space physically and vocally, and my desire for women (and female bodied people) was not only allowed but celebrated and even encouraged. It was interesting to have straight cis women be attracted to me just by changing my clothes, again even off stage. In many ways this speaks to how desire is constructed within a heteronormative "straight" binary.

When I was hired as an assistant professor at Marlboro College, I now had the opportunity to offer a drag course that was steeped in theory and practice (embodiment). Marlboro College has a radical pedagogy where faculty create or co-create courses that they are interested in teaching, and students take whatever classes they want to fulfil their senior thesis (a plan that is unique to them). I was so excited about the opportunity to teach the course that I wrote up a course description in my first semester. By the following academic year, Nelli Sargsyan was hired as an anthropology professor with a focus on auto-ethnographic research. As I mentioned earlier, I was not only interested in the conversation between theory and practice, but also interested in how drag might change, affirm, or deeply question all the participants' relationships to their gender(s) and gender performances. We utilized auto-ethnography by having students write weekly about a current or former experience performing or not performing their current or assigned gender. The focus was on actions and lived experiences. For example, one cis woman noticed at lunch that she only allowed herself to eat a salad in order to stay thin. By noticing, she could then make a different choice and/or note how her body felt conforming to taught dominant "beauty standards." Also, Nelli's PhD research focused on queer Armenian artists, so she also had a deep knowledge of gender and queer theory. She immediately agreed to co-teach the course, although it was not until winter break that I learned she had never seen a drag show.

In December we watched a local drag queen performance that included banter that was self-hating and misogynistic. This had never been my experience. The queens I previously saw onstage were smart, sassy, and unabashedly confident in the expression of gender(s) and their desire for men. In short, they were fierce. I think it is important when teaching a drag course to acknowledge and address how drag performance can be problematic. Drag performances can restate the binary and replicate forms of sexism, racism, ableism, *et cetera*. It was important to Nelli and me that we find drag kings and queens who moved away from harmful drag and drag performances that were exclusionary.

Over winter break, Nelli and I worked and reworked different resource lists to build our syllabus and shape our course for the Spring 2017 semester. We agreed to start the course with Queer Indigenous Theory, including chapters from *Queer Indigenous Studies* (Driskill et. al. 2011) and Maria Lugones's (2008) article "The Coloniality of Gender." We also utilized multiple chapters from *The Drag King Anthology* (Troka, Lebesco, and Noble 2002), which intertwines critical race, ethnicity, gender, sexuality, and feminism though the voices of drag king performers and scholars. As we read each other's academic sources, we quickly became aware that we had too many. Together we mapped our semester with some of the following guiding questions: What consequences can a failed gender performance have? What consequence can disrupting gender performance have? How does drag allow us to re-imagine and queer gender? Whose sexual and gender desire is allowed? Does one need to feel safe to publicly identify as genderqueer, non-binary, or trans? What potentialities does drag have to en/act erotica and queer desire?

In addition to written sources, we incorporated short YouTube clips, documentary films, and drag performances into the syllabus. The film *Screaming*

Queens disrupted the Stonewall story of the first LGBTQ+ resistance to police brutality while also centering trans women stories (2005). YouTube series *The What's Underneath Project* interviewed genderqueer, trans, and non-binary people about their journey with clothes and fashion.

Since this course emphasized embodied practice, we began each class with a short mindful meditation and warm up exercises that then lead to discussion about assigned video clips and articles. We also incorporated Augusto Boal's embodied methodology. One example was the application of Boal's Image Theatre with Qwo-Li Driskill's article, "Stolen from Our Bodies: First Nation Two-Spirit/Queers and the Journey to a Sovereign Erotic" (2004). This combination was one of the most potent moments in our course as it provided an opening to speak to the weight and harm carried by those of us who fall outside the straight heteronormative binary.

In addition to theory, it was important to allow our collective knowledge, perspectives, and experiences about gender, sexuality, and desire into our discussions. The following course description was posted on our website:

Drag: History, Politics and Performance
   This survey course will explore the history of drag performance across a variety of sociocultural and political settings. We will examine the uses of drag through reading ethnographic research and multiple mediums: From Kabuki Theatre to *RuPaul's Drag Race*. This course will interweave queer Indigenous studies, feminist anthropological theory, gender theory, queer theory, and trans theory to examine and interrogate gender, gender roles, and gender performance. Each course participant will develop their own drag persona as a form of embodied ethnographic research/inquiry into these various theories.

As mentioned earlier, we intentionally began the course with Queer Indigenous Studies to expand students' ideas and notions about gender and sexuality. Our college and classroom were on Abanaki and Wabenaki land and it was important for students to understand that these Nations, along with other Native nations, have/had different ways of thinking and enacting genders. As far as we know (much has been lost due to genocidal efforts since 1492), there are no gender pronouns in many Indigenous languages. Also, generally speaking gender, sexuality, and spirituality are intertwined and not separate categories. Most importantly, these Indigenous nations do not organize their homes, work, governance, *et cetera* based on gender. Rather, they organize their communities based on people's strengths, gifts, and spiritual paths. In other words, there is not a gender hierarchy or a gender binary. Your value is/was based on how well you treat/ed others and how you contribute/d to your community[2].

We listed the course under theatre, anthropology, and cross-discipline fields. On the first day of registration the course was filled with a waiting list despite the fact it was not a required course. We also had three alumni who wanted to take the class. I think this speaks to the need to have an informed community to explore gender and desire and to also act on those desires. In the end, we had five students who identified outside the binary, two "feminine" gay men, and a few queer women while the majority of the class were cis straight women of different ethnicities. As I mentioned earlier, I identify as a genderqueer dyke without a partner or children, and my colleague Nelli identifies as an Armenian American straight cis woman who is married with kids. In fact, her kids would end up coming to our drag rehearsals later in the course. (I still have this great image from one of our rehearsals where Nelli was dressed up as Freddie Mercury breast-feeding her two-year-old toddler.)

I found Nelli's presence served as a "safety gap" that turned out to be helpful. Even in this queer classroom space, it seemed that my gender and sexuality sometimes made the students uncomfortable, even the gender queer/non-binary students. This was often demonstrated by the amount of push back and even visual upset I received from students versus how students relaxed to Nelli.

Not only did I embody queer realities, but I could also deeply engage in theory to deconstruct my own gender "failings," fluidity, and identities. At the same time, I had been exploring and honoring my own gender and queer desire for decades, while some of our students were tentative, protective, unsteady inwardly and outwardly (and rightfully so). Ultimately, theory and embodiment could be overwhelming, confusing, or upsetting for the non-binary students. Certainly, any of us outside the heteropatriarchy have experienced pain and shame for who we are and who we desire/love. In academia, we are often trained to be objective, and yet feelings are often what show up in a classroom when you deeply dig into gender, gender performance, and trans history.

In addition to teaching, I also filled the role of artistic director, coordinating PR, tickets, transportation, costumes, props, set pieces, sound design, tech workers, reserving theatre spaces, creating the show program, and much more. In addition, I was the director, which put me in the role of consistently asking students to step up and follow through with rehearsal dates. Nelli became the "cheerleader mom" who told the students how much she loved them, while I was up at 11:00 pm after working all day, for example, to help the emcee (a gay staff member) to be his campy fun self when he's not on stage (he clammed up in rehearsal).

What worked

We created a classroom climate that allowed students to take risks and to begin formalizing what they wanted to explore or say about gender. At the beginning of our first class, the students created the guidelines and parameters for the classroom environment and they stayed true to that commitment. When it came to sharing their pieces, everyone was supportive and also willing to give constructive feedback. It was also helpful for the students to witness their two professors in their process of creation and co-creation. We both had ideas for solo pieces and a duet but recognized there were too many pieces and not enough time to develop and/or rehearse them. Nelli and I ended up performing *All Out of Love* by Air Supply. We wore bright orange and lime green leisure suits with fake fur for our chest hair. We sang our lines while performing synchronized moves that became more melodramatic as the song intensified. At one point we were on our knees, squeezing Visine into our eyes to help us cry as we held one another for emotional support. The piece ended when we recognized that we are attracted to each other and we began a seeming rebound relationship.

Nelli and I also worked on the music for a Queen tribute with the song *Bicycle Race* as the through line. In the process of choosing specific Queen songs, I learned that while in Armenia Nelli saw the rock video for *I Want to Break Free* that was banned in the United States by MTV. In that video all the band members are dressed in drag with mixed gender signifiers. The cast was influenced by the music video, adding mustaches and fabulous wigs for our final piece. For the final group piece, both faculty and students were able to create whatever persona they wanted with the one unifying element of bright colors. All eighteen of us performed the Queen montage which opened with *We Will Rock You* and closed with *We Are the Champions* (changing the word "losers" to "haters"). The overall show, titled *MC Drag King, Queens and Much More* was flexible, allowing for dance, poetry, skits, multiple languages, lip sync, tricycle riding, and more. It was queer in the most liberatory way, and the crowd loved it. The entire cast was super happy and pleased with their results and by the audience's response. The Dean of Faculty said it was his favorite show and would sing *All out Love* to Nelli and me weeks after the performance. We also did an encore performance at the dinner for graduating seniors.

What didn't work

Surprisingly, for our first run of the course, it went really well. That said, there were challenges with the title of the course, the amount of work assigned, students' lack of experience with performing and/or devising new material, unexpected absences, and the pressure to perform off campus.

The title of the course did not work. When I first began imagining the course, I had the working title *Deconstructing Gender through Drag* but changed it when I created the list of theatre classes for the Marlboro College web page. I titled it *Drag History, Politics and Performance* because I imagined doing a deeper dive into "drag" theatre history. Needless to say, the course title was listed well before Nelli and I decided to co-teach the course.

Beginning the course with Indigenous theory and frameworks did not work. Students shared that because it was radically different than "Western" theory, it was therefore confusing and even off-putting. Interestingly, they wanted to read Judith Butler's work at the beginning of the course (1996). When we debriefed the course at the end, the non-binary students felt the course title was misleading despite our syllabus description and framing of the course on the first day of class.

What we also learned is that we did not have enough time to get through all the theory we assigned and that we had even less time to develop our performance pieces. In addition, we needed to decide the order and transitions for the entire show, which included two large numbers at the opening and closing. The lack of time had a greater impact on the performance since a majority of the students had never acted before, which created additional stress and ultimately less polished pieces. Also, out of eighteen actors, I was the only one who had actually performed drag on stage. At the beginning of the course we had students anonymously answer a group of questions that included sharing their fears about the class. The most consistent fear they had was that they would produce a terrible piece that would be then witnessed by an audience. As theatre artists, we know this is a common fear for new actors. My main methodology to reduce fear is repetition and positive feedback, so that the actor, even if nervous, has the piece deeply in their body. This is difficult-to-impossible to do when things become rushed, when there is not much time to work and rework the pieces.

During our rehearsal process, a late spring flu started spreading throughout the campus and we ended up losing actors for many of our group rehearsals. We had eighteen actors and seventeen pieces with many costume changes, light and sound cues. Ultimately, we had only one rehearsal where everyone was present. Needless to say, this did not help people's fears about performing, and I did not have sufficient time to continue coaching those less experienced performers to move away from common stage errors (such as looking at the floor versus the audience).

In addition to our performance at the college, I also coordinated a performance downtown at Hooker-Dunham Theatre. At the beginning of the course, I checked in with Nelli and the students about utilizing our performances as a fundraiser for the local LGBTQ+ non-profit organization, Out in the Open (formerly Green Mountain Crossroads). My rationale was that drag originated in the trans/queer community, so it made sense to give back to the LGBTQ+ community. We were graciously given a theatre space for free, so that all the proceeds went to Out in the Open. Overall, the performance was a success and we were able to raise nearly $800. That said, it was a big endeavor to organize and transport students, props, costumes, and food to this new theatre space. What was more complicated was trying to fit our eighteen-actor show on a ten- to twelve-foot stage with one entrance. The "back stage" was about fifteen inches deep with a very rough rock wall that contained no lights. We had to buy headlamps to be able to navigate the narrow and potentially dangerous rock wall. We also had very little technical support with only two student technical theatre workers who had never been in this theatre. We spent hours reworking our transitions and some of the action on stage. For example, performers needed to have someone push their tricycle over big cables onto the stage and in the process one actor slammed their knee into a brick wall as they peddled while other bikes careened around them. It was dangerous, as we nearly careened off the stage and into the audience's laps. In addition, there wasn't a green room or dressing room but rather a big open space that was usually the office space. Despite all the new changes and the crowded stage, the performance went off without a hitch. By the end, we were exhausted from a full day and night and the hours of loading and unloading props, costumes and set pieces back at the college. I still question whether this was the best choice for the faculty and students. It put greater pressure on the new performers and created a great deal of labor on everyone's part to remount the show in a new space with little support.

What I would recommend

Slow down the process, and honor our elders. Both Nelli and I agreed that creating two linked classes—critical theory and a drag lab—would work best. Students would be required to take both courses if they wanted to perform, while the critical gender and queer theory course would be open to everyone. Within the course, I would increase the time spent discussing the intricacies of gender, sexuality and desire. I would expand the discussion about our genders beyond pronouns, and explore with students the ways we do or don't identify around gender (e.g., non-binary, genderqueer, cis, etc.). It is also important to talk about sexual identity and queer desire, how gender is in relation to sexuality, and/or how gender often troubles these categories. We are aware that Butches/Bois, genderqueer dykes, and effeminate men (fabulous sissies) are more likely to be attacked (verbally or physically) for their gender presentation rather than their sexuality *per se*. All that said, it is trans women of color who are at most risk of violence that can often lead to murder. Many transgress these rigidly constructed gender lines, and we often pay through our very bodies. It is important to have these sometimes difficult and complex conversations with students while co-creating equitable, compassionate, celebratory spaces to explore our own genders and sexual desire.

Additionally, queer students need to know how their ancestors resisted and fought back (through poetry, direct action, *et cetera*) against oppressive institutional gender and sexual norms. Ultimately, this generation has been a part of deep and complex conversations about gender; in some cases they are ahead of the academy. I believe we need to be willing to learn and adopt some of their language. At the same time, we need to honor all the queer elders in the Two-Spirit/LGBTIQ+ community for their courage and resiliency. These elders have witnessed and lived through violence without one single law to protect them while also watching their chosen family die from genocidal efforts and, more recently, the AIDS (plague) epidemic.

I would suggest that we incorporate a queer history into our theatre history and dramatic literature classes, so as to not leave out the queer student who will inevitably take these classes. It is important to us to see our lives reflected back to us, and we need stories that go beyond the self-hating, closeted, lonely, and victim narratives. We need to teach that queer communities, including Two-Spirit communities, have always resisted the subjugation of their queer bodies and queer desires. Through the centuries we have fortified a brilliant resiliency that is part of our ancestral lines. We have been here since the first humans were born into this world. For this reason, we need to move away from dominant narratives that see queer folk as an anomaly–only 10 percent of the population. I beg to differ, as the closet still remains fairly locked down by institutionalized transphobia, heterosexism and a "sexaphobic" (Justice 2010, 108) settler regime.

End results

This class created a community of learners willing to test out theory in front of live audiences. The students were genuinely invested in the work of the course and broke open their ideas about gender. They absolutely found ways to re-imagine gender both on and off stage. Throughout the process there was generative conversation, deep and difficult questions that expanded our thinking, and the final performance in which everyone shined. In the end, it was a gift to work closely together to create final performances that both celebrated our collective labor and benefitted our communities.

Notes

1 Dyke has a positive meaning that was created by the Jewish poet Judy Graham to include her working-class upbringing while fighting for the end of classism, racism, and homophobia.
2 This insight comes from Robyn Fernis and Corey Taybor who were interviewed by Qwo-Li Driskill ("Aesegi Ayetl," 2011, 103–104).

References

Bergman, S. Bear. 2006. *Butch is a Noun*. San Francisco: Suspect Thoughts Press.
Bornstein, Kate. 1991. *Hidden: A Gender: A Play*. [Place of publication not identified]: K. Bornstein.
Bornstein, Kate. 1995. *Gender Outlaw: On Men, Women, and the Rest of Us*. New York: Vintage Books.
Butler, Judith. 1996. "Performative Acts and Gender Constitution." *The Twentieth-Century Performance Reader*. Edited by Michael Huxley and Noel Witts. New York: Routledge, 120–34.

Driskill, Qwo-Li. 2011. "Aesegi Ayetl: Cherokee Two-Spirit People Reimaging Nation." In Driskill et al., 97–112.

Driskill, Qwo-Li. 2004. "Stolen from Our Bodies: First Nation Two-Spirit/Queers and the Journey to a Sovereign Erotic". *Studies in American Indian Literatures* 16 (2): 50–64. www.jstor.org/stable/2073950.

Driskill, Qwo-Li, Chris Finley, Brian Joseph Gilley, and Scott Lauria Morgensen, eds. 2011. *Queer Indigenous Studies: Critical Interventions in Theory Politics and Literature*. Tucson: University of Arizona Press.

Justice, Daniel Heath. 2010. "Notes Towards a Theory of Anomaly." In *GLQ: The Journal of Lesbian and Gay Studies* 16 (1–2): 207–242.

Lagones, Maira. 2008. "The Coloniality of Gender." *Worlds & Knowledges Otherwise*. 1–17.

Screaming Queens: The Riot at Compton's Cafeteria. 2005. Directed by Susan Stryker. Frameline.

Troka, Donna, Katheen Lebesco and Jean Noble, eds. 2002. *The Drag King Anthology*. New York: Harrington Park Press.

13 The "best" bad idea

Decentering professional casting practices in university productions

Maria Enriquez

As theatre educators, our teaching approaches draw from our training programs and experiences as practitioners. Additionally, the theatre departments we work in commonly replicate professional working models as an unquestioned methodology while preparing students to enter an undeniably competitive field. This is most visible through the process of college and university production work. From the pre-production planning to post-mortem wrap-up, the steps taken for delivering plays and musicals to educational communities closely resemble those found in regional theatres across the country. However, the professional theatre world has come under increased scrutiny for its long-standing history of marginalizing people of color. This raises the question: how beneficial is it for students and theatre programs in higher education if decision-makers continue to unquestioningly replicate a professional model that is facing increased criticism for its dismissive and counter-productive approaches to ethnoracial and cultural equity? My research examines the relationship between professional and university theatre programs and its impact on students of color, and follows how I deviated from a universally accepted production practice in order to address issues of ethnocultural and international representation.

In his essay "The Best Actor for the Role, or the Mythos of Casting in American Popular Performance," Brian Herrera traces a history of casting practices, and how they shape one of the foundational and universally accepted beliefs in both professional and non-professional theatre: that "the quest for the best actor remains an ideal worth pursuing." His work tracks how casting the "best" actor is believed to be based in equity, artistry, and meritocracy, and the ways those justifications are used "to sustain a perhaps illusory sense of affinity" (Herrera 2015, 7). However, material and economic consequences—specifically for minority actors—press against the rationalization for casting the best actor. This tension is clearly seen in the 1991 casting controversy surrounding *Miss Saigon,* in which white actor Jonathan Pryce was cast as The Engineer in the UK production and wore eye prosthetics and bronzer in a performance of yellowface for the ethnically specified Eurasian role. The Asian American community and US Actors' Equity Association protested the production's transfer to Broadway, but show producer Cameron Mackintosh defended the casting decision with the argument that the role should be filled by "the right actor, whatever race they were" (Bunbury 2016). Equity conceded, and in an industry-affirming act, Pryce won the Tony for Best Performance by a Leading Actor in a Musical.

The politics of choosing the best actor in professional theatre—a topic that Herrera notes has eluded historical inquiry until recently—is part of a larger, ongoing conversation about the ramifications of the casting system. At the 2015 Carnaval of New Latinalo Work at DePaul University, then *HowlRound* Director P. Carl leveled criticism towards regional theatres' employment practices during his opening remarks,

> The numbers don't add up. Our stages, our theatres, our institutions, still don't look right. They do not represent who we are as a country of rapidly shifting demographics. They are not a reflection of the complexity of the American story.
>
> (Carl)

A study conducted between 2006 and 2011 by the Asian American Performers Action Coalition (AAPAC) demystified the statistics of hiring practices on Broadway and in large NYC non-profit theatres, which illustrates Carl's remarks of employment inequity. The AAPAC's startling findings on the breakdown of working actors were as follows: 80 percent Caucasian, 14 percent African American, 4 percent Latinx, 2 percent Asian American, and 1 percent Other (AAPAC). By comparison, the population breakdown for NYC was 33 percent non-Hispanic white, 28.6 percent Hispanic/Latinx, 25.5 percent African American, and 12.7 percent Asian. AAPAC's research shows significant disproportions between the casting of white actors versus non-white actors, which is alarming when considering the potential percentage drop in the number of artists of color in non-metropolitan regions of the country. *Casting A Movement: The Welcome Table Initiative* (Syler and Banks 2019) documents the interventions that theatre practitioners, administrators, and scholars are making to address the representational disparity. Regional playhouses are being called upon by groups like the LTC, AAPAC, Project Am I Right?, and CastandLoose, along with the recently closed Alliance for Inclusion in the Arts, to address the institutional neglect toward minorities. The last decade has witnessed increased outcries against instances of whitewashing and erasure on professional stages.[1]

Building upon the important conversations that are happening in the professional realm, I consider the complicated politics underlying the concept of the "best" actor and what this means for higher education. We have been taught as practitioners the importance casting holds for a show's success (and its reflection on the person making those decisions), and yet, we absorb into our pedagogy a fairly ambiguous process that wields considerable power. To clearly delineate what I refer to when I use the term the "best" actor, I include two specific components: talent (real and perceived) and the subliminal factors that can sway a casting call. While it can be acknowledged that assessments of talent will always be partly subjective (talent is in the eyes and ears of the beholder), there are measures used to determine ability and technique, which factor into determinations of talent—musicality, dance precision, clarity of objectives and richness of given circumstances, etc. In addition to talent, there are other influencers on how a person's audition is received. They can include clothing choices, resume listings, audition material selections, or general likeability (did the auditionee appear friendly?) that practitioners are trained to unconsciously or knowingly pick up on. These cues signal to a casting director the level of experience and professionalism an actor has, and subsequently, their desireability as a potential cast member.

As Herrera points out, these "weeding" mechanisms have real, economic consequences in the livelihoods of working actors of color. Decision-makers scanning for these indicators of "good" or "bad" auditions, which then lead to perceived "right" or "wrong" casting choices, ultimately act as a gateway for who is and is not represented onstage. Adding to this tension is the question of transparency regarding those elusive factors that subliminally influence a casting director's determinations. Herrera identifies the search for actors with the "It" factor, and Marvin Carlson describes "the invisible presences of the past roles of individual actors" that haunt the expectations for a current production (Carlson 2001). These intangible elements may sway casting directors' decisions to unconsciously favor white actors who can replicate past performances given by previous white actors—creating an unintentionally racist system that is imperceptible in the moment of casting decisions due to its argued subjectivity and perceived fairness. Despite the indeterminable nature of casting and its material consequences on working actors—as evidenced by the employment disparities found in the AAPAC's collected data—these practices have remained largely uncritiqued and widely accepted as inherent to the process of finding the best actor.

This established praxis in the professional theatre world presents a dilemma for theatre programs in university settings. Herrera points to how the enduring principle that "university theatre productions should meet professional (or peri-professional) standards" can prevent schools from producing culturally rich plays for fear of not having ethnically specific actors to fulfill the roles (Herrera 2015). As an educator, I have observed how this rationale creates a cyclical problem; roles are not readily available that showcase student actors of color, who are then unable to develop performance skills deemed necessary to be featured onstage, which further limits the school's offerings of culturally diverse works and creates a vacuum of performance opportunities for inexperienced minority actors.

Even when universities select productions designated for actors of color, the philosophy of casting the best actor can sabotage departmental intentions for creating diversity onstage. Recent college and high school productions at Kent State University and Ithaca High School drew national attention when students protested the deployed casting practices for their respective productions of *West Side Story* and *The Hunchback of Notre Dame*. In the case of Kent State, student complaints of non-Latinx students being cast in *West Side Story*'s three Puerto Rican leading roles led to the School of Theatre and Dance canceling the September 2018 production. Theatre major Bridgett Martinez, who was cast as the Maria understudy after losing the role to a white student, described her shock at the casting choices, "Once I read (the list) again and I really saw ... all of the casting choices, I was just blown away because it was not correct ..." (Gutierrez 2018). She explained on the local WKSU public radio station that her reason for protesting extended beyond not getting the role for which she auditioned, and was part of her larger concern about the number of auditioning Latinx students who were passed over in favor of white students for the Puerto Rican ensemble. "If they didn't have this diverse cast in mind, and they didn't think that we as the Latino students could fulfill these roles, then why would they continue on with the show in the first place?" (Gutierrez 2018) Fellow Kent State theatre major Viviana Cardenas argued that for *West Side Story*, "there are more things that need to be considered" (Gutierrez 2018) than casting solely based on talent. The department held a town meeting to provide students the opportunity to vocalize their concerns, resulting in the decision to cancel the production and replace it with *Children of Eden*. The new production, a musical retelling of the Book of Genesis, is not a Latinx-centered narrative like *West Side Story*, and its selection relinquished the school from any obligation for ethnically specific casting. Students who auditioned for *West Side Story* were recast in *Children of Eden*, however, the possibility for substantial Latinx representation was squelched when no Latinx students were cast in leading or supporting roles.

This example highlights how the pressures of casting the "best" actor limits theatre departments seeking ways to expand representations onstage. However, de-centering these casting practices serves to challenge the long-established history of university theatre programs emulating professional models and serving as a pipeline into the field. The emergence of university theatre programs correlates with the growth of regional theatres, and shows how these training programs are uniquely intertwined with their professional counterparts. The regional theatre surge during the 1960s prompted increased focus on "professionalism" in terms of performance and design production, "The thrust toward quality was uppermost...This was also a period in which better known and more experienced talents were introduced into the regional theatre. As a result, the quality of the work improved significantly during this period." (Zeigler 1972, 199–200) Professional theatres expanded in numbers across the country, and following that growth was the need for trained actors with more advanced skill sets beyond community theatre.

The imbricated relationship between regional theatres and university programs is evident in the establishment of the US Office of Education's

Arts and Humanities branch, followed with its two-part developmental conference on February 3–6, 1966, and May 26–31, 1966. Documented in the *Educational Theatre Journal's* special issue *Relationships Between Educational Theatre and Professional Theatre: Actor Training in the United States*, the conference explored how a mutually beneficial relationship between professional and academic theatre could be fostered. A February convening involved theatre educators exploring the established practices of theatre training and shaping the future of actor training programs. The first phase of the conference affirmed the belief in "the indissoluble link between theatre's educators and its practitioners: the areas of preparation and performance are interdependent; one relies on the other for purpose, meaning, and continuity" (Graham 1966, 316). A May convening invited institutional leaders from professional regional and New York theatres to join the theatre educators to bridge the professional and academic spheres, and to build a network that could lead to increased interchanges between them. The forty participants included Heads of Departments from geographically scattered programs like Columbia University, Yale School of Drama, Ohio University, University of Minnesota, and UCLA, and theatre company representatives from the Actor's Studio (NYC), the Guthrie Theatre (Minneapolis), Playhouse-in-the-Park (Cincinnati), and The Theatre Group (Los Angeles), along with the Director of Actor's Equity, Robert Loper. This conference was crucial in laying the structural groundwork and providing the methodological template for emerging theatre programs in higher education.

The alignment of university training programs with theatre companies was done with the intention of transitioning students into the theatre field. As such, professional companies were expected to

> provide the models of excellence in performance for theatre in colleges and universities. ... When [they] undertake professional training, moreover, it means that the professional theatre should serve as a consultant in planning training programs, a source of teachers, a means of furnishing intern experience, a reviewing body, and a resource for employment.
>
> (Graham 1966, 321)

The two-part conference established the working relationship between universities and regional theatres, and created a pipeline that was dictated, in large part, by the standards established in professional theatre. However, in doing so it allowed a working model with an ongoing history of excluding artists of color via casting and season selections to imprint a template onto newly establishing college programs. Significantly, the only mention in the *Educational Theatre Journal's* report regarding students or actors of color was a small outlier that offered a brief guiding principle for higher education. "Universities and colleges must realize the value of, and their responsibility to, integration. Talent in theatre is always at a premium; theatre, therefore, because of prejudice, conservatism, or whatever, cannot afford to ignore entire races of people" (Graham 1966, 354). This brief synopsis from the two-part conference highlights the developing mid-twentieth-century blind spot regarding issues of ethnoracial and cultural representation in academic theatre. The admonishment that talent take precedence over "prejudice, conservatism, or whatever," centers the priority of casting the perceived best actor in university production work over addressing biases and calling for equitable inclusion.

Contemporary criticisms of regional theatre's ongoing struggles with ethnoracial representation begs for a reevaluation on the role of university production work in relation to the professional field. Low enrollment numbers of minority students during the earlier decades of developing theatre programs certainly contributed to this institutional tunnel vision regarding those featured on university stages. However, the profession's long history of ignoring non-white bodies requires an examination of how those biases may have infiltrated production work in higher ed.

The incorporation of new methodologies that dismantle homogenized spaces and are responsive to current conversations within the field are all the more urgent as an increased number of diverse student populations continue to enter into college theatre programs. While national tracking data on ethnic enrollment in theatre programs is intermittent, the helpful study *Race/ Ethnicity Trends in Degrees Conferred By Institutions of Higher Education, 1980–81 through 1989–90* (Table 13.1) shows how the percentages for most minority students increased towards the end of the twentieth century (Aud et al. 2010, vi).

This data demonstrate how student populations have and will continue to change as more people of color enter college programs. An increase in diversity heightens the responsibility of theatre departments to address the educational needs of all of their students, including during production work. The inherited practice of overlooking or tokenizing students of color fails them on pedagogical and humanistic levels, and sets up theatre departments for

Table 13.1 Race/ethnicity trends in degrees conferred by institutions of higher education, 1980–1981 through 1989–1990

Fine/performing arts degrees	Bachelor's degrees in 1980	Bachelor's degrees in 1990	Master's degrees in 1980	Master's degrees in 1990
African American	1,835	1,416	267	246
Asian/API	788	1,377	160	266
American Indian/ Alaskan Native	187	163	22	35
Hispanic/Latino/a/x	779	1,059	132	143

potential casting embarrassments that can be scarring for their students—a probability that increases as more non-white students study theatre.

Informed by the historical imbrication of professional theatre and higher education, the conversations currently happening in the field, and my own sensibilities as a Latina director, I have intentionally dislodged finding the best actor as the overriding priority during the casting process. In full disclosure, this shift came about after I was deeply troubled by an earlier production I directed at Penn State Harrisburg, which ended up featuring an all-white, four-person cast. For that show, three students of color had auditioned. There were various reasons why I did not select them (lack of experience, questions about whether they could play the role, and scheduling conflicts), but I later realized that during the entire casting process I unthinkingly circled back to an internalized need of casting the actor who had what I perceived to be the best audition. During a talkback event after one of the shows, a local theatre-maker openly praised the production, saying that I had "cast the show perfectly." That compliment bubbled my discomfort to the surface as I realized that I was participating in a system of erasure for the sake of pursuing professional standards. Unhappy with the disparity that decision yielded, I asked myself: *What happens if I don't adhere to the same winnowing process used for actors in professional theatre?* In my own wrestling with how to intervene on behalf of our non-white and international students, it became clear to me that one clear way was to dislodge the ideology of casting the "best" actor as the singular pursuit, and instead, to widen the value system that underpins casting practices in higher education to prioritize equitable representation. For the next university production that I directed, I instead re-prioritized the goal of ethnocultural representation to have shared importance as casting the "best" actor.

My intention to amplify ethnocultural representation in production work was further influenced by, and in response to, the unique student demographic of the university in which I work, Penn State Harrisburg. Situated in Middletown, PA (population almost nine thousand), the small college is adjacent to the state capital, is surrounded by Pennsylvania farmlands, and has a modest undergraduate population of thirty-nine hundred. Many students are first generation college students from rural PA communities. However, PSH is also a surprising hotbed for international students. In the 2016–17 school year, there were approximately 716 international students out of the nearly 3,900 total undergraduate students, or roughly 20 percent of the student population. Of these seven-hundred-plus international students, the largest majority were from Asia. Over three hundred students from China arrived to PSH that school year. Additionally, the Latinx population in Lancaster County has neared fifty thousand residents, and accounts for over 50 percent of the total population growth in the last five years.

Harrisburg and Lancaster County's growing minority populations, combined with the close proximity to four major cities (NYC, Philadelphia, Baltimore, and Washington, DC), makes Penn State Harrisburg an appealing option for students from urban areas. This creates a unique situation for this small college in rural Pennsylvania as it becomes an increasingly diversified space for racial, ethnic, and cultural visibilities and exchanges.

Due to an uptick of hate crimes targeting the international and Muslim communities in Central PA following the then-recent 2016 presidential election, I felt it was necessary to produce a show that touched upon themes of difference and acceptance while still being accessible to a college population. This was further necessitated by the growing presence of non-white and LGBTQ groups on campus. The music director and I agreed that the content of *Avenue Q* was an ideal choice, as the R-rated *Sesame Street* story focuses on recent college grad, Princeton, and his struggles to find his purpose in life while meeting a diverse group of human and puppet characters. I understood that the show's success would require a unique combination of performance abilities from the cast: acting, singing, and puppeteering. PSH had no Theatre major or minor at that time, making the audition process a guessing game of who would turn out and what performance experience students would have. Also, as a first-year faculty member directing PSH's first musical in a newly built 375-seat theatre as part of the university's fiftieth anniversary festivities, I felt the pressure to direct a strong show to justify the recent allocation of resources to the fledgling theatre program.

In addition to the cast requirements of live human characters played by actors and puppet characters manipulated by puppeteers, *Avenue Q* has very specific casting needs for the human characters Christmas Eve and Gary Coleman—which serve the production's critique of racial politics and inequities in the United States. The Christmas Eve character critiques the exaggerated stereotypes of Asian women that permeate stage and film (Kim in *Miss Saigon*, Bloody Mary and Liat in *South Pacific*, all the characters in *The Mikado*) and the Gary Coleman character is a fictionalized extension of the real life actor who experienced financial and personal hardship following childhood fame. As such, it is imperative for the roles to be cast with Asian/Asian American and black actors. In the original 2003 Broadway production, Asian American actress Ann Harada played Christmas Eve, and Trinidadian-born American actress Natalie Venetia Belcon played Gary Coleman, with the remaining characters portrayed by white actors.[2] No ethnoracial specificities are required for the remaining characters, and professional productions typically following the casting path of its Broadway predecessor. The show's casting need for two actors of color sets an admittedly low baseline for cultural-ethnic representation onstage. However, a quick search of online videos reveals cringeworthy university performances of white actors performing yellowface for the role of Christmas Eve, illustrating the challenge some colleges face in fulfilling that casting requirement.

In order to draw a more diverse casting pool, I modified our audition process to be less intimidating for novice actors. The standard monologue was discarded—which is a typical staple for filtering out less experienced actors from the rest. Instead, auditionees were asked to tell a brief auto-biographical story of a happy time in their life and sing Happy Birthday as part of the singing audition. I also made assurances on the audition notices that no prior theatre experience was needed. Fortunately, we had a small presence of students of color at the auditions, which allowed me to seriously consider two appropriate students for the role of Christmas Eve; Zihang—a freshman international student from China, and James—a freshman US student whose parents are from South Korea. James, an unorthodox choice for Christmas Eve, delighted in auditioning for the role, and said that all he had to do was to imagine the mom from the TV show "Fresh Off The Boat."[3] Zihang (whom I will now refer to by her self-selected English name, Sky), faced two major challenges: a language barrier, as she was in the early stages of learning English, and a complete unfamiliarity with theatre performance and production. It became evident that the large and technically-demanding role of Christmas Eve would have been overwhelming for her to perform, and it would have been irresponsible for me to put her in that position. James, with his spot-on comedic timing and acute understanding of the character's performativity of Asian stereotypes, subsequently was cast as Christmas Eve—which made for a fascinating critique not just of ethnic, but also gendered Asian stereotypes.

This left the question of what to do with Sky? There was only one supporting role left, Bad Idea Bear #1, and the music director urged me to cast another student with a stronger audition who had extensive choir experience and some production credits on her resume. He reasoned that Sky did not have a strong singing voice and the other student had a more commanding presence onstage. By those measures, he was right. I believed the Bad Idea Bear role was one that Sky could grow into with practice, but the question was: should she be given the opportunity if there was a "better" actor? The reality is that Sky was (1) a freshman, with (2) zero theatre experience, who (3) was learning English. From that vantage point, well-worn casting options for this situation seemed clear: create a minimal/non-speaking role for Sky, cast her in an understudy role, or ask her to be a part of the production in another way, such as backstage crew, and encourage her to audition for the next show. This would include Sky in some way, while allowing the standard of casting the best actor to remain.

However, this solution troubled me. *Avenue Q* provides opportunity for black and Asian/Asian American actors in the roles of Gary Coleman and Christmas Eve, but at the same time, it risks tokenization once those roles are cast. This underlying pressure to strive towards a production aesthetic that looks and feels professional risks leading college directors to treat actor bodies, significantly actors of color, as dispensable based on production needs. Here, I recall my own experiences as an undergraduate theatre student in a rural Ohio college being heavily recruited for our college production of *West Side Story*, only to be ignored for later productions like *Singin' in the Rain* and Yeston and Kopit's musical *Phantom*. In the end, I bypassed the quest of casting the "best" actor (the student who most clearly displaced the aesthetic of a professional actor) for Bad Idea Bear #1. Instead, I prioritized a more accurate representation of our college's diverse demographic to be reflected onstage. I ended up casting Sky as Bad Idea Bear #1, and offered the other student the opportunity to be a part of the production team as assistant director, which she declined. In this case, greater representation of the international community meant dislodging the standard of maintaining a professional aesthetic and casting "the best actor" in an academic theatre production.

The decision to include Sky and this new approach to casting led me to reevaluate the ways that production work can be reframed as a pedagogical practice that supports the individual needs of students (as opposed to thinking about how students can service the needs of the production). This resulted in me making additional changes that I would not have otherwise made if I had not cast Sky. Five students of color auditioned for *Avenue Q*, and of those five, I cast four. The fifth student, a first-year international student from Ghana named Tomi, stepped into the role of assistant director—which proved to be invaluable during rehearsals. Sky needed additional support as a result of her experience as a new international student. Tomi, who had a shared understanding, helped Sky to acclimate to her Bad Idea Bear role as well as to the generalized theatre culture. My position as a US citizen created an inherent disconnect in my understanding of the struggles and questions of an international student. However, Tomi immediately recognized commonalities with Sky despite them hailing from two different continents, and she volunteered to be Sky's mentor during the rehearsal process. Tomi's strong handle on the English language and previous theatre experience allowed her to tutor Sky on theatre basics such as the layout of a script, line memorization and pronunciation, and staging conventions that would have been time-consuming to cover during rehearsals. In an added and unforeseen benefit, Tomi and Sky provided emotional support for each other, as the only two production participants who understood the challenging acclimation process for international students. Tomi was able to relate to me how Sky was coping with the difficult task of managing her full classload on top of the rehearsal schedule. At one point, I reduced Sky's rehearsal schedule so she could catch up on a class she was falling behind on based on the feedback I received from Tomi. In many ways, Tomi served as a cultural translator for me and Sky, and created a space for mutual learning. As a director, I was able to gain freedom by shifting casting priorities to make space for an equally important and long-needed goal of having greater representation on and offstage—in this instance, an increased visibility of the substantial Asian/Asian American and international populations on our campus.

As educators navigating the changing demographics of the twenty-first century, it is all the more important that we critically evaluate our historical legacy of theatre professionalism and education, and how it has negatively impacted our university stages and students of color. The recuperative and pioneering work from scholars like Herrera, Angela Pao, Brandi Wilkins Catanese, and others who interrogate the phenomenon of casting can guide the everyday practices of decision-makers in higher education. A failure to deconstruct the casting of the best actor as the default, pinnacle goal in university production work risks further alienating non-white students, as well as binds educators who wish to expand representation in their departments. The time is ripe for us to explore how we can go beyond replicating professional models to actively shape our university productions as a reflection of our student populations and society, and as an imaginitive space where all can belong.

Notes

1 The TheatreWorks production *The Motherfucker With the Hat* (2011), the Shakespeare Theatre Company production *Much Ado About Nothing* (2011), and the La Jolla Playhouse production of *The Nightingale* (2012) are a few examples of contested productions.
2 The remaining actors were John Tartaglia (Princeton/Rod), Stephanie D'Abruzzo (Kate Monster/Lucy the Slut), Rick Lyon (Nicky/Trekkie/Bad Idea Bear), Jennifer Barnhart (Mrs. T./Bad Idea Bear), Jordan Gelber (Brian).
3 Based on chef Eddie Huang's 2013 autobiography *Fresh Off The Boat*, which details his Taiwanese American family's acclimation to the United States in the 1990s. The TV show is significant in being the first sitcom on a major network to star an Asian American family since 1995.

References

The Asian American Performers Action Coalition. "Ethnic Representation on New York City Stages" Report. www.aapacnyc.org/stats-200607–201011.html. Accessed 11 November 2019.

Aud, Susan, Fox, Mary Ann, and KewalRamani, Angelina. 2010. *Status and Trends in the Education of Racial and Ethnic Groups*. US Department of Education. Washington, DC. July. p. vi.

Bunbury, Stephanie. 2016. "Jonathan Pryce on the controversy that almost sunk *Miss Saigon.*" *The Sydney Morning Herald*. September 26. www.smh.com.au/entertainment/movies/jonathan-pryce-on-the-controversy-that-almost-sunk-miss-saigon-20160926-groc7a.html. Accessed 11 November 2019.

Carl, P. 2015. "Carnaval 2015 Opening Remarks." July 23, 2015. *HowlRound*. https://howlround.com/carnaval-2015-opening-remarks. Accessed 11 November 2019.

Carlson, Marvin. 2001. *The Haunted Stage: The Theatre as Memory Machine*. Ann Arbor: University of Michigan Press.

Graham, Kenneth L. 1966. "Special Issue: Relationships Between Educational Theatre And Professional Theatre: Actor Training in the United States." *Educational Theatre Journal*.

Gutierrez, Lisa. 2018. "*West Side Story* Dumped after Kent State Students Criticize Casting of Non-Hispanics." *Kansas City Star*.

Herrera, Brian Eugenio. 2015. "The Best Actor for the Role, or the Mythos of Casting in American Popular Performance." *Journal of American Drama and Theatre*. Vol. 27. No. 2. Spring. https://jadtjournal.org/2015/04/24/the-best-actor-for-the-role-or-the-mythos-of-casting-in-american-popular-performance/. Accessed 11 November 2019.

Herrera, Brian Eugenio. 2017. "'But Do We Have the Actors for That?": Some Principles of Practice for Staging Latinx Plays in a University Theatre Context." *Theatre Topics*, vol. 27, no. 1, pp. 23–35, esp. p. 24.

Syler, Claire, and Daniel Banks. 2019. *Casting a Movement: The Welcome Table Initiative*. London: Routledge.

Zeigler, Joseph Wesley. 1972. *Regional Theatre: The Revolutionary Stage*. Minneapolis: University of Minnesota Press.

Part IV
Communities
Applying theory

14 Life first
Interdisciplinary placemaking for the theatre

Jen Plants

As a tool for dramaturgs, the value of theory simply cannot be assessed as something separate from practice. Theory expands or limits possibilities, impacts what we see and how we see it, frames distinctions in praxis, and opens gateways to clarify values. How then can it be separate from artmaking itself? Without theory, dramaturgs are simply observers.

Any artificial distinction between theory and practice also constrains what is conceivable as theory itself, as any theory that might involve actual practice is off-limits. However, what if the work of the dramaturg is to explicitly deny this distinction? What if theory led dramaturgical practice? What if placemaking were the theory to secure the unity between practice and theory, and the dramaturg was the linchpin?

Placemaking fosters abundance and innovation, and its key to success in the theatre lies in the interrogation skills of the dramaturg. But what is placemaking, and what are dramaturgs doing if they're not making places already?

In her 2017 book *Essential Dramaturgy: The Mindset and the Skillset*, Theresa Lang considers dramaturgy not only as a noun, but more importantly, as a verb. "When we shift from noun to verb and see the role as inextricably linked to the action, it becomes clear that dramaturg is something one does; it is simultaneously a process, practice, the person, and the outcome. Its very title requires an acknowledgment of this active nature." If dramaturgs are actors—in the sense that they take action—like directors who direct or designers who design, how is that action defined in a profession where the inability to clearly define the work is often an inherent value of the work itself? For Lang, the central action is succinctly put: "to dramaturg is to curate an experience for an audience" (Lang 2017, 7) Dramaturgs, then, do not practice dramaturgy (like lawyers practice law). Dramaturgs curate. A question arises, though: don't curators already do that?

Curation implies the selection, arrangement, and interpretation of what already has been created. In dramaturg Norman Frisch's 2003 definition, curation is the process of finding an "appropriate presentational format for the subject under investigation" and the search for the best pairing of "form and content in a work." (Thomson 2002, 237) Dramaturgs are to frame the creative work in the best existing form (rather than inventing a new one). This understanding of dramaturgy as an advanced search-and-find then locates its practitioners as the only vital participants in the performance-making process who are considered doers and not makers, ultimately rendering much of the action, impact, and possibilities of dramaturgy invisible. However, if placemaking is what dramaturgs do, then the work of dramaturgy is both visible and experiential, making the theatre a material site to celebrate liveness.

Placemaking, as defined by Mark A. Wyckoff of the Michigan State University Land Policy Institute, is "the process of creating quality places that people want to live, work, play, and learn in." Since the genesis of this people-first design approach in the 1970s that prioritizes lived experience over hierarchical design theories, urban planners, architects, and artists have pushed the ideas of scale, process, and the dynamic needs of specifically defined communities to the forefront of considerations in making public spaces. Put more simply, Danish architect Jan Gehl lays out a definitive three-step process to placemake: "First life, then spaces, then buildings—the other way around never works" (2017). In the largest and most venerable performing arts institutions, the most common way of making theatre—filling a pre-existing place with life—is entirely "the other way around." The making of a place, then, requires conceptualizing an experience separately from the constraints of pre-built environment.

Theatre historian David Wiles writes in *A Short History of Western Performance Space* that "analysts of theatre have been slower than analysts of modern art to perceive how far meaning is a function of space, and how performance in the second half of the twentieth century" (and I would argue right on into the twenty-first century) "has been the product of a particular aestheticizing environment." Put more simply, Wiles notes that no space is actually empty as "the myth of the black box as an inert container has been too strong" (Wiles 2009, 258). A foundational truth of placemaking is that the truly "empty" space is a myth.

Applying such a truth directly to dramaturgy raises a question about what kind of space a theatre is, then: Is the theatre a public place or a private place? Private places generally erect barriers to entry, and the barriers to entering a theatre—from restrictions to who is physically able to enter the building, to economic barriers limiting who can afford to buy a ticket—tell us that the theatre is most definitely not entirely open to the public. In fact, theatres often specifically pride themselves on being artistic "homes": homes for comedy, homes for drama, a home for family values musicals, a home for queer performance, et cetera. A home is the polar opposite of a public place. Home is private—only a select few have the right to a feeling of ownership and power within its walls. Others may be allowed in, but those others always need an invitation. Institutions may think of themselves as public-facing, but even a fresh welcome mat every season is not an open door to anyone who wants to enter.

If an institution purports to belong to a community as its home, why is it frequently so difficult to assemble a group of people who look like and represent the actual community into the rooms where an institution wants them? The theory of placemaking frames a future that could leave behind a history of exclusion by changing the ways institutions utilize power and presence. As Stephani Etheridge Woodson so keenly observes in *Theatre for Youth Third Space: Performance, Democracy, and Community Development*, "belief and enthusiasm in our work is not enough" (Woodson 2015, 232). If dramaturgs frame their work as places to be made, the tyranny of "space" is at an end.

Theatre as both a process and an event is capable of creating a "third space" beyond the binary of public/private. Distinct from home (first space) and school/work (second space), third spaces leverage community capital to foster inclusion. Leveraging actual as-it-exists community capital and practicing radical inclusivity are the subtextual keys to success in this call to action. Dramaturgically, creating a third space requires leaving the buildings we call "homes" to physically go and meet the communities we want to serve and actively interrogate who is being excluded by "buildings first" philosophies. Radical inclusion will never be realized by staying home and putting together the right guest list for a party we're throwing for ourselves.

The people who are not in audition and rehearsal rooms, audiences, classrooms, artistic offices, and faculty meetings do exist—they are simply elsewhere, and we need to go to those "elsewheres" to build lasting inclusive relationships. Put more simply, a friendship that takes place exclusively at your home and never in public and never even at your friend's home is not a friendship at all. A strong friendship is not site-specific. Lasting relationships require portability. Where are the people who are not in the room? Why aren't we where they are?

In *The Abundant Community* by John McKnight and Peter Block, competent communities are identified by three qualities: they "focus on the gifts of their members" by amplifying individual capacities and skills; they "nurture associational life" by supporting shared affinity groups not based on consumerism or transactional relationships; and they "offer hospitality, the welcoming of strangers" (McKnight and Block 2012, 67). These particular qualities require authentic engagement, which cannot be done from an office, a stage, or a rehearsal room. Fostering competent communities requires embracing elsewhereness.

Ultimately, as argued by Roberto Bedoya, executive director of the Tucson Pima Arts Council:

> Much of the national discourse on creative placemaking is caged in an understanding of 'place' as the built environment. Indeed physical places like artists' live-work spaces and cultural districts benefit from creative placemaking. But to understand the term—and the practice—solely in terms of the built landscape is to miss the complete picture. Creative

placemaking is much more than what manifests physically within the built environment. Before you have places of belonging you must feel you belong—to a community, a locale, or a place.

Performances may fill a theatre with a curated imitation of life, but they don't make a place. As much as we try to convince ourselves that moving around the metaphorical deck chairs is an act of making, we haven't made a place if the rules of the space lead decision-making. What is fundamentally different about theatrical experiences in a space where all that changes—both materially and philosophically—is the play being performed? The dominant American theatrical practice is not placemaking, but rather "spaceclaiming."

Spaceclaiming positions an institution (which we intuitively read as a physical space) at the center of everything like the Sun King at Versailles. Spaceclaiming is throwing a party, though perhaps fabulously and thoughtfully created, to which only the best and the lucky are invited. Those lucky few then can roam the institution as they would the Hall of Mirrors at the palace, mirrors explicitly designed to reflect the images of those few already in attendance. Institutions literally put art in boxes and give artists a handful of evenings (and afternoons on the weekends) to claim space within them, ever hopeful that the "invitations" are popular enough to demand a good price in the marketplace.

Spaceclaiming even undermines the act of curating, as an already built environment comes with already built values, and though you might be lucky enough to see yourself in the Hall of Mirrors, your view is still framed by the institutional power confirming its superiority. Ultimately, spaceclaiming is akin to planting a flag on the moon—inherently exclusionary and of value for an audience only as passive observers (neither of which are qualities which make for particularly moving theatrical experiences).

There are alternative ways of thinking and doing, new language to put life first, new metaphors to deny institutions power solely through their materiality. As in all good dramaturgy, these ways are best understood as questions (built from hard truths) that provoke actions that move theory to practice.

#1: Who is not in the room?

Racism in institutional settings is just one of the systemic forms of exclusion that people think can be solved just by talking about it. Imagine if we took that same approach to hunger: If we just participate in enough conversations and forums about hunger, we'd surely solve the problem without taking any kind of action to actually feed people at all! Acknowledgment and exposure of historic and current systems of exclusion is the first step on the road to inclusion, but radical inclusivity requires immediate, collective action—not another meeting.

A simple question can help focus efforts of equity, inclusion, and diversity: Who is not in the room? Often perversely difficult to answer clearly in a way that serves anyone beyond the asker, "Who is not in the room?" purposefully creates an expected binary: there is "us," and there are "others," but this question flips the script creating others out of those already in the room, forcing acknowledgment of the exclusionary limitations of spaceclaiming. Who are you making this work for and why are they not in the room with you?

Storycatchers Theatre in Chicago, Illinois, works with court-involved youth to support them in telling their own stories through musical theatre. Since 2017, the company's work has also included collaborating with the Chicago Police Department. Acting workshops held on neutral territory (in Chicago History Museum, for example—a place made for the examination of history) bring officers in training and Storycatchers participants together to enact scenarios from both the perspectives of the youth and the officers. As reported in the *Chicago Defender*, in a 2019 workshop, "'Why don't I have any real power?' sang dozens of Chicago Police recruits and justice-involved youth in a chorus. Facing them, another group of young adults and recruits chanted, 'Protect and serve! Protect and serve!' (Nabong) Only by bringing together all the key stakeholders—in a place made for the collective examination of the past—can we effectively utilize art to build community.

This sense of the theatre (or those in power) as "the other" and the focus on others as the "us" you're trying to support is key. Don't count who's in the room before you begin—lead with these outward-looking questions instead:

- What existing communities of people are we trying to serve and to support?
- What existing organizations and groups in our community are potential stakeholders in this project?
- Who then *should* be in the room?

#2: What places have already been made?

Ultimately, theatres are just spaces unless we actively make them places.

The good news is that abundance does not need to be manufactured, as any community is already abundant in resources. Limited empirical knowledge, lack of geographical awareness, and preconceived notions of what *should* matter, rather than celebrating what actually does matter, prevent the already well-made places of the community from being visible.

In *The Trash Project*, a 2009 production by choreographer Allison Orr and Forklift Danceworks in Austin, Texas, employees of Austin Solid Waste Services came together with sixteen garbage trucks to create a movement and musical performance on an abandoned airport runway. A grand space for expanding notions of scale already existed in communities, as did performers, artists, and audience members from traditionally marginalized groups. Orr had to go to those places, not simply issue an invitation that centered places she already felt at home. The ultimate performance was a grand feat in placemaking, examined in the 2012 documentary *Trash Dance* by filmmaker Andrew Garrison.

Building on McKnight and Block's properties of abundance, once you've identified who is not in the room, embed elsewhereness as a value by asking yourself:

- Where are the gifts of those not in the room most visible?
- Where are the places where those not in the room exchange those gifts?
- Where are places in the community that welcome strangers?

#3: How many "what's" can be included?

Interdisciplinary work is inseparable from effective placemaking, but what gets counted as interdisciplinarity needs to be reframed.

Theatre artists often assume that just by working in the theatre that they are naturally interdisciplinary, but true interdisciplinarity requires assembling different practices, motivated by diverse factors, that lead to a variety of answers to the question: "What do you do?" If everyone's answer to the "what" question is "I make theatre," then no matter the methodologies employed, the discipline is the same.

Looking to organizational consultant (and viral Ted Talk presenter) Simon Sinek's "golden circle" provides an unexpected frame to determine how interdisciplinary a project actually is. Imagined as a bullseye, the golden circle puts "Why do you do what you do?" at the center. "How do you do what you do?" rings the why, and the final question "What do you?" encircles them both at the far edges of the target. Sinek posits that organizations spend a great deal of time on these outer two circles—the how and the what—when they need to start with the "why" bullseye at the center and then align their values and resources to serve that target. If this is not also representative of the work of dramaturgy, then what is?

This is not to say that theatre artists are lacking because of their singular "what," but to fill that "what" circle with more answers, you must seek partners and stakeholders who share the same "why" while they pursue a different "what." Interdisciplinary work acknowledges "elsewhereness" as a researchable and knowable reality. Those elsewheres include intellectual spaces, ways of questioning, branches of knowledge, but also—and most importantly for placemaking—literal elsewheres, places that are physically outside of the built environments of theatres and performing arts centers that are so often called homes by those who already work and thrive there.

Amrita Ramanan and Alison Carey at Oregon Shakespeare Festival continue to develop a new language of "greenturgy" as a way of "framing the importance of environmental focus to artistic directors, board members, and other gatekeepers" (LMDA). At a Festival "inspired by" the works of William Shakespeare (not "focused on" or "beholden to"), located on land that is often under threat from wildfires, Ramanan and Carey have framed a mission that by design requires working with diverse fields of inquiry including science, social justice, business, and government—all to make theatre inspired by Shakespeare that is responsive to the needs of the environment.

Places designed by single discipline-driven methodologies frequently result in inward-looking final products whose form and functions are limited and pre-defined. After identifying the why, you'll want to seek those who share your why by asking:

- Who else in the community shares the same why for the work you're doing?
- Where and how can you meet to exchange the gifts of your collective "what's"?

If there isn't a place for that exchange, the place you need to make is clear.

#4: How do you know that?

Only interrogation of assumptions can defeat both our blindspots that lead to "it has always been done like this" thinking. This interrogation requires self-examination and radical honestly as much as anything else.

- How do you know what the gifts of your community actually are?
- Have you been to the places to bear witness to them?
- Have you been to places in your community where you are a stranger?

Digging deeper:

- How do you know who your community is in the first place?
- What methodologies have you used to identify and classify unique populations within your community?
- How do know what methodologies to use?

Most importantly:

- How do you know what place needs to be made?

"Life first" thinking puts the buildings last, and the life of the art and the collective lives of a community's citizens at the forefront of all decision-making.

Case study: *Hunger/Here*

In 2017, at the University of Wisconsin-Madison, I led a group of Interdisciplinary Theatre Studies graduate students (and a few select undergraduates) in a course about making a community-based performance project in an educational setting for young audiences. The specific content of the performance itself is topics-based (focused on state educational curricula and community concerns) and changes each time the course is taught. Led by the statistic that food insecurity is an issue for one in five Wisconsin children (Heckman), the performance was designed to examine the impact of hunger and food insecurity in our community. The resulting devised theatrical event *Hunger/Here* performed at area schools, on the university campus, and at the Dane County Juvenile Detention Center. Below is an overview of how *Hunger/Here* tackled the four key questions of placemaking as dramaturgy. Rather than a comprehensive analysis, selected specific answers to those questions are offered here as representative of the project's process and outcomes.

#1: *Who is not in the room?*

For *Hunger/Here*, our cast and creative team comprised those enrolled in the course. The list of who should be in the room was grouped into three categories:

- The targeted audience (young people in grades 6–12)
- Those who are currently food insecure
- Those who are involved with the material processes of food justice and food delivery systems

Once a list of who should be in the room is made, there's another question to provoke more inclusive thinking. As those in the room cannot contain all the knowledge of a community's abundance of human resources:

- Who might help us identify more "who's" for our list?

Participants can then identify where on the list they might feel connected and where they have some work to do. Voluntary self-disclosure about who is in the room might then happen informally, but it is not required. In the case of *Hunger/Here*, participants shared that they were all currently food secure, but fears related to past and potential future issues related to hunger varied immensely. Alternatively, participants could have been led by curiosity, rather than self-disclosure of lived experience (and what they lacked). The obvious question follows either path: Whose story do those in the room have the right to tell? The first step to finding that answer requires going elsewhere.

#2: *What places have already been made?*

Students then selected groups, people, and places for individual research. Investigative approaches focused on listening and observation via interviews and site visits.

Interviews as research are often implicitly framed as opportunities for someone of great privilege to listen to and learn from someone of little privilege, and site visits in this context can also be another sort of "poverty tourism." This kind of framing not only centers the experiences of those already privileged and in power, but it also exploits another individual's trauma and/or lack of privilege for the sake of a vicarious lesson. This is an anathema to fostering empathy.

Interviews instead are designed to foster relationships. Conversations should be led by curiosity and a desire for the interviewer to invest—not take from the interviewee. Interviewers are expressly not journalists. They are guests asking questions to guide service. What might art be able to provide to the interviewee to help address a problem, reveal a hidden story, correct a misconception, or engage a community in problem solving?

The best interviews are always done in person, focus on examining the "what" of the interviewee and are conducted in places where the interviewer is not "at home." For *Hunger/Here*, student interviewees included:

- A currently homeless person who one student had a non-transactional relationship with well before the start of the project
- The former head of a major regional food pantry
- A local high-school teacher running a food pantry at their school

Students were also each assigned a location for site visits to research performed behavior and physical patterns in food-related spaces. Students observed and recorded details of each site including its objects, gestures, sensory elements, and patterns of action and topography. Site visits included the following collectively identified elsewheres:

- A food pantry at a local community center
- A university dining hall
- A grocery store

Lastly, rehearsals, performances, embodied research, and the class itself were held in multiple locations so elsewhereness was embedded from the start. Participants held workshops in a community center's afterschool program and at the Dane County Juvenile Detention Center in order to listen to the voices of young people we wanted to serve, in places where we were the guests.

#3: How many "what's" can be included?

The mobility required in valuing elsewhereness leads participants to discover individuals and groups in their community doing different "what's" for the same "why." The "what" for *Hunger/Here* was making an original piece of theatre to be performed at area schools and community centers, and the "why" was to build awareness of food insecurity and hunger in Dane County, Wisconsin—awareness that would engage young people to seek active solutions to the problem. However, a project does not have to be devised to have a community-based "why." Every play should have a "why" centered in its community. Without such a center, the project can never hope to do anything but spaceclaim.

For *Hunger/Here*, the other "what's" we found included:

- Qualitative Economics: A research project of a qualitative economist at the university focused on why some individuals and families who are food insecure were not utilizing food pantries. This work gave us access to the voices of those struggling with hunger where individuals were anonymous and had been compensated for their labor.
- Food Pantries: As one example, the university (run and staffed by students) food pantry literally opened its doors to us for a site visit to examine the logistics of both accessing and maintaining such a resource.
- "Making Justice": A community-based arts learning program for at-risk and court-involved teens partnered with us so that workshops and performances could be held at the Juvenile Detention Center.

You can be assured that no matter your community, there are groups and/or individuals concerned with the same "why" as you. Who is not in the room? Who is already doing the work?

#4: *How do you know that?*

Mobility is a value inherently excluded by the materiality of institutions, but if dramaturgy is placemaking, then utilizing the materiality of the pre-built as a place (or form) becomes simply a choice, and new forms (or places) often need to be invented.

- How do you know the theatre you have is the best place to present your work?

Making the *Hunger/Here* creation process actively mobile introduced portability as a central value right from the start. Simply rehearsing in various locations, presenting in-progress material as scratches to diverse audiences gave participants empirical knowledge of the geography of their community by visiting already made places and listening to the voices of those who share the same values and who are already performing the "why" of the work. You don't know how to make a place until you know the places the community already values (or fears).

Hunger/Here was ultimately performed:

- In classrooms at area schools
- At the Dane County Juvenile Detention Center

- On the university campus, for young people residing at the Dane County Shelter Home

Generous artmaking assumes only this: that communities are abundant already in resources, knowledge, and places. Developing your artistic home into a well-made place open to and valued by your community is an assumption that requires continual interrogation. How does your work foster third spaces and not Halls of Mirrors?

None of these questions to support placemaking can ever effectively be answered in isolation, as the process of placemaking resembles Sinek's bullseye target more closely than a consecutive series of steps. Not just provocations for creation, these questions are calls to make places that matter to a community *as it actually is* and to decenter institutional control over a community's already abundant resources. This is not to say that existing institutional structures are never the best place for a particular theatrical project, but rather this is a call to question the values built into the materiality of the theatre itself. Up until opening night, potential audiences are the most important people not in the room. Those we purport to serve are the friends we only see when we choose to invite them over.

Not until we center the lives of our desired audiences will we know what spaces are required and what buildings need to be built or avoided to make non-transactional places that people "want to … play and learn in." The acknowledgment of spaceclaiming as the dominant form of making theatre is the first step in transcending it, putting buildings last and making the life of the art what matters most. Let us take up Woodson's challenge: "Neither public art, in general, nor community-based theatre is inherently good work. We must make it so" (2015, 232).

References

Bedoya, Roberto. 2016. "Belonging: A Cornerstone of Placemaking in the Region." *Creative Exchange.* July 29, 2016. http://springboardexchange.org/belongingrobertobedoya/. Accessed 11 November 2019.

Deer, Holly L. "Addressing Environmental Topics in Theatre by Using Greenturgy." *HowlRound Theatre Commons.* Accessed October 1, 2019. https://howlround.com/addressing-environmental-topics-theatre-using-greenturgy. Accessed 1 October 2019.

Gehl, Jan. 2007. "Open Space: People Space." In *Open Space: People Space,* 3–9. London: Taylor & Francis.

Heckman, Nick. 2016. *A White Paper: Hunger & Food Security in Wisconsin and Dane County.* www.publichealthmdc.com/documents/foodSecurityWhitePaper.pdf. Accessed 11 November 2019.

Lang, Theresa. 2017. *Essential Dramaturgy: The Mindset and Skillset.* New York: Routledge.

LMDA. "2016 Bly Grant Recipients." https://lmda.org/2016-bly-grant-recipients. Accessed 1 October 2019.

McKnight, John, and Peter Block. 2012. *The Abundant Community: Awakening the Power of Families and Neighborhoods*. San Francisco: BK, Berrett-Koehler Publishers, Inc.

Nabong, Pat. "Through Theatre, Justice-Involved Youth and CPD Recruits Put Themselves In One Another's Shoes." *Chicago Defender*, August 26, 2019. https://chicagodefender.com/through-theatre-justice-involved-youth-and-cpd-recruits-put-themselves-in-one-anothers-shoes/. Accessed 11 November 2019.

Sinek, Simon. 2013. *Start with Why: How Great Leaders Inspire Everyone to Take Action*. London: Portfolio/Penguin.

Thomson, Lynn M, ed. 2002. "Norman Frisch." Interview. *Between the Lines: The Process of Dramaturgy*, 273–299. Toronto: Playwrights Canada Press.

Wiles, David. 2009. *A Short History of Western Performance Space*. Cambridge: Cambridge University Press.

Woodson, Stephani Etheridge. 2015. *Theatre for Youth Third Space: Performance, Democracy, and Community Cultural Development*. Bristol, UK: Intellect.

Wyckoff, Mark A. 2014. "Definition of Placemaking: Four Different Types." *Planning & Zoning News* 32 (3). http://pznews.net/media/13f25a9fff4cf18ffff8419ffaf2815.pdf. Accessed 11 November 2019.

15 Growing applied theatre

Critical humanizing pedagogies from the ground up

Beth Murray

Overview

Joining the effort toward decolonizing applied theatre curricular spaces, *Cotton & Collards: Unearthing Stories of Home through Kitchens & Closets* (2015–2016) was a local and global community multi-event project involving artists and educators eliciting stories of home catalyzed by clothing and food histories. The ten community sites all served youth, inside and outside schools. Each used art/s in response to the question: "What's the relationship between our food, our clothes and our earth?"

In the southeastern United States, where the project originates, cotton and collard greens evoke stories across generations and geographies. These two crops—one for food, the other for clothing—are potent symbols and ubiquitous objects. Cotton fields and mills dot the landscape as blurred relics, with long fallow fields covered by housing developments and unrazed mill buildings repurposed as breweries and condominiums. Collard greens, appearing on every self-respecting southern cuisine menu, first traveled to the United States as seeds with European immigrants. The culinary preparations for this hearty green leaf arrived with enslaved West African victims of the Middle Passage who became cooks in southern kitchens (Davis and Morgan 2015, xi). The clothes people wear and the food they eat weave complex stories of home.

Each of the ten participating sites—local and global—stepped in with either food or clothing as an entry point. Inquiry events unfolded across eighteen months, designed and executed at each site culminating with curation at a local museum and on a closed social-media space. This chapter centers on two project sites: "Stories from Seeds" with fourth graders at Chambers Elementary School and "Coming to the Table" with seventh graders at Foothills Middle School.[1] In conversation with the foundational theories of Paolo Freire's *Pedagogy of the Oppressed* (1970/2000) and Augusto Boal's *Theatre of the Oppressed* (1992), current critical applied theatre perspectives filter project actions through constructs of citizenship, self-reflection, common good, and varied publics (Giroux 2014). Productively operationalizing both the promise and confines of applied theatre's realities, as opposed to its idealized intentions (Snyder-Young 2013), analysis elevates tiny and tentative (Balfour 2009) as richly real (Emdin 2016) inquiry spaces.

Underpinning

In interviews about critical pedagogy, seventeen self-identified post-secondary critical pedagogues in Mary Breuing's (2011) research consistently named Paolo Freire, revolutionary Brazilian educator and *Pedagogy of the Oppressed* (1970/2000) author/creator, as an influence. Yet, when asked to define critical pedagogy, responses splintered. Magnetic terms like "liberatory" and "revolutionary" fall poetically from lips, yet also elude consistent action. Freire encouraged context-driven reflective adaptation of his ideas. "To evaluate almost always implies readjusting and reprogramming. For this very reason, an evaluation should never be considered the final step of a particular process" (Freire, 1998, 7). In *For White Folks Who Teach in the Hood*, Christopher Emdin (2016) writes as an academic recalling "readjusting and reprogramming" as a beginning math teacher in an urban school. A pivotal "a-ha" came when, Emdin saw joyful, engaged students in a cypher circle spitting rhymes during free time. The contrast with his disengaged math class prompted Emdin to reflect on the hip-hop circle as what Freire would call a "culture circle" (p. 63), then reconceived his pedagogy built on students' cultural assets and affinities in creating "reality pedagogy" for a specific context.

The *Cotton & Collards* project set out to be a legible act of reality pedagogy, shaped by Freire's problem-posing approach where "the point of departure of the movement lies in the people themselves," and that "the movement must begin with the human-world relationship."(Freire 1970/ 1993, 85) Cotton and collard greens, materially and symbolically, welcomed critical perspectives on race, class, gender, and geography, albeit gently. Striving toward "conscientziação" in Freire's native Portuguese—translated clumsily as "awareness" and colloquially as being/getting "woke" (Kelley 1962 SM45)—we hoped to hold space for participants "learning to perceive social, political and economic contradictions, and to take action against the oppressive elements of reality" (Freire 1970 [2000], 35) on some level. The initiative kicked off locally with a professional-development workshop facilitated by a museum educator and me, a theatre education/applied theatre scholar/artist. We led game and image-centered activity guided by Augusto Boal's *Theatre of the Oppressed* (1985) and *Games for Actors and Non-Actors* (1992). We then toured a museum exhibit on the region's evolution from cotton farming to urban living, and visited the historical collection in the main library. We encouraged teachers to build generative, relevant inquiries using arts-based approaches in concert with primary source material.

The project design problematized applied theatre's capacities. In James Thompson's (2009) article, "Performance affects: Applied theatre and the end of effect," the author contemplates the actual impact of applied theatre work in war zones and refugee camps, in response to decades of literature claiming—perhaps over claiming—effects of "giving voice" and "effecting transformation" for disenfranchised peoples. Thompson advocates instead for a brighter focus on affect, rather than effect. Spelling out tensions in work by scholars and artists doing "liberatory" and "transformative" applied theatre, Michael Balfour (2009) highlights inherent contradictions in arts-based work trained on a politics of intention. He pushes for tiny change. "In resisting the bait of social change, rehabilitation, behavioral objectives and outcomes, perhaps (and it is a small perhaps), applied practice might more readily encounter the accidental, and acknowledge that what applied theatre does is not always linear, rational and conclusive in its outcomes, but is more often messy, incomplete, complex and tentative" (Balfour 2009, 357). Dani Snyder-Young's (2013) book title—*Theatre of Good Intentions* provides a cautionary moniker for applied theatre work claiming social change and transformation without sufficient evidence. Snyder-Young reinforces the call for specificity, challenging the field to identify and build upon what theatre can do well, and remain honest about what it can't. Judith Ackroyd (2007) troubles the evolving parameters of applied theatre interpreted by some as progress and by others as increasingly exclusionary and ill-defined. Ackroyd further points out the ironies of applied theatre programs claiming social-justice aims while housed in publicly and privately funded theatres and universities dependent on capitalist structures for survival. On this richly troubled terrain, the *Cotton & Collards* project embraced Balfour's promise of "tiny" and aimed to focus local through the idea of home.

In the critical feminist reflective memoir *Belonging*, bell hooks (2009) meditates on the return to her childhood home in rural Kentucky in the sunset of her parents' lives. Each chapter originates in a specific strong sensory memory—like tobacco, her grandmother's quilts, the hill of her childhood yard. From these simple places and artifacts, hooks weaves memory, theory, research, story, and metaphor to distill critical questions about power and justice relevant in and far beyond hooks's Kentucky homeland. "We create and sustain environments where we can come back to ourselves, where we can return home, stand on solid ground, and be a true witness" (hooks 2008, 120). In "witnessing" as a researcher, I employed qualitative methods through field notes, participant observation, artifact collection, and target semi-structured interviews. Many of the qualitative data collection methods functioned also as simply doing/implementing/supporting the work at each site, as/if needed or requested in helping participants "witness" their own home stories. Thus, sometimes my research presence was peripheral if not external, or after-the-fact of creation. Other times, I toiled alongside the teacher and students creating and teaching and learning, and the notes waited for later. No two sites followed identical pathways. Leveraging hooks's notion, cotton and collard greens appeared literally, figuratively, and nominally across the varied sites as each class opted to pursue a "what we eat" or a "what we wear" inquiry trajectory. Following are case thumbnails of two sites' activities. Both began with food.

Coming to the table

At Foothill Middle School, guided by a seventh-grade social studies teacher and a succession of two theatre teachers, students embarked on a semester-long inquiry with an entry point on the collards side of the research question, wondering about food. The teachers settled on the theme of coming to the table because it provided a concrete, familiar way in, but also bore the potential for historical and metaphorical explorations. In planning, the teachers envisioned an exploration guided by the ways and reasons people have to come to the table, literally and figuratively, across time and geographies. Ubiquitous tables became an equalizing, accessible entry point.

The work was primarily housed in the social studies classroom, with a last-period group called "Advisory." The first activity introduced coming to the table. Each student painted a plate that answered: "What do YOU bring to the table?" Some plates depicted particular skills like musical notes or sports equipment, others signified qualities like a yin-yang symbol or a peace sign. Still others created compelling abstractions. Following the whole-group art activity, the teacher charged students to form inquiry groups and propose their own activity about coming to the table. Some wanted to dance, some to write and speak poems, and one envisioned a play. Others proposed creating short films, websites, and interactive games. Another group wanted to research the history of collard greens. Quickly, the full group proposed hosting a festival, where each contribution could be celebrated. The theatre teacher's involvement centered on performance aspects: rehearsing the play and supervising tech elements. The social studies teacher convened and coordinated the festival event, and I helped where asked.

Guests—parents, grandparents, students, teachers, administrators—attending the festival found the school lobby set with a sign that read "Coming to the Table" followed by an event itinerary. There the collards research team offered a tri-fold display with collard-green facts and images. Flanking the collard facts on either side were a tasting table and a survey table. The tasting table featured two types of collard greens, one prepared by a student's grandmother, the classic way with smoked ham hocks and vinegar, and the other prepared by a student's chef father with a fusion flair incorporating Korean kimchee elements. At the survey table, two students sat with a giant kettle, paper leaves and some pens. They asked passers-by "What do you put into YOUR collard greens?" Participants wrote answers on the leaves and put them in the pot. Answers ranged from "hot sauce" and "brown sugar" to "auntie magic" and "love." The remaining lobby tables displayed the what-do-you-bring-to-the-table plates.

Just off the lobby perched a video camera primed to capture table-related stories from willing participants. The sign pointing to the makeshift stairwell recording studio read: "Tell us what YOU bring to the table." There a pair of middle schoolers prompted and recorded informal sharings, one-on-one.

Inside the auditorium, scheduled events unfolded. The play came to fruition, entitled "Table Tales," chronicling the past, present and future lives of a magical time-traveling table that finally speaks its cumulative insights warning people to listen to one another. An array of poems, songs and dances—some of which grew from the theme and some of which the students simply wanted to share—appeared in the sequence. Middle-school students who created web-based materials curated them backdropped with a gigantic screen. One pair led a virtual tour of their website, page by page, closing with an invitation for the audience to revisit and "let us know what you think" at a future time. Another pair hosted their interactive table quiz questions inviting audience members to participate on their devices in real time. A four-minute interview-style film appeared in which teachers and students answered: "What does a table mean to you?" The early and primary entries were students speaking in a busy school hallway. Answers were concrete (a place to eat and work), abstract (table means family, tradition, celebration) and in between. The concluding entry featured the school's media specialist saying: "I bring a love of story to the table." A blooper reel immediately followed, which was almost equal in length to the film itself. Following the event, the author visited and interviewed the two collard-green cooks, the grandma and the chef, to include their perspectives, images and recipe secrets in the exhibit.

Stories from seeds

At Chambers Elementary School, a fourth-grade teacher and I also entered the inquiry through the food side. That class explored stories linked to the land by looking closely at their physical school and the foods—the vegetables—of their families and friends. This "Stories from Seeds" inquiry lasted three weeks and began in that late-May curricular limbo affectionately known as "after testing."

The first activity started with small-group collective map drawings of the school, from memory. On large sheets of brown paper, fourth graders negotiated—with words and markers—how their school looked from a bird's-eye view. The instructions were purposely vague, hoping to tap what students prioritized. Almost every group began with desks. One group's map included a detailed parking lot, highlighting their classroom teacher's parking space having been recently named the school's "Teacher of the Year." Another went into great detail on the cafeteria. Aside from a couple of trees, the outdoors were unrepresented. As a group, the students looked over each other's maps and generated a list of things they knew about their school, and things they wondered about their school. The known items came easily and focused on purposes, materials, procedures, and rules. The wonderings required a little prompting, then broke open with constructive brainstorms, like: "Who was Frederick Chambers, anyway?" and "When was this school built?"

Following question generation, the group walked the school grounds inside and outside, observing with all their senses, cataloguing even more questions. The challenge of "making the familiar strange" (Geertz 1973) set purpose for the walk, serving as ethnographers of their own lived surrounds:

> "What is up with those giant boulders? Did you ever notice those?"
> "Look. There are more."
> "Was that always a park next to our school?"
> "I never noticed that fence before. Where does it stop?"
> "The grass is bigger than the building."
> "We forgot the playground on our map!" and on and on.

Students realized they were missing important things, like land and plants and histories of people. Upon returning to the classroom, leaders prompted students to individually draw and label what they think the land where Chambers Elementary currently sits was like previously, at any point in history. The array of visual theories included dinosaurs grazing, farmland, a small town, a little building and some homes, a smaller school, a gigantic store, and an alien spaceship-landing site.

A few children actually interviewed Frederick Chambers III, son of the school's namesake. They learned many things through Mr. Chambers's stories, including that their school rested on a former cotton field and that the adjacent county park was built on land gifted by his family, also formerly cotton fields. He recounted stories of scouting adventures on the land, including climbing on an old stone house that, years later, someone "discovered" and made news. The idea that the earth could help people tell stories undergirded the next class task: to plant seeds. The seed smorgasbord invited one self-selected packet per child filtered only by the criterion that the plant grew something familiar to the student. Some chose collard greens, others beans or okra or peppers or chard or cilantro. Most read the instructions, quickly realizing their seed supply far exceeded their tiny pot of soil. An old-fashioned seed swap ensued with the extras. They nurtured the seeds. The plants grew. Each student created "story seed" interview questions to ask a family member, elder, or friend about their vegetable in an effort to gather stories through purposeful receptive listening.

The students sowed questions, then harvested stories. Some stories were like recipes, with an elder describing how to make okra or use cilantro. Some stories were memoir nuggets "those are the long beans we ate in my country" or "cabbage in the grocery store just isn't the same ..." Some stories were tiny revelations. One fourth grader reported that when she sat with her mom, placed the plant on the table and asked: "What do you remember about jalapeños from when you were a little girl?/"*¿Qué* *recuerdas de los jalapeños cuando eras una niña?*," her mom just stared at her. When the fourth grader pressed, asking her silent mom what was wrong, Mom answered: "You never ask me questions like this." Then mom smiled, and answered.

As a culminating activity, students created original stories based on anything the interviews inspired, then shared the stories in class. In truth, time ran short and writing the stories became homework. At sharing time, some students simply recounted their interviews. Others used their interviews to create original stories, both fiction and non-fiction. Some opted not to share, but listened to the stories of others.

Curation

In the last eight months of the eighteen-month inquiry, the *Cotton & Collards* exhibit opened at the partner museum, in two cumulative installments. Simultaneously, the effort was curated on social media for the closed group of participants and supporters. Museum and cyber curation included an overview video with clips and/or still-image representation of every project with guiding headers and brief captions. Each project completed had its own section that elaborated highlights through artifacts, images and descriptions. The representations were sometimes youth-created artifacts (e.g., painted plates, drawn maps), story-capture images (e.g., photos, video stills of performances) and artistic distillations of activity (e.g., word collages based on student talk or festival participant collard-green recipe secrets).

What's so critical about these pedagogies?

Noted critical theorist Henry Giroux's voluminous body of work routinely calls capitalist, educational, religious, and political systems to ethical task for working at cross-purposes to their stated missions. These contradictions, according to Giroux, are established and expand exponentially, calling for a radical interruption through "critical education" and "educated hope." Says Giroux:

> At stake here then is more than a call for reform. The American public needs to organize around a revolutionizing ideal that enables people to hold power, participate in the powers of governing and create public institutions and discourses capable of explaining and reversing chronic injustices evident everywhere in society.
>
> (2014, 83)

Giroux's initial sentences are a call to critical arms, and a warning about damage to democracy ignoring such a call insures. Translating Giroux's transformational intentions to concrete assessments, the *Cotton &*

Collards project humbly shrinks from claiming a contribution toward such systemically-thorough ends. However, reading to the closing sentence of Giroux's paragraph, hope emerges, concrete and small.

> Democracy requires, at the very least, a type of education that fosters a working knowledge of citizenship and the development of individuals with the capacity to be self-reflective, passionate about the collective good, and able to defend the means by which ideas are translated into the worldly space of the public realm.
>
> (2014, 84)

Here we consider the *Cotton & Collards* project's two profiled sites borrowing Giroux's aspects: citizenship, self-reflection and passion for common good, and examination of how ideas translate to the world.

Working knowledge of citizenship

Exemplary critical pedagogues maintain learning spaces as social microcosms, with students as the citizenry—even when the content covered has seemingly nothing to do with revolution. Thus, the content is in part, daily classroom commerce. Increasingly, the academic literature would describe this routine rehearsal for democracy as "humanizing pedagogies." In the 1970s, Freire explained humanizing pedagogies as those that liberate students to be more fully human, more fully their actualized selves in their fight against oppressive forces. However, more recent iterations of humanizing pedagogies charge educators and institutions with fostering dialogic humanizing contexts with, between, and among students, such as Django Paris' (2017) work in humanizing literacies pedagogies and Maria del Carmen Salazar's (2013) work in humanizing teacher preparation pedagogies. Citizenship asks humanizing questions like: How do I belong? How do others belong? To whom am I beholden, and on whom can I depend to foster belonging?

An important element toward belonging was agency in shaping the inquiry. We challenged participants to build belonging through what was often ungraded arts-based inquiry activity. At both sites, tasks were more open and organization messier and louder than usual school tasks. However, both case sites included teachers skilled at fostering agency in and among students. Time set parameters. The festival date determined what would be completed in the "Coming to the Table" inquiry. "Stories from Seeds" squeezed itself between the end of testing and the last day of school. The extra-curricular nature was both freeing for open-ended inquiry and slightly diminishing with respect to prime curricular real estate. The liminality both cohered the groups and marginalized the activity outside normal school bounds. In this in-between space, each site created a citizenry of creative practice.

Self-reflection on balance with passion about the common good

In the same phrase, Giroux advocates self-reflection and concern for the common good. Individuals balance self and shared world critical awareness as distinct yet symbiotic competencies. At both sites, individual, small and large group reflection occurred routinely. Talk of worlds beyond selves embedded in each site's activities. The nature of this talk relied more on the questions asked than on the art activity undertaken. "Coming to the Table" fostered repeated reflection opportunities around identities and individual strengths. This began with the plate activity where students painted their strengths, and carried through the preparation activities to the festival itself. The seventh graders repeatedly asked two questions: "What do you bring to the table?" and "What does a table mean?" Answering "What do you bring to the table?" happened literally when students made plates and sought variations on collard recipes or sent out questions via websites, then figuratively when students decided which way they wanted to participate in the festival preparations. Such a pointed line of questioning united the group as a community, but kept the focus largely on the citizens of the room. Answering the second question "What does a table mean?" nudged the inquiry slightly outward and productively off center, evidenced in the video and the short play. Both pointed to perspectives beyond the singular, hinting at plural histories and futures. While the "Coming to the Table" inquiry was artistically generative, the questions remained steady with answers varying on a theme, as opposed to evolving. Thus the "common good" remained fairly insular to the group and festival attendees.

The "Stories from Seeds" inquiry stayed closer to the overall *Cotton & Collards* research question linking food to the earth and home. We aspired to keep generating more and deeper scaffolded questions. While these questions root in food, the same sequence, adapted slightly, could pertain to cotton and clothing. The progression roughly flowed as:

- What does your school look like from memory?
- What does your school look like while walking around?
- What do you wonder about your school?
- What do you wonder about the earth around your school?
- What do you imagine about the earth around your school at different times?
- Who might have interacted with that earth?
- What about the earth around your food?
- How does that food grow?
- Where do you get that food now?
- What can you learn about the earthbound food through the voice of an elder?
- What can be passed on from that elder's interview?
- What else …?

Both projects grounded in personal assets as an entry point, yet the elementary project remained more limber to pivot reflection—individual and group—between the familiar and the world beyond the classroom. The "common-good" possibilities faced outward through the school, into students' elders and the community. They also stretched across time. Conceptions of a common good remained preliminary, but promising. Cotton's potency as a practical symbol of oppression locally and globally could open a productive critical pedagogy door, for wherever cotton goes, oppression follows—even to the present day (Beckert 2015). The concreteness that sharecroppers picked cotton where students currently play, study and test opened dynamic critical pedagogy possibilities for balancing self-reflection with understandings of challenges to the common good. Alas, the school year ended.

The curation elements—both on-line and in museum—represented a reach toward collective reflection. While most groups paid most attention to their own initiatives in these public/published spaces, seeing their own work in the context of other work inquiring similarly broke through borders and boundaries on some small level. Again, when conceived, intentions included local and global partners in dialogic inquiry throughout. In reality, sites remained distinct except for teacher professional development and curation steps. Although short of the perhaps-too-ambitious dream, shared museum and social-media curation spaces fed the idea of common-good questions; each site quilted a facet. Future designs could involve sites more actively in curation, as it is a cross-mode, cross-art, cross-site reflection with public-facing, common-good-expanding storytelling opportunities.

Examination of how ideas are translated in the public realm

In *Remapping Performance: Common Ground, Uncommon Partners*, scholar-artist of socially-engaged theatre, Jan Cohen-Cruz (2015), describes "uncommon partners" in community-centered collaboration as

> brought together by commitment to a common, social concern. When performance is part of such a project, they may or may not include the creation of a show, take place on a stage, direct themselves to established audiences, or even be recognizable as performance, but they rely deeply on aesthetic training, methodologies and mindset.
>
> (2015, 1)

The *Cotton & Collards* project, over and over again, embodied Cohen-Cruz's qualifying description. It set out to build with uncommon partners—with the museum, with each location, with each international colleague, and across partners—inviting artistic inquiry, without making a culminating performance the presumed end, but also not discouraging it. While the limits on time yielded limits on activity and depth, the curation forced the asset-centered articulation of each site's activity, no matter how small or large, preliminary or polished it initially seemed. The museum exhibit and social-media element prompted analysis that yielded rigorous attention to honoring each contribution, each step, each place, each voice, each idea, each intention. Additionally, the curation step required multimodal storytelling by artifacts, images, few words and no live performance, both complementing but also productively inverting many traditional theatre processes, yet sharing a "common thread in socially-oriented performance commitment to place and to locally significant action" (Cohen-Cruz 2015, 1).

The events called "performance" or "sharing" for an audience at each community initiative read most legibly as theatre. When theatre, dance, and poetry enlivened the middle-school stage, that was considered theatre. When a student interviewer catalyzed and collected video stories in the stairwell studio at the "Coming to the Table" festival, that was considered theatre. The summative storytelling/sharing for the elementary schoolers punctuated "Stories from Seeds" and involved standing before others who eventually clapped; that was considered theatre. By frequency numbers and program focus, the middle-school project generated more ostensible theatre activity. However, considering the same projects using Boal's spect-actor (1992) concept as a lens, the elementary students' work flowed more episodically, allowing and encouraging participants to inhabit varied perspectives; to "walk in someone else's shoes" (Heathcote 1984) for a time; to both express and receive fluidly. With the middle-school inquiry, once a student established a role in the impending festival, energy went toward animating that role which would culminate in the event.

While neither group used forum theatre or role-based improvisation with each other's stories, interesting role-playing and performing occurred outside a consciously theatrical frame or strategy. Richness lingered in micro-theatre moments imbued with a sense of active audiencing and rooted reflection, often in informal exchanges. Embodied conversations wove between Chambers Elementary students: walk-running and describing their own school grounds; sharing vegetable and garden memory stories while planting seeds. Similarly, Foothills Middle seventh graders, who systematically avoided being on stage, unknowingly fostered performative spaces in the lobby as they told the story of collard greens to single visitors at a time, cajoled them to taste collard greens and tell/write collard-green recipe secrets, then steered collard paparazzi toward Grandma L., who attended the event alongside her renowned greens. "Coming to the Table" participants reflected back on their work in video-recorded interviews. Many spoke as emerging advocates and activists, touching on and even connecting the artistic and social ("Even though we were not always ready for rehearsal, I think we should do more stuff like this. We had to work together. Every seventh grader should have to do this.") as well as the artistic and ecological ("I would like more people to visit our website and share what they bring to the table, like their food and their ideas."). The idea of assuming an advocate's register for an imagined audience was both an act of theatre and an act of community-focused advocacy.

Playback Theatre (playbackcentre.org) is an applied theatre approach in which stories from a public audience are improvisationally re-enacted for the larger audience, either by a company or by the audience themselves. Linda Park-Fuller (2003), a company member, contemplated the strategies at play in balancing stories and representation in such a context. She forwards the idea of "audiencing the audience" and acknowledges its alignment with Boal's spect-actor concept (1985), both aspiring to shift the audience role from passive to active, from fixed to varied, fluid. While not an effort anything on the scale of Playback Theatre, the tentacles of the *Cotton & Collards* project shared the multiple, layered, shifting dynamic of trying to cultivate, represent, honor, and question peoples' real stories. While the "Coming to the Table" and "Stories from Seeds" efforts within *Cotton & Collards* both carried a consonance and a dissonance between intention and action, we aspired to work within a realistic view of what theatre can do and what it can't, by artistically centering responsiveness, smallness, and home stories.

Home

The project title, "*Cotton & Collards*," stuck more than the tag line "*Unearthing Stories of Home Through Kitchens and Closets.*" This was true in the museum, in print, and in conversations between participants. Homeness, however, was everywhere in theory and practice. The term "applied theatre" is a continuing discourse of creating and contesting an academic home for theatre work outside traditional theatre spaces (Ackroyd 2007). Paulo Freire's and Augusto Boal's anchoring works, *Pedagogy of the Oppressed* and *Theatre of the Oppressed*, respectively, spoke of and to social injustice in their Brazilian homeland. The bell hooks critical feminist memoir relied heavily on ideas of memory and home. Thomas, Snyder-Young, Balfour and Cohen-Cruz cautioned against applied theatre works that literally and/or figuratively colonize the homelands of "partners" through well-intentioned feats of "transformative" theatre. In essence adopting a critical pedagogy effectively means making space for participants to be at home with challenging home—the known, the familiar, the taken-for-granted.

It is worth pondering that Freire's and Boal's important "... of the Oppressed" works, on which critical applied theatre pedagogy finds firm foundation, are both manifestos exhorting action at and about injustice at home, but penned from a distant political exile. Sometimes small, humble, local, responsive efforts shrink further when imagined alongside revolutionary artistic and pedagogical acts prompting exile. Reliance on literal fidelity to such guides, without adaptation to context and circumstance—as called for repeatedly in both books—poises critical pedagogues to recreate or falsely create the conditions and positions of 1970s Brazil, casting oneself as the benevolently radical Boal or Freire. Most of us have not earned such a home place, nor is such an orientation uniformly applicable. The questions follow, often unvoiced. Is this liberatory enough? Is it revolutionary enough? Are the questions too hard, or not hard enough? Who exactly is the oppressor in this instance? Uh-oh, is it me?

"Humanizing pedagogies" powerfully cite Freire and call out historical practices justifying one identity group as more human than another in curriculum's center stage. Critical pedagogues work to highlight and dismantle these dehumanizing systems. Meanwhile defenders of the systems dismiss critical pedagogues as hypocritical grandstanders with elite seats inside the very systems they critique. All sides entrench. Re-reading Freire reminds us of his call for *"mutually* humanizing pedagogies" (1970, 56). This co-inquiry idea allows no one the comfort of unbridled power, nor the paralysis of victimhood, but rather eludes the binary and calls all to "free your oppressor and yourself" (44). Elizabeth Ellsworth (1989) recounted her own journey in a university course designed to examine and confront patterned and public injustices on her campus as complex, messy, necessary business. Ellsworth set her critical pedagogue's agenda not as a knowing liberator poised to grant theorized justice, but rather as a privileged agent implicated in the struggle to:

> become capable of a sustained encounter with currently oppressive formations and power relations that refuse to be theorized away or fully transcended in a utopian resolution—and to enter into the encounter in a way that owned up to my own implications in those formations and was capable of changing my own relation to and investments in those formations.
>
> (1989, 308)

Thirty-plus years ago, Ellsworth forwarded working through "repressive myths of critical pedagogy." Almost fifty years ago, Freire implicated everyone as responsible and beholden to one another, and the shared definition of pluralized "common good" grounded in revolutionary humanizing strategies and orientations. "In a world saturated by hegemonic narratives, neoliberalism, and cultural products reinforcing the status quo" (Snyder-Young 2015, 135) was the *Cotton & Collards* project a baby step toward revolution, or a slightly frilly maintenance of mainstream ways? Can anything—artistic or not—unfolding through a public university, a donor-dependent museum, and within the walls of two public schools ever challenge systems of power and habits of human and environmental oppressions? This project is neither poised to answer such questions, nor to avoid them. It is merely a step that, once taken, reveals ever-increasing possible next steps and ethically-bound possibilities. As Freire points out "pedagogy will be made and remade" in conversation with the struggle (1970 [1993], 48).

Note

1 All names are pseudonyms in accordance with the university human subjects protocols established for this research project.

References

Ackroyd, Judith. 2007. "Applied Theatre: An Exclusionary Discourse?" *Applied Theatre Researcher* 8: 1–11.

Balfour, Michael. 2009. "The Politics of Intention: Looking for a Theatre of Little Changes." *Research in Drama Education: Journal of Applied Theatre and Performance* 14 (3): 347–359.

Beckert, Sven. 2015. *Empire of Cotton: A Global History*. New York: Vintage.

Boal, Augusto. 1985. *Theatre of the Oppressed*. New York: Theatre Communications Group.

Boal, Augusto. 1992. *Games for Actors and Non-Actors*. London: Routledge.

Breuing, Mary. 2011. "Problematizing Critical Pedagogy." *The International Journal of Critical Pedagogy* 3 (3): 2–23.

Cohen-Cruz, Jan. 2015. *Remapping Performance: Common Ground, Uncommon Partners*. London: Palgrave Macmillan.

Davis, Edward H. and Morgan, John T. 2015. *Collards: A Southern Tradition from Seed to Table*. Tuscaloosa: University of Alabama Press.

del Carmen Salazar, María. 2013. "A Humanizing Pedagogy: Reinventing the Principles and Practice of Education as a Journey toward Liberation." *Review of Research in Education* 37 (1): 121–148.

Ellsworth, Elizabeth. 1989. "Why Doesn't This Feel Empowering? Working through the Repressive Myths of Critical Pedagogy." *Harvard Educational Review* 59 (3): 297–325.

Emdin, Christopher. 2016. *For White Folks Who Teach in the Hood… and the Rest of Y'all Too: Reality Pedagogy and Urban Education*. Boston: Beacon Press.

Freire, Paolo. 1970/1993. *Pedagogy of the Oppressed*. London: Continuum Press.

Freire, Paolo. 1998. *Teachers as Cultural Workers: Letters to Those Who Dare to Teach*. Oxford: Westview Press.

Geertz, Clifford. 1973. *The Interpretation of Cultures*. New York: Basic Books, 1973.

Giroux, Henry A. 2014. *The Violence of Organized Forgetting: Thinking Beyond America's Disimagination Machine*. San Francisco: City Lights Publishers.

Heathcote, Dorothy. 1984. *Collected Writings on Education and Drama*, Edited by Liz Johnson and Cecily O'Neill. London: Trentham Books.

hooks, bell. 2008. *Belonging a Culture of Place*. New York: Routledge.

Kelley, William Melvin. 1962. "If You're Woke You Dig It." *New York Times*, 20 May 1962, SM45.

Paris, Django, and H. Samy Alim, Editors. 2017. *Culturally Sustaining Pedagogies: Teaching and Learning for Justice in a Changing World*. New York: Teachers College Press.

Park-Fuller, Linda M. 2003. "Audiencing the Audience: Playback Theatre, Performative Writing, and Social Activism." *Text and Performance Quarterly* 23 (3): 288–310.

Snyder-Young, Dani. 2013. *Theatre of Good Intentions: Challenges and Hopes for Theatre and Social Change*. New York: Springer.

Thompson, James. 2009. *Performance Affects: Applied Theatre and the End of Effect*. New York: Springer.

16 Up close and wide awake
Participating in Anna Deavere Smith's social theatre

Stephanie L. Hodde

Facing the noise: Urgency for participatory responses

Playwright and cultural provocateur Anna Deavere Smith contends with a noisy world; she knows that artists like her must inspire "a will to communicate large enough to carry over the noise" (1993, 81), devoting attention to intimate qualities and contradictions of human experience. Moreover, by listening to the noise, her documentary performance practices allow audiences to consider who authorizes the commotion, and who willingly resists by vocalizing their own response. In groundbreaking, verbatim plays like *Fires in the Mirror: Crown Heights, Brooklyn and Other Identities* (1993), or in recent works like *Notes from the Field: Doing Time in Education* (2016),[1] Smith moves away from spectacular truths to create a mixed bag of human meanings, prompting similar testimony projects such as David Hare's *Stuff Happens* (2003) concerning the Iraq War, or Tectonic Theater's *Laramie Project* (2000) about a Wyoming town's response to a hate crime. Smith claims how uncertain meanings promise new political and theatrical terrain:

> Many people assume that political life is theatre. The theatre is created to illuminate the truth. What truth is our political theatre illuminating? True theatre is not only text and subtext—it is a vast mélange of contradictions and paradoxes, associations and disassociations.
>
> (2000, 151)

As a college professor, jumping into any sociocultural mélange with undergraduates can be tricky to navigate. Still, when I first introduced Smith two years ago in a course entitled "Artistic Responses to Social and Political Issues," I was urged to do more than just teach her documentary performances as responses to issues; I felt I also owed my students, as civic participants, to present Smith's pedagogical theory and practice as social tools, especially after reading the *New York Times* review of the Public Theater's production of *Julius Caesar* a month before the Fall term, "Hard Truths or Easy Target? Confronting the Summer of Trump

Onstage," which pointed out the uncanny resemblance of our sitting president to Shakespeare's title character. Brantley, Greene, and Soloski further stated that American theatre has a problem because "politics has become more incredible than anything the stage can deliver" (2017, 1). Referring to the production's characterization of Caesar as a misguided plutocrat—not unlike the "tycoon, television star and now head of state" Donald Trump— they worried whether reigning political media could be eclipsed by any creative attempts at sociopolitical drama.

Prompting this "who can deliver" moment, these *New York Times* critics reckon with growing national anxiety over "media spectacle," a phrase Douglas Kellner adapts to reassert Guy Debord's "society of the spectacle" for digital capitalism where, to our detriment, political news spends public attention on entertainment. In the case of this US populist presidency, news spectacle from Washington now saturates mainstream news syndicates Twitter and Instagram with outlandish narratives that surely entertain, but also dislodge, rather than cultivate democratic concerns. For me, this juncture between staging American culture and staging American politics seemed critical to teaching Smith. It re-ignites an age-old debate over theatre's role, whether it questions or even redirects the ways we think and learn about our sociopolitical reality. On our first day of class I ask my students, are dramatists motivated to teach or incite? Is theatre a mirror or a catalyst?

As a professor of English at Virginia Military Institute, where I teach dramatic literature, writing, and cultural rhetoric to cadets, Smith's intimate pedagogy and verbatim techniques afford students access to their own intimate and investigative paths, ways to access emotional incomes and openings in social character. VMI is one of the oldest of its kind, a state-supported, liberal arts college where cadets go to learn tradition, but also skills and habits of mind for service and civic engagement. Since its founding in 1839, VMI faculty have developed "citizen-soldiers" for both military and civilian lives. Our contemporary moment creates an arguably crucial time for cadets to identify more closely with others—and thus extend themselves across borders real or imagined, of their own or others' making. This chapter considers Smith's pedagogy of social theatre as a vehicle for students to inhabit a kind of flexible inclusion through intimacy with other's accounts.[2] In particular, I sketch my thinking for teachers and theatre practitioners wanting to use Smith's dialogic, emotional approach to frame and explore verbatim practices that embrace human potential through ethnopoetic performance. I discuss her work in light of the "affective turn"[3] influenced by theories of social discourse and educational theatre, all which inform her performance rhetoric as one that moves beneath and between social events to activate participatory, polyvocal discourse. Performances such as Smith's *Doing Time in Education* and *Twilight: Los Angeles, 1992* model techniques for students navigating social crisis, especially as adaptive counteractions to more distanced, defensive, or uniform responses. As evidence, I share instructional choices for the "Artistic Responses" course, particularly students' responses to a "Creative Adaptation" assignment, where students imitate the rhetorical strategies of American playwrights. Students get close as they attempt to inhabit the liminal process of voicing others with fluid, empathic intent. In their novice performances they attempt to locate not solutions, but rather, as Smith encourages, the creative process of becoming human "inside the problems, or the crisis" (1994, xxiv).

On the road: Smith's territories for teaching

Smith's contributions to civic dialogue have shifted potential for American performance artists and audiences in the public sphere. Over thirty-plus years, Smith's seminal field project, "On the Road: A Search for American Character" documents some of the most compelling human crises and conditions plaguing our time—urban uprisings and identity politics (*Fires in the Mirror; Twilight: Los Angeles, 1992*), the role of the Presidency (*House Arrest*, 1995), health care (*Let Me Down Easy*, 2008), and recently, the school to prison pipeline (*Doing Time in Education*, 2017).[4] In each live exploration of other's words, she examines, as David Savran suggests, "how identities are consolidated and performed in a nation grown increasingly fragmented" (1999, 238). As Smith recalled of her artistic road trip's beginnings with college friends, "we wanted to see America and to make sense, each in our own way, of what to do with all the breakage and the promise" (2000, 3). Talking to Americans, making hundreds of individual "character" contacts, Smith found her expansive project still required an intimate process—a way of being close with those giving, telling, and witnessing a nation's happenings. Inviting closeness often begins for Smith by posing three questions:

> Do you know the story of your birth?
> Have you ever been falsely accused?
> Have you ever been close to death?[5]

Moving interviewees to speak at length, Smith heard, recorded, and most astonishingly, performed solo the poetic discourse of others' dramas. She thus pioneered social theatre, initiating both a dialogic "verbatim" pedagogy and wider participatory stage for contributing voices. Though not the first post-war dramatist to do so, Smith galvanized documentary theatre to unpack political spectacle in "all its specificity and contradictions" (Parenteau 2017, 20). As Smith notes, her work authorized artists and audiences to leave "safe houses of identity" (2000, 23) because, "reality is more varied than anything I was seeing on the stage. I was trying to enliven the stage" (2006).

For Smith the theatre professor, building a participatory stage required engaging students and fellow colleagues. In a keynote speech to the 1993

Association of Theater in Higher Education, "Not So Special Vehicles," she forecast young people's responsibility to become boundary crossers and humble students of society, calling for fellow professors to prepare students beyond the stage: "We need to educate people who can move from place to place" (Smith 1995, 87). At that time, I was a graduate student in education and performance at the University of Illinois at Chicago. Smith's practices for social theatre became serendipitous tools—ones that helped me access a more connective, participatory way of knowing in a multi-voiced society full of crisis, what Dwight Conquergood once defined as "knowing how," and "knowing who" (2002, 146), or what Shannon Jackson foresees as "interpublic coordination" (2011, 9). Motivated by Smith's process, I ran dramatic writing workshops with pregnant high school students at Nicola Tesla High School, worked with a writing group of homeless adults near our Southside campus, and wrote my dissertation on an expeditionary perform-ance project, "Girltopia" composed by Latina girls with Redmoon Theater's Dramagirls.[6] Even when I left the city for the quiet Blue Ridge Mountains of Virginia, I found a new place to practice Smith's dialogic, verbatim practices with clients and caseworkers in a domestic violence program. None of these social theatre projects, however, helped me grasp how Smith might inspire real encounters for undergraduate cadets at a small state-funded military college.

Any teacher who considers Smith's praxis as a platform for classroom creative inquiry should question whether students less versed in dramatic lit-erature, performance, or even cultural discourse can emulate her ethnopoetic expertise. Should we also ask whether artistic pedagogies like hers can shift student efforts or perspectives toward social inquiry? Smith delivers crit-ical knowledge through felt realities; yet, this exercise may not be an easy diet for youth fed on (T)ruths or quick fixes, or with students trained in a military corps mindset. Allison Forsyth's reading of Smith's performances (2009) suggests that this need to "get real" may be a tall order for younger generations who may have been "anesthetized" by media's version of reality, and thus disenfranchised from more authentic voices. Critics of Smith's work have questioned the linguistic focus of her performances and their impact on audiences; even Smith herself asks: "can the talk make anything happen, or is it just one more thing we consume?" (2000, 41). But I argue Smith's dialogic methods for listening and delivering her interviewees activate a dra-matic *learning through* talk, for herself, participating voices, and eventu-ally her audiences. When called an impersonator of others' stories, Smith countered, "if anything, they give me a voice" (Syme 2016, 7). Making her-self a vessel for shifting perspectives, Smith shows us how to make room for dissent, debate, but most sustaining, creative contact with diverging vantage points, or as performance theorist Erin Hurley claims, ways for "letting us know that we are by letting us feel that we are here" (2014, 3). I hoped her pedagogy could inspire my cadets to act as social bricoleurs by dwelling in how uncertain, how plural and yet how resonant any participating insights about human crisis can be.

Making the strange familiar: activating emotional intelligence

With less theoretically prepared students in a sophomore-level rhetoric and performance class, it seemed best to feel our way through Smith's genre of dramatic talk, rather than begin with cultural "messages," as one cadet assumed after reading online about *Twilight* as a response to the LAPD's altercation with Rodney King. This student knocked on my office door, and politely admitted his hesitations: "Major Hodde, Can I talk to you? I'm thinking about joining the police force—I can't tell with Smith how I'm going to feel about reading this play." We talked for a while. I asked him to give Smith a read-through first to consider how her monologues bridge broad swaths of public concern with urban unrest, and offer generous social and emotional vocabularies that might give him more ways to connect than he expected.

Smith's vocabularies of affect start in her fieldwork. Each subsequent interview offers new emotional intelligence inside unwieldy events, thus new social and co-relational exchanges within epic problems. Confessional response in late 1980s television culture—particularly the public trial, interview testimony, and press conferences of the O.J. Simpson, Clarence Thomas, and President Clinton trials—taught Smith to study individual voices in play with larger political systems, gaining her more intimate voices within a political spectrum, such as with President Clinton in *House Arrest* (1997). Before my students attempt verbatim playwriting, as I'll show later, we listen to and discuss excerpts from *Twilight: Los Angeles* (1992) and *Doing Time in Education* alongside other methods for shaping verbatim material, such as Moisés Kaufman and Tectonic Theater's "moment work" (2018). Each method exposed students to a full affective sense of another's poetics (strong moments, cadences, repetitions, gaps, and juxtapositions in speech), and how doggedly listening to these patterns might complicate social experiences and networks. Furthermore, when students and I review recordings of Smith's edited performances, we think about what it means to be another's interpreter, to act as public vessel for a precious human message, to want to create dramatic affect, and to only have three minutes to do it.

To uncover "the lack of opportunity and resources for young people" (Smith 2019) living in impoverished situations with *Doing Time*, my students practiced listening close to those voices forgotten, and those responsible on the school to prison pipeline. Grounded in four geographical areas, Smith's interviews carry voices of a system's disarray, along with a tenacious resourcefulness dwelling in that very system's cracks. We listened to Smith portray Denise Dodson, an interviewee who studies her civic participation while serving twenty-three years; she comes to know herself as a citizen, conscious of her part in a larger political whole:

The more I talk the better I get.
What is expected of me as a citizen,
to make better living arrangements for everyone as a whole ...
I wish the teachers would see the children as little people.

(*Doing Time*, Second Stage 2016)

Smith illuminates a woman affected as adult and child, inmate and citizen, one resigned and hopeful. Denise seeks to change her role, educate her community and shift policy "arrangements." Juxtaposing felt realities, Smith also talked to official personas such as Sherillyn Ifill, President of the NAACP Defense Fund. As the play's prologue, Ifill frames the trigger-happy responses of an America prone to epic rather than sustainable decisions:

We make big investments. Big bets.
Criminal justice system at the expense of education.
That's what we call policy. The investments we decide to make.
There's a lot of heaviness in the country, a lot of pain ...
It takes epic moments for us to take the red pill.

(*Doing Time*, 2016)

My students hear how repeated utterances of "investment" and "expense" in educational policy testify to multiplying emotional identifications, real consequences of disappointment, and policy shame.

With these examples, Smith shows an epidemic social problem on a different scale, intervening in participants' felt realities *before* they become news. When I asked my students to analyze how Smith's approaches reach beyond the stage, they concluded that Smith builds emotional knowledge through intertextual connections, what I might call "aesthetic outreach." By doing so she unearths sentiments through other artists' research, such as in Jesman Ward's historical novel, *Sing, Unburied Sing.* Her piece on Ward's story, "Ghost Whisperers" (*NYT Book Review*, 2018) ponders how younger generations are tied to Mississippi's Parchman prison. Smith contemplates Ward's character Jojo, a young man who fends for himself and witnesses for others: "It seems as if Jojo is not paying attention at school, but he is. He is incredibly vigilant. He sees through his teacher's makeup to the bruises and wonders if she gets beaten like his mother does" (2018, 12). Before teaching at VMI, I spent three years as a domestic violence counselor, and these encounters taught me to listen to how felt realities present a fuller, more resilient social presence in traumatic predicaments. Rather than focus on how difficult lives report as data, such as IEPs, police reports, or by way of circumstantial scars—Smith convenes with Ward to warn official documenters that the data don't reveal everything. Rather than tally marks or list events, Smith suggests we follow the emotional vigilance of incoming voices: "The ear might be a better way of finding those resources than looking at numbers on a spreadsheet. And it takes a certain kind of ear" (2018, 14).

Before doing their own verbatim research, my students listened for these same resources, starting with their own voices. Choosing one of Smith's questions noted earlier, such as, "tell me the story of your birth," or "have you ever been falsely accused?" each student conducted an unrecorded, fifteen-minute interview with a classmate, following guidelines for listening with an ethnopoetic ear to jot down their partner's salient speech, what linguist and educator Courtney Cazden calls "strong lines" worth punctuating, juxtaposing, or repeating, as if a refrain.[7] I then read their collection of edited monologues aloud to the class as an unbroken utterance, leaving interview pairs anonymous. You could have heard a pin drop. They were rapt, recognizing themselves, but also hearing what others could make more familiar. Bodies were still, some eyes were even closed, listening to each take on a disoriented beginning, perhaps a difficult home environment, a complicated choice, a regretted exchange. Cadets have little space for sharing intimate concerns—and the classroom becomes no exception. Because they abide by stringent, institutional codes of honor and military corps rules, emotional realities or individual takes on social reality can be a challenge to share. Despite this, Smith gave us a springboard for venturing into a dramatic potpourri, what social theatre educator Gallagher recognizes as a means for "affective real-feeling knowing" (2014). By magnifying and hearing their

Figure 16.1 Students inhabit interviewees' talk in their *Twilight* performances. Photo by Stephanie L. Hodde.

own and others' felt connections, students loosened their grip, ready to intervene in the process of how social assumptions, and ultimately political conditions, harden (Figure 16.1).

Students get closer—inhabiting social performances

> We were confronted,
> It was so hard to confront the brutality.
> Definitely eye-opening.
> So much has been forgotten, 'ya know?
> I didn't realize 36 people died.
> *Our memories are so short.*
> We're so used to school shootings, violence ...
> Just a statement about where we are now.
>   (M., 2018)[8]

When it enters our consciousness, social theatre can be an unsettling gift. "Our memories are so short," exclaims Ron Niette-Garcia, a property manager and owner of Alta Vista Realty in Antioch, California, now in his fifties. My student, M., speaks for Ron in "Blind Belief," a monologue of her interviewee's experience in Los Angeles, 1992. Ron's exclamation unsettles M.'s classmates from a tunneled sense of current events, of what's being done or undone as racial tensions ramp up in cities like Baltimore, or even an hour away in Charlottesville, Virginia. During post-discussion one student wondered, "Why are Americans going in circles?"

I had already framed Smith as an inheritor of crucible moments in our democracy, moments that require a critical imagination to permeate existing social material, to question what's messy and unmade about real events.[9] Course thematic units such as "Social Crisis," "Neighborhoods," and "Work" carried us between events represented by Smith's *Twilight*, Tectonic's *The Laramie Project* and *Laramie Project—10 Years Later* (2010) and Lynn Nottage's *Sweat* (2017)—to earlier witch hunts with Arthur Miller's *The Crucible* (1953), or lingering effects of segregation with Lorraine Hansberry's *A Raisin in the Sun* (1959) and Bruce Norris's *Clybourne Park* (2010). Reading these artistic responses to social events gave students ways to compose their own intimate affects in the above mentioned "Creative Adaptation" assignment. Everyone was asked to compose an original monologue or scene modeling dramatic techniques from one playwright. M's "Blind Belief" was one of three student monologues constructed from new interviews in response to *Twilight: Los Angeles 1992*. Students edited and performed their interview transcripts, but also brought additional felt meanings through author notes and post-performance reflections.[10] Hoping to engage Smith's "more complex emotional language" (1994, xxv) than merely than "us versus them," my assignment suggests they accept a more intimate social encounter:

Some professors of drama will argue that adaptation as a class exercise is a moot point. The playwright already said what they needed to say, didn't they? What are we fooling with? What you are fooling with is a chance to dig more deeply inside the mind of a playwright who provoked you and left you wondering what else might happen, how you might take up their practice or social inquiry.

(Hodde, 2018)

For "Blind Belief", M. asked Smith's three questions after tracking down a friend's relative (Ron) who was present in L.A.'s city limits during the unrest. She grounds his response to the "birth" question by highlighting local beginnings:

We lived in Antioch, CA- the Bay area
Working for Safeway grocery stores.
Uhh, not really sure …
Uh, born into a lower class Mexican Latino family,
Son of an illegal immigrant—
A farm worker.
My mother was a US citizen.
Humble beginnings, humble upbringing
But does not mean low quality …
that's important.

(M., 2018)

In her monologue's exposition, M. explained that her interview "offers insights from an individual who has had twenty-six years to reflect on these events." Our follow-up discussion together revealed what M. learned:

Imitating A.D-S. allowed for a deeper learning process. We were connecting the past to the present. People we interviewed have had over a decade to process it, there's that big time gap. It's like asking "Do you remember where you were?" On 911? It had a deeply personal impact on so many people nationally. It *felt like* a personal attack—on an idea of America. *Twilight* was focused on a community but also had that same feeling. It was talking to everyone paying attention in other cities.

(Interviews, M. 2018)

Connecting to national dialogue, M. witnessed how we can close a felt gap of time, how returning to an earlier social trauma might influence responses now. By selecting "we" in her edited version of the interview and "we" in her reflection, she seems to cross a boundary that Smith defines as: "*We* means moving from me to us" (2000, 72). In concert with Ron, her interviewee,

M. inhabited someone else's return to the moment of Rodney King, and so "woke up to" other generational and cultural perspectives.

Later in the monologue, M. uses Smith's strategy of punctuating an interviewee's verbal cadences and textures. She creates rhythm in Ron's nominalizations (founda*tion*, retalia*tion*, realiza*tion*), as well as his reflective pauses, marking his shifts from the event to social reckonings:

> When I saw the video of the beating ...
> It was so brutal and vicious
> It rocked my *foundation*
> Blind belief in police
> Then the riots broke out, the *retaliation* ...
> It compounded the *situation*
> The riots, breaking into stores, the fires and everything ...
> It wasn't a way to solve the situation
> It was really the start of America's *realization*.
>
> (M., 2018)

M. shared how editing and performing helped connect her with Ron's powerful pauses:

> During those ellipses, what did I want to communicate to the reader, audience to show him thinking in those pauses? Either that he didn't know or remember, or that he didn't want to say, or was searching for substitute words. Or, they could just show the effort to recall and articulate what it meant in that moment, or even now.
>
> (Interviews, M. 2018)

Another student, B., recalled timely cop stories based on riding city beats with his father and other Bay Area officers, found he could assemble what it felt like to patrol for safety but have limited options: "All we could really do was hold the line" (Interviews, B. 2018). He elaborated in his follow-up interview:

> I've always tried to wrap my head around work in public safety ... I've been around my Dad for twenty-five years ... even though you can't speak *for* their experience, an unspeakable thing, I was still trying to put myself out there through writing. It's almost a collection of voices, things they deal with a on a daily basis—they see a lot in this cycle of Oakland and Berkeley. Police are stuck in the middle. They can't say "Hey, we're not going to respond."
>
> (Interviews, B. 2018)

My third student, E., who had family ties to Los Angeles, but no immediate way to speak about the 1992 events, sought to re-experience events with her father, who had lived through those days in his twenties as a student at SoCa Institute of Architecture. As E. shared later of her Dad, Jorge,

> He'd say, 'I don't really like to talk about it.' So it was eye-opening to me, to hear his different identifications. We can think about the immigrant story too. 2nd of three kids. His family came from Spain to Canada, arrived in Los Angeles, 1969. His Dad bought a machine shop downtown, whatever building he could afford.
>
> (Interviews, E. 2018)

E.'s monologue, "The Rampart," recalls Jorge's experience with fellow students:

> We called it the Civil Unrest
> Not this L.A. riot thing
> Hombre, we were scared
> and pissed off.
> They moved the trial out to Silicon valley away from the riots
> Ughh,
> I remember
> I was at lunch in Downtown one day with my friends
> Sky was black from smoke.
> We were drinking coffee between classes.
> A man
> A black man
> came running down the street (...)
> They choked him
> Till he passed out or maybe worse
> Closest I've been to death
> They took to the streets
> The people, hombre, the people to the streets
> "The Rampart" was what we called them
> The Rampart, the corrupt police
> Didn't do anything but make it worse...
>
> (E., 2018)

After witnessing these student performances, classmates felt frustrated that neither L.A. authorities nor onlookers could clarify a big (T)truth for who was to blame, or who could solve any urban center's social ills. Still, as Gallagher, Mealey and Jacobson (2018) argue, exploring felt experiences helps students balance their wish to represent objective reality, and their need to complicate meanings connected to a vast range of feelings about it. E. got to re-sense and then articulate a confrontational moment in her father's character, whom she knows to be a "respectful, quiet man, very conscientious." She seemed to help her "Dad" locate himself in L.A.'s social memory as he watched strangers being abandoned by the authorities. This wake-up call prepared his own attitudes toward local workers as a future architect:

> Having him retell it, remember it, really brought out his relationship to that period, to the city now. Doing this interview made me realize how my Dad was formed by living through this event, how he treats others with a certain sense of respect, more so than others I know.
>
> (Interviews, E., 2018)

Future acts for social theatre

If we heed Anna Deavere Smith's call to step out into what's real and "know the issues differently" (2000, 81) we must help students cultivate dialogic affect by listening to their own fluid selves in relations with others. Mid-semester I took my class to see several talks by Pulitzer Prize–winning playwrights Suzan-Lori Parks and Paula Vogel, hosted by our next-door neighbor and equally tradition-steeped institution, Washington and Lee University. My often overtired cadets woke up when Parks started jamming on her steel guitar, singing in a throaty voice an account of how she and her fellow passengers had practiced "radical inclusion" on the airplane ride to Roanoke. And, when Vogel spoke to them about "The Art of Tolerance," she noted that in light of democracy's social experiment, "theatre is a training and a mindset, a way to process," a way to articulate our "getting over our resistance, fear, loathing" of shifting ideas and identities. Like Smith, Vogel seemed unconcerned with instability; rather, she suggested that as participants in an artistic process, we figure out how to manifest identity as an unfixed thing, a continuously estranging process, and confront *how we change*. Her talk's uniting gesture became, "All of us have things to come out about" (Vogel 2018).

Notes

1 Verbatim theatre is a preferred category for artists who aim to document spoken words and real lives. Smith, who uses only the words from actual transcripts for her monologue plays, developed verbatim theatre as a critical performance term within documentary and investigative theatre. Many reject "documentation" as an authorial, ethnographic position. See Parenteau's article in *American Theater* (2017) discussing current categories for factual theatre.

2 I began using this term social theatre to teach Smith's pedagogy as inclusion via intimacy after listening to Suzan-Lori Parks talk about practicing "radical inclusion" as an artist at a "Diversity" talk at Washington and Lee University's Mudd Center for Ethics in 2017.

3 The affective turn was critical theory's response in the 1990s to mounting political and economic trauma, in which the loss of the subject left little room to discuss emotion or bodily affect. Educational theorists and social dramatists picked up a linked response, the "social turn" (James Gee; Kathleen Gallagher) to revalue literate discourse and creative knowledge as socially constructed and felt production. See also Erin Hurley (2014) and Kathleen Gallagher's writings (2014) on Clough (2008).

4 Johnathan Kalb (2001) reviews her series of linked projects as a play on Kerouac's *On the Road*. Many reviewers have noted the metaphor of travel within Smith's work as an act of discovering the territories and dialogues between self and other.

5 I adapt these questions slightly from Smith's original wording. See her discussion in the introduction to *Fires in the Mirror*. Although she notes she no longer needs these questions to prompt poetry from her interviewees, the spirit of them remains in her listening ear.

6 Dramagirls was an outreach program for adolescent girls to express themselves through spectacle theatre until their parent company, Redmoon Theater, closed its doors in 2015. I performed with and ran outreach for Redmoon before studying their expeditionary performance practices in 2003.

7 I use my training in educational discourse, particularly Courtney Cazden's (1988) sense of "strong lines" to help students realize the potential of Smith's ethnopoetic editing practices like repetition and juxtaposition.

8 Student's names are anonymized in this way throughout the chapter.

9 Critical imagination is an inquiry tool in "questioning a viewpoint, an experience, an event, and so on, and in remaking interpretive frameworks based on that questioning" (Royster, Jones and Kirsch 2012, 19)

10 Evidence was drawn from both student monologues and initial "exposition notes" they turned in with their creative adaptation assignment. After the term's end, I requested and held informal interviews with three students, asking them to reflect on their purposes and processes for exploring Smith's intimate, verbatim approach.

Reference

B. "War Zone." 2018. Student Monologue. Lexington, VA: Virginia Military Institute.

Brantley, B., Green, J., and Soloski, A. August 16, 2017. "Hard Truths or Easy Targets? Confronting the Summer of Trump Onstage." *New York Times*, Theater 1.

Cazden, Courtney B. 1988. *Classroom Discourse: The Language of Teaching and Learning*. Portsmouth, MA: Heinemann.

Clough, Patricia Ticiento and Halley, Jean O'Malley, eds. 2007. *The Affective Turn: Theorizing the Social*. Durham, NC: Duke University Press.

Conquergood, Dwight. 2002. "Interventions and Radical Research." *Drama Review* 46 (2): 145–156.

E. "The Rampart." 2018. Student Monologue. Lexington, VA: Virginia Military Institute.

Forsyth, Alison. 2009. "Performing Trauma: Race Riots and Beyond in the Work of Anna Deavere Smith." In *Get Real: Documentary Theater Past and Present*, edited by Alison Forsyth and Chris Megson. London: Macmillan, 140–150.

Gallagher, Kathleen. 2014. *Why Theater Matters: Urban Youth, Engagement and a Pedagogy of the Real*. London: University of Toronto Press.

Gallagher, Kathleen, Scott Mealey, and Kelsey Jacobson. 2018. "Accuracy and Ethics, Feelings and Failures: Youth Experimenting with Documentary Practices of Performing Reality." *TRIC, RTAC* 39 (1): 58–76.

Gee, James. 1992. *The Social Mind: Language, Ideology and Social Practice*. New York: Bergin and Garvey.

Guinier, Lani and Anna Deavere Smith. 2001. "Rethinking Power, Rethinking Theater: A Conversation Between Lani Guinier and Anna Deavere Smith." *Theater* 31(3): 31–45.

Hansberry, Lorraine. 1959. *A Raisin in the Sun*. New York: Vintage Press.

Hare, David. 2005. *Stuff Happens*. New York: Farrar, Straus and Giroux.

Hodde, Stephanie. 2018. Course Syllabus. "ERH 203: Artistic Responses to Social Issues," Virginia Military Institute.

Hurley, Erin. 2014. *Theaters of Affect: New Essays on Canadian Theater*. Toronto: Playwrights Canada Press.

Interviews. April 2018. Recorded by Stephanie Hodde with students M., B., and E. for "ERH 203: Artistic Responses to Social Issues," Virginia Military Institute.

Jackson, Shannon. 2011. *Social Works: Performing Art, Supporting Publics*. New York: Routledge.

Kalb, Johnathan. 2001. "Documentary Solo Performance: The Politics of the Mirrored Self." *Theater* 31 (3): 13–29.

Kaufman, Moisés. 2014. *The Laramie Project and The Laramie Project: Ten Years Later*. New York: Vintage Books.

Kaufman, Moisés, Barbara Pitts McAdams, Leigh Fondakowski, Greg Pierotti, Andy Paris, Kelli Simpkins, Jimmy Maize, and Scott Barrow. 2018. *Moment Work: Tectonic Theater Project's Process of Devising Theater*. New York: Vintage Books.

Kellner, Douglas. 2017. "Guy Debord, Donald Trump, and the Politics of the Spectacle." In *Spectacle 2.0: Reading Debord in the Context of Digital Capitalism*, edited by M. Briziarelli and E. Armano. London: University of Westminster Press: 1–13.

M. "Blind Belief." 2018. Student Monologue. Lexington, VA: Virginia Military Institute.

Norris, Bruce. *Clybourne Park*. 2011. New York: Faber and Faber.

Nottage, Lynn. 2017. *Sweat*. New York: Theatre Communications Group.

Parenteau, Amelia. 2017. "Fact: Documentary Theater Aims Beyond Stage Realism to Grapple with Reality Itself." *American Theater*. September 2017: 24–27.

Parks, Suzan-Lori. "One Million Suggestions." Mudd Center Ethics Series Lecture, Lexington VA: Washington and Lee University. https://columns.wlu.edu/opportunities/mudd-center-for-ethics/. Recorded February 8, 2018.

Richards, Sandra. 1993. "Caught in the Act of Social Definition: On the Road with Anna Deavere Smith." In *Acting Out: Feminist Performances*, edited by Lynda Hart and Peggy Phelan. Ann Arbor: University of Michigan Press: 35–53.

Royster, Jacqueline Jones, and Gesa E. Kirsch. 2012. *Feminist Rhetorical Practices: New Horizons for Rhetoric, Composition, and Literacy Studies*. Carbondale: Southern Illinois University Press.

Savran, David. 1999. *The Playwrights Voice: American Dramatists on Memory, Writing and the Politics of Culture*. New York: Theater Communications Group.

Smith, Anna Deavere. "Anna Deavere Smith Pipeline Project." n.d. www.annadeaveresmith.org. Accessed 11 November 2019.

Smith, Anna Deavere. 1993. *Fires in the Mirror: Crown Heights, Brooklyn and Other Identities*. London: Anchor Books.

Smith, Anna Deavere. 2018. "Ghost Whisperers." *The New York Review of Books*, LXV 4, March 2018.

Smith, Anna Deavere. 2016. *Notes from the Field: Doing Time in Education*. Second Stage, American Repertory Production. Recording, accessed at New York Public Library for the Performing Arts, NCOV 4133.

Smith, Anna Deavere. 1995. "Not So Special Vehicles." *Performing Arts Journal* 17 (2/3): 77–89.

Smith, Anna Deavere. 2000. *Talk to Me: Listening Between the Lines*. New York: Random House.

Smith, Anna Deavere. 1994. *Twilight: Los Angeles, 1992*. New York: Anchor Books.

Smith, Anna Deavere. 2006. Women in Theater Interview by Linda Winer. *Newsday*, CUNY TV Recording. Season 3, ep. 3, accessed at New York Public Library, 2019.

Syme, Rachel. 2016. "Anna Deavere Smith Contains Multitudes." *New Yorker*.

Vogel, Paula. "The Art of Tolerance." Mudd Center Ethics Series Lecture. Lexington, VA: Washington and Lee University, October 16, 2018.

17 Tricksters in the academy

"Find the gap, then look for the people"

Susan Russell and Kikora Franklin

Susan

I found Kikora early in my teaching career at Penn State, and we quickly discovered that one of our meeting places was outside our departmental circle. We did not belong, and we knew it. We confronted systems of power, sometimes we dodged them, sometimes we adapted, and sometimes we complied with systems and got to work changing them from the inside. When we finally began to unpack our intersecting experiences of life, art making, and teaching and learning, which we did while writing this chapter, we called ourselves Tricksters. We belong inside this archetypal framework because we were and are disruptors, boundary crossers, benders and breakers of rules, and every culture, even the cultures of theatre and theatre education have Tricksters in their midst.

In claiming the Trickster narrative, I discovered that we used our outsider position to frame the methods and practices that sustained our art and created our lives as educators and activists. The Trickster is an insider/outsider, visible and invisible, present and absent, and a Trickster's observational position is his/her/their strength. From an observational position, Kikora and I would look for obstacles to our personal, artistic, and social justice missions, and then we would watch the obstacles "playing out" through people and the systems of power he/she/they "illustrated." When you do this kind of Trickster due diligence, you can choose to be visible or not, and both approaches work when observing, confronting, dodging, and adapting. Confronting a system might look like leading faculty conversations about race, gender, sexual orientation, mental health, and educational equity. Dodging a system might look like using storytelling and dance to create those very conversations in our local communities. Adapting to a system and working from the inside to change it might look like creating artistic engagements for middle and high school students where school administrators can hear how these topics affect the everyday lives of their young people. Kikora and I have practiced all of the methods above, sometimes as insiders, sometimes outsiders, and have created more Trickster methodology.

Trickster methodology is not for everyone. Insider/outside positioning is not comfortable, and Kikora and I have been very uncomfortable not belonging, but we found great comfort in our friendship and our unified mission. Once we decided to do the work, the slippery slopes we constantly navigated became what we looked for, and if we were slipping into invisibility in our department, we knew we had found a gap that needed to be explored. There was an upside to becoming invisible in our department; the more invisible we were to our colleagues, the more *visible* we were becoming in our communities. We disappeared from School of Theatre productions and could be seen at a middle school, or a high school, or a community home for girls, or a women's shelter, or an elder care facility. We disappeared from theatre classrooms and could be found in bio-behavior health, athletics, engineering, law, and science classrooms. We disappeared from Penn State entirely and could be found working with hospitals, businesses, and community organizations. We became a bridge between our theatre school and the human beings who live around it, and our work elevated the importance of the arts at Penn State. We were inside a School of Theatre, but outside its definition of theatre making, and in looking back on our ten years of collaboration, I know we could not have done the work we did if we had been inside the Theatre department circles.

Kikora and I are two different women from two different generations, with two different perspectives of the world earned through navigating a myriad of differences. We differ in race, sexual orientation, motherhood, religion, et cetera. Although Kikora and I see, hear, and respect our differences, the system of power we operate in and through is the same. We did not come to this truth easily. This chapter is a story about discovering resilience, determination, and joy in the academy.

Kikora

In 2003, my husband and I packed up our then one-year-old son and our pet chow, and moved from Smyrna, Georgia, away from the home we had so proudly bought just one year prior—a brick split-level home with a white picket fence—and headed north. My husband was headed back to school to pursue a graduate degree in Acting, and I was set to teach dance in the same department. Our plan was to be in one place for the duration of his graduate program, then move to New York, Los Angeles, or wherever opportunity led. Little did we know that opportunity would present itself in the very place we were headed, State College, Pennsylvania, home of the Nittany Lions and The Pennsylvania State University. Since 2003, I have taught students from all majors and backgrounds across the university. In the past sixteen years I have worked with students who major in dance, go on to receive graduate degrees, and become professional dancers, and others who enroll in dance to get a respite from rigorous academic life.

In teaching such a wide range of students, I learned to appreciate the impact a dance class can have on the confidence, joy, and overall health of a student. However, as a Trickster in the academy, it is this very observation that is both the reward and challenge. At the beginning of my teaching career, I loved the *feeling* of observing students' hard work and successes in class. I enjoyed hearing their immediate, positive feedback. However, as an Assistant Professor working towards tenure, I wondered how I would quantify the work I was doing. How would I demonstrate my real, measurable value to students and more than that, my value to the academy? Wouldn't it be great if I could just have students report that taking my class was a major factor in "increasing their confidence, joy and overall health," and let that be the end of it? But the academy, then and now, requires more. It asks us to calculate, measure, explain, and validate what we do and how we do it.

Susan

Kikora and I share the experience of being an artist inside the academy, and we have spent a decade re-defining how our department thinks about theatre. That's a bold statement, but I can see changes in the cultural climate of our department via the attention to what and how our students are taught and why we are teaching what we teach. I am an actor and an academic inside a conservatory-based department, which created gaps in my departmental identity, but those gaps were revealed to me as a graduate student in a MA/PhD Theatre Studies program, so I was prepared for this constantly surprising void. Simply put, my MA/PhD program positioned performance as a line of thinking to theorize or historicize, and the human beings who created theatre were not visible in the conversation. When I was hired at Penn State, this line between performance and intellectual rigor was firmly in place, and the line itself became something I confronted, dodged, or adapted to every day until, in true Trickster fashion, a gap opened up. This gap opened up in my university at large, and the gap was communication.

For the past eight years, I have been teaching "Creative Communication" in our various Colleges, and at this moment in 2019, I have taught CC in every college and almost every department on our University Park campus. In these interactive workshops, I use performance and playwriting skills to help people translate information into a story that can be understood by anyone in the room. My goal in these workshops is to help people tell stories about not just what they know, but why what they know is important to them. I have visited all twenty-three of our Commonwealth campuses offering communication workshops about Dignity, I have taught storytelling to all 8,000 first year students all at once, and I have taught storytelling to eight second-year medical students between rounds at our local hospital. I have taught storytelling at middle schools to address bullying, and I've taught storytelling at high schools to help students talk about mental health.

I've built a storytelling course for first year students called Moral Moments, and this course in emotional intelligence, cultural awareness, and critical thinking is now offered on five Penn State campuses.

My approach to communication has gotten the attention of scientists here at PSU, especially in life sciences and material sciences, and student and faculty scientists have embraced my actor identity in ways theatre studies has not. When I work with scientists, I use the word "performance" in all of its context and content, and when they start taking on the identity of "actor," they begin to open up to the process I teach. They learn and apply skills that define communication and storytelling, they watch others learn and apply the skills, then they agree as a group to practice their skills with others. Scientists are very honest about their fears. Their major fear is being reductive, and I tell them, "Simplifying is clarifying, and clarifying is good for you and the information." I have discovered that asking engineers, lawyers, business majors, and scientists to make communication choices *everyone* can understand connects the individuals to their information in very personal ways. When information becomes personal you are building a bridge to the listener and inviting them over. Simplifying, clarifying, and focusing on the story is the definition of a seasoned actor, which I am. I am also a seasoned teacher, and the lines between the two no longer exist.

Kikora

While the term Trickster accurately describes how Susan and I maneuver in academia, there is a purposeful and necessary shift that takes place once we enter the sacred space of our classrooms. As we begin the work of engaging students, Susan and I know that we must earn their trust. To do so, we cannot wear our Trickster hats. Thus, the first imperative for me as a teacher is to bring my most authentic self into the space and I ask the same of my students.

My teaching is grounded in an embodied approach to dance and movement that asks students to fully engage mind, body, and spirit. The teaching philosophy I draw upon derives from Total Dance/Dancical Productions, Inc. of Atlanta, GA, the source of my artistic training and education. I was immersed in dance and performing for over twenty years at Total Dance, under the direction of my mother, Terrie Ajile Axam, a dancer/choreographer and performer. In addition to that, I attended an international elementary school where I learned alongside children from nearly every corner of the globe. In *my* ten-year-old world, difference was the norm. Diversity wasn't a "thing," it just *was*. My early exposure to arts, dance, and cultural diversity greatly impacted my worldview, which in turn, impacted my pedagogical practice.

My teaching philosophy acknowledges the rich cultural and historical underpinnings that are intrinsically connected to the physical and embodied nature of dance. I embrace the idea that dance does not exist without the culture and history that birthed it, and it is important for students to learn and understand this. My dance and arts education background are also based in principles termed the "Total Dance Concept," a term coined by my dancer/ educator-mother. This concept includes values such as: (1) Teaching to the total person (valuing the whole individual and recognizing each student's contribution); (2) Equally valuing process and product; (3) Emphasizing technical proficiency and human integrity; (4) Viewing dance as a meaningful tool of communication that is used to transmit culture, and (5) Building safe and respectful learning communities.

The additional methods I employ to bring my teaching to life I term an "Africanist Performance Paradigm." This approach embraces a West African based and holistic view of people and the arts. It is well documented that in traditional West Africa, dance, music and the creative arts rose to the highest level possible and these arts were fully integrated into the lives of the people for value beyond entertainment. Dance scholar Lynne Fauley Emery, author of *Black Dance in America* states, "… music was one of the most highly developed of the arts…dance could be of recreational or secular nature and in one way or another pervaded all of African life…" (Emery 1972, 2). Within an Africanist Performance Paradigm, value is placed on human connectivity, community, and the breadth of human existence. In traditional West Africa, the expressive arts involve all members of the community and work in concert as a service to the community. Scholar Geneva Smitherman states in her book, *Talkin and Testifyin*, "The traditional African worldview conceptualizes a cosmos, which is an interacting, interdependent, balanced force field. The community of men and women, the organization of society itself, is thus based on this assumption … the fundamental requirement is active participation of all individuals (Smitherman 1977, 108).

In *Engaging Performance, Theatre as Call and Response*, author Jan Cohen-Cruz writes about the "call and response of theatre," a phenomenon that occurs in the cultural aesthetic of the African diaspora and thus lives within the Africanist Performance Paradigm. Cohen-Cruz cites Smitherman who defines call and response as "spontaneous verbal and non-verbal interaction between speaker and listener in which all of the speaker's statements (calls) are punctuated by expressions (responses) of the listener" (1977, 104). Cohen-Cruz elaborates on the concept and states:

> Translated to engaged performance, call and response foregrounds the many opportunities for inter-activity between a theatre artist and the people involved in the situation in question. … the call may be initiated from a community, and the response may come from the artist, who then sets forth a new call directed to an audience. The overall process of such must be reciprocal and must benefit the people whose lives inform the project, not just promote the artist.
>
> (Cohen-Cruz 2010: 19)

Cohen-Cruz's concept of a call and response that exists between the community and artists and layers in between describes the nature of my work with students at the university, colleagues like Susan, and people in the broader community.

Susan

The beautiful narrative above opens a conversation about teaching and learning and the structured freedom both require. Like Kikora, my mother was "in the business," and it was a business to her. She was a concert soprano who worked alone in every regard, and she raised me to be that, too. I was also an actor, and this is where things got confusing because acting requires collaboration and community building. I had a twenty-five-year nonstop professional career as a singer/actor being any "body" a director wanted in any play a producer wanted to produce. But I was conflicted when it came to being the actor part of singer/actor and I didn't know why until the final years of my performing career.

My final job as a singer/actor was as a swing in the Broadway production of *The Phantom of the Opera*. From 1999 to 2002, I was responsible for nine roles. My job was to replace a missing male or female cast member, sing his/her/their assigned harmonies, walk his/her/their blocking, and accomplish his/her/their stage craft tasks without anyone knowing I was not the "real" actor in the role. If I was on for an ensemble member, I was invisible and that was my job. If I played Carlotta or Madame Giry, I was visible as Madame Giry or Carlotta, but to management and audiences alike, I was not the "real" actor who was supposed to "be" these leading roles, so I disappeared. No matter how good my performance was, I could not be the "real actor," and although I was doing all the tasks perfectly, I could not "be" real and the audience's disappointment in my visibility, or invisibility, became a conscious burden. I didn't have access to information about realness or a skill set to think about it, but I remember the first moment I began wanting to know what the burden was and who taught me to carry it.

I realized I was taught to do what the playwright and director dictated, and I was taught how to make my complicity look real, and I realized neither skills had anything to do with realness. In *Phantom*, it was said that you only get two performances that are your own, your first and your last, and I experienced that first-hand. After my first performance as Carlotta, I was congratulated by the PSM for a wonderful performance, and then I was told to show up the next afternoon to work on the performance they wanted me to give, which was a replication of Judy Kaye's award-winning performance from 1988. Perfecting this performance from the past would be "real" to this company, its producers, and its audiences; if I perfected Judy Kaye's performance and was awarded a six-month leading actor contract, I would be a real Carlotta. A Trickster awakened during that rehearsal at The Majestic, and this identity helped me begin to connect with my real self on stage and off.

When I entered grad school, I entered as a singer/actor, and all the theories, the histories, the literature and criticism that defined the academic discourses of theatre were brand new to me. As an outsider in my theatre studies program, I began trying to connect with the academy in personal ways. I asked questions like, "Where are the acting theories written by actors?" "What does an acting theory do for actors?" "And BTWs, where are all the actors?" I'm sure these questions were reduced to the narcissism historically attached to my profession, but I really wanted to know where *I* was inside all the information. I had to choose a starting place, so I looked for names of actors, any names, and this simple act led me to the grand narrative of my theatre studies research: actors are invisible. When this awareness began popping up in my research, and when I dared to begin researching the visibility of actors in theatre studies, my advisor offered me some guidance by saying "Never admit you are an actor if you want to be taken seriously by the academy." Much to her surprise, and I suspect delight, everything I wrote about, thesis and dissertation included, and everything I have ever done and said, including this chapter, has circled my actor self.

I'm not an academic, I am an actor who slipped inside the academic circle, and from my outsider position, I have observed the academy drawing lines of separation in order to make decisions about, as musical theatre historian Bruce Kirle says in *Unfinished Show Business*, "Who is in charge?" Like an actor, I ask questions that start with "what if?" What if lines of separation drawn by the theatre studies academy are active in the teaching of the discourse? What if the provenance of a discourse, its time, place, and space of history is stabilized by the words used to define what the discourse *is*? What if looking for the actors, the human beings accomplishing the tasks that define theatre craft, is like looking for the citizens inside a civilization? I look for people, the human beings telling stories inside history and theory, and more than anything, I seek ways for human beings from the past and the present to be seen and heard in their own words. I am listening to the stories people tell, and in doing so, I am discovering what authenticity and realness mean.

Kikora

Like Susan, I came to the realization that I am a dancer and educator who found her way inside the academic circle. The academy was new and exciting terrain, however, I longed for a connection to the world that was outside of the "ivory tower" of the university. I wanted for my work in academia to touch the lives of people who might not make their way to campus.

At the start of extending my work into the community, I was disenchanted with what appeared to be a lack of resources, people, and opportunities to engage with diverse cultures, people, and spaces. I asked myself two questions: (1) What is the problem? (2) Do you have any way to help solve the problem? The problem as I saw it was that there was little to no space for conversation, interaction, and exchange with people from different backgrounds. I felt isolated and lonely. I eventually determined that in order for the community to reflect what I desired, I must *take action*. Opportunities emerged and led to collaborations with Susan and others in the State College, Pennsylvania, area.

In 2006, a district Learning Enrichment teacher invited me into Mt. Nittany Middle, one of two middle schools in the State College Area School District. I was asked to teach weeklong residencies in West African dance. The idea was to provide students with a diverse arts experience that they might not otherwise receive. This opportunity was a win-win as there was a need in the local schools, and I found an outlet for my newly inspired focus, bringing arts and dance into the local community. Through the dance residencies, we foregrounded art, culture, and performance from multi-cultural perspectives in an effort to contribute to a more inclusive learning experience for students. The invitation for me to teach was the community's call, my acceptance of the invitation was the response.

In 2009, we expanded the West African dance workshops beyond the middle school to the entire State College School District and ended up with over two hundred student participants. Our program consisted of sessions where young learners engaged in dance, drumming, poetry, and literature. We also discussed local and global social justice issues. That inaugural year, with the help and support of many people, we managed to teach workshops, have costumes sewn, and prepare for and complete a performance. The residencies at the middle school became very popular amongst the students, enrollment increased year after year. We decided that we would form a company of students called *Roots of Life* that would meet consistently and perform throughout the community.

Over the past ten years, we have worked with hundreds of students, performed for thousands of people, and impacted an extraordinary number of lives. We also expanded our work to include individualized mentoring and service opportunities for students. Perhaps more than anything, students in Roots of Life find community; some of the students call our group a second family. Students consistently comment about how they are enriched by the inclusive nature of our mission. Jonathan, a former Roots of Life member, credits his experience in the group with much of his personal growth and his connection to community. After participating for over five years, he said, "Our group was multi-cultural, encompassing people of black, European, Asian, Latino and mixed cultures. We used our differences and special talents to create a group that was able to share cross-cultural connections to the community around us." Jonathan's articulation of his experience is directly connected to the outcomes we state and envision for Roots of Life.

Susan

Kikora's work in our local school system has been transformational for so many young people. Just as Kikora's focus has been with middle and high school students, my work has taken me deep into the various Penn State educational communities. The more I work with faculty and students in law, medicine, engineering, business, and science, the more they sound like the young people Kikora and I work with in middle and high school. It turns out that everyone wants to be seen, heard, and understood, and everybody wants to be real and authentic. These commonalities connect Kikora's and my work on a foundational level, and in seeking the elusive "something more," this something might be found in the experience of telling a story.

There was a moment in my *Phantom* career when I started seriously grappling with realness. The cast was called in early to get notes from the production supervisor. Getting notes was a daily occurrence in *Phantom*, and at every show, there was a possibility of nine sets of notes coming at you, which you were expected to apply to the next show. We were always being watched, assessed, scrutinized, and given re-directions, but we were rarely addressed as a collective. We arrived at 5:30pm, two hours early, and were told to sit in the audience of the Majestic Theatre. We were told by the supervisor that we were not "doing our job." The Supervisor said, "Your job is to make it look like the first time *every* time." He went on to say, "I don't know how you are supposed to do that, but you had better do it tonight." Then he left us there to figure out how to do what he wanted, which was to be real.

Theoretically, you can be real only once, as Peggy Phelan so eloquently unwraps in *Unmarked*. Actors depend on a skill set to make the moment look like it's real-ly happening, and if you simulate realness enough, you lose the ability to recognize "real" if it happens. I jumped feet first into the possibility that I could connect my PhD training in theories of representation to other disciplines. I used Henry Ford's "special purpose machinery" to frame my ability to execute nine independent and interdependent sets of tasks as a swing in *Phantom*. I invited Michel Foucault's narratives of docility-utility in *Discipline and Punish* to speak to the note-giving practices of corporate performance, and I used my experiences playing Carlotta, which was based on replicating acting choices from the past to question whether *Phantom* is "live" theatre. Fascinated by possibilities, I created acting exercises to explore semiotics, phenomenology, queer theory, Marxism, and deconstruction, and Michel de Certeau's discussion of space and place in devising classroom performance projects.

All my students read and discuss theory, and I teach general education courses as well as undergraduate and graduate MFA theatre students. Theory is an extraordinary way to look at thinkers and thinking, and if human beings, actors included, don't know what is or has been written about how we became who we are, they cannot collaborate with their culture, they can only succumb to it. I finally began to understand the word collaboration, and it came to mean doing your homework about yourself, your culture, and all the cultures around you, and being human is not a solo performance.

Kikora

Susan's ideas of collaboration, realness, and authenticity are central to her work and to mine as well. These values directly relate to the Africanist Paradigm I rely on in my teaching. A call and response element continued to emerge as I moved forward in my artistic-community journey with the Roots of Life Performing group. In 2010 a seventh-grader saw our flyer calling for "all those interested in drumming, dancing, speaking, and writing," and showed up. He had no real experience performing, but he had an open mind and a willingness to learn. When he started with us, he was shy. He had just started to embrace himself as a dancer/artist when we received an email from his mother expressing her concern for her son's social and emotional well-being. She informed us that another student in the program was accused of bullying her son and that they had just moved from their home due to this bullying.

I prided myself on providing a safe learning environment for all of the students who work with us. I was faced with a situation that could potentially put one or more students in an uncomfortable (at best), and/or dangerous (at worst) situation. I was faced with having to address this potentiality before continuing with rehearsals. I spoke directly with the student who had been accused of bullying and explained firmly that all students must respect each and every person with whom we were working. More than that, I expressed that I expected for him to engage *all* people with respect. This proved to be the right thing to do.

That year, Roots of Life joined forces with Susan. As part of this engagement, we collaborated with Penn State students to perform for the annual Cultural Conversations festival Susan directed. It happened that the theme of the festival that year tackled the issue of bullying in schools. Susan attended our rehearsals and we all participated in exercises centered on the theme of bullying. To work through this difficult topic, the group of about twenty students formed a circle and engaged in discussions about moments where they experienced bullying and how that felt. We also asked students to think and write about ways they could display empathy and stand up for themselves and others. Some students chose to share their writing while others kept it for themselves. We used material from those discussions and the writing exercise to develop choreography and movement for the final presentation.

Throughout the process, the two young men who had trouble interacting with each other worked together and performed on the same stage. By the end of the process, the two had become friends. The process, in this case, was just as important—if not more—than the final product/performance. Through their shared experience in the process, the young men were able to discover more about themselves and build a connection with one another. The young man who had first come into the group as a shy seventh-grader continued to participate in the group until he graduated from high school. Today, as a college student, he walks with his head high and is a great role model to other young students. He credits his positive experiences in Roots of Life with much of his growth.

Susan

Kikora and I realized early on we had to let the kids teach us how to do this work, and I think vulnerability is key to teaching at every level. Teachers must ask for help, and Kikora and I, though strong teachers, have always asked students to help us teach. I learned to ask for help the year Cultural Conversations was telling stories about bullying. I was asked by a local school system to help the teachers and administrators figure out why the junior high students were being so mean to each other. Since these kids were hurling insults, I figured they needed communication skills, but more than anything, I knew they needed to be heard. I tasked them with building a question they wanted to ask the principal, a serious question, which I promised to let them ask him in person. I divided them into groups; each person had to articulate a problem and create a question out of it, and then the whole group had to agree on "the one." We narrowed the list of questions to ten. It then took thirty minutes for one hundred thirteen-year old kids to agree on the one question they would ask: "How am I supposed to succeed in a world where I am afraid to fail?" I invited the principal to join us, and when he heard this question, his intake of air was audible. We saw him look around the cafeteria at all the signs that said, "Failure is not an option." We saw him pause, we witnessed the moment a principal become part of a community.

Creating community is key to any classroom situation, but creating community is a skill. Part of building community is understanding what your goals are and then being open to finding professionals to help you achieve them. I always have school counselors and mental health professionals in the room, and Kikora and I work together because we fill in some gaps in each other's skill sets. This is collaboration, community building, *and* collegiality and we had to learn it. For the human beings I work with, concentrating on being open to a surprise and staying willing to learn something new has been a welcome relief from all the stress of not knowing what to do with all the people in the room. Maybe being open to a surprise and being willing to learn something new is the art of being real, and maybe this is where teaching and learning begin.

Finale

As Tricksters in the academy, we have found our space or created it where it did not yet exist, while remaining true to who we are as artists and humans—a feat that has not always been easy. Perhaps the ultimate triumph for us as the Tricksters is shedding the label of "insider/outsider" and inviting ourselves to take a seat at the "academy" table. Throughout our years we asserted our right again and again to become a part of an expanded vision and definition of arts as theory, practice, and pedagogy within the university. With the ever-changing world we face, we have remained committed to ensuring that our arts practices include as many voices as possible, that we make space for new ideas, and that we engage students in real, authentic ways. Our goal remains to use the arts to create meaning, to educate, and to effect positive change—whether it is in a university classroom, at a local elementary or middle school, in the community, or beyond.

References

Cohen-Cruz, Jan. 2010. *Engaging Performance, Theatre as Call and Response.* New York: Routledge.

Emery, Lynn Fauley. 1972. *Black Dance in the United States from 1619–1970.* Palo Alto, CA: National Press Books.

Foucault, Michel, Sheridan, Alan. 1977. *Discipline and Punish.* New York: Random House.

Kirle, Bruce. 2005. *Unfinished Show Business: Broadway Musicals as Works-in-Progress.* Carbondale: Southern Illinois University Press.

Phelan, Peggy. 1993. *Unmarked.* London: Routledge.

Smitherman, Geneva. 1977. *Talkin and Testifyin.* Detroit, MI: Wayne State University Press.

Welsh-Asante, K. 1985. "Commonalities in African Dance: An Aesthetic Foundation." In Asante, M. and K. Asante (Ed.) *African Culture: The Rhythms of Unity.* Westport, CT: Greenwood.

Index

Note: Page numbers in *italics* indicate figures and in **bold** indicate tables on the corresponding pages.

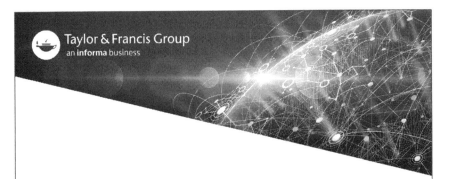